MznLnx

Missing Links Exam Preps

Exam Prep for

Mathematics for Economists

Simon & Blume, 1st Edition

The MznLnx Exam Prep is your link from the texbook and lecture to your exams.
The MznLnx Exam Preps are unauthorized and comprehensive reviews of your textbooks.

All material provided by MznLnx and Rico Publications (c) 2010
Textbook publishers and textbook authors do not particpate in or contribute to these reviews.

MznLnx

Rico
Publications

Exam Prep for Mathematics for Economists
1st Edition
Simon & Blume

Publisher: Raymond Houge
Assistant Editor: Michael Rouger
Text and Cover Designer: Lisa Buckner
Marketing Manager: Sara Swagger
Project Manager, Editorial Production: Jerry Emerson
Art Director: Vernon Lowerui

Product Manager: Dave Mason
Editorial Assitant: Rachel Guzmanji
Pedagogy: Debra Long
Cover Image: Jim Reed/Getty Images
Text and Cover Printer: City Printing, Inc.
Compositor: Media Mix, Inc.

(c) 2010 Rico Publications
ALL RIGHTS RESERVED. No part of this work
covered by the copyright may be reproduced or
used in any form or by an means--graphic, electronic,
or mechanical, including photocopying, recording,
taping, Web distribution, information storage, and
retrieval systems, or in any other manner--without the
written permission of the publisher.

Printed in the United States
ISBN:

For more information about our products, contact us at:
Dave.Mason@RicoPublications.com

For permission to use material from this text or
product, submit a request online to:
Dave.Mason@RicoPublications.com

Contents

CHAPTER 1
Introduction — 1

CHAPTER 2
One-Variable Calculus: Foundations — 5

CHAPTER 3
One-Variable Calculus: Applications — 7

CHAPTER 4
One-Variable Calculus: Chain Rule — 19

CHAPTER 5
Exponents and Logarithms — 23

CHAPTER 6
Introduction to Linear Algebra — 27

CHAPTER 7
Systems of Linear Equations — 37

CHAPTER 8
Matrix Algebra — 51

CHAPTER 9
Determinants: An Overview — 68

CHAPTER 10
Euclidean Spaces — 73

CHAPTER 11
Linear Independence — 86

CHAPTER 12
Limits and Open Sets — 89

CHAPTER 13
Functions of Several Variables — 97

CHAPTER 14
Calculus of Several Variables — 108

CHAPTER 15
Implicit Functions and Their Derivatives — 119

CHAPTER 16
Quadratic Forms and Definite Matrices — 127

CHAPTER 17
Unconstrained Optimization — 133

CHAPTER 18
Constrained Optimization I: First Order Conditions — 140

CHAPTER 19
Constrained Optimization II — 148

CHAPTER 20
Homogeneous and Homothetic Functions — 152

Contents (Cont.)

CHAPTER 21
Concave and Quasiconcave Functions — 161

CHAPTER 22
Economic Applications — 168

CHAPTER 23
Eigenvalues and Eigenvectors — 178

CHAPTER 24
Ordinary Differential Equations: Scalar Equations — 196

CHAPTER 25
Ordinary Differential Equations: Systems of Equations — 213

CHAPTER 26
Determinants: The Details — 228

CHAPTER 27
Subspaces Attached to a Matrix — 241

CHAPTER 28
Applications of Linear Independence — 252

CHAPTER 29
Limits and Compact Sets — 258

CHAPTER 30
Calculus of Several Variables II — 269

ANSWER KEY — 296

TO THE STUDENT

COMPREHENSIVE

The *MznLnx* Exam Prep series is designed to help you pass your exams. Editors at MznLnx review your textbooks and then prepare these practice exams to help you master the textbook material. Unlike study guides, workbooks, and practice tests provided by the texbook publisher and textbook authors, *MznLnx* gives you **all** of the material in each chapter in exam form, not just samples, so you can be sure to nail your exam.

MECHANICAL

The MznLnx Exam Prep series creates exams that will help you learn the subject matter as well as test you on your understanding. Each question is designed to help you master the concept. Just working through the exams, you gain an understanding of the subject--its a simple mechanical process that produces success.

INTEGRATED STUDY GUIDE AND REVIEW

MznLnx is not just a set of exams designed to test you, its also a comprehensive review of the subject content. Each exam question is also a review of the concept, making sure that you will get the answer correct without having to go to other sources of material. You learn as you go! Its the easiest way to pass an exam.

HUMOR

Studying can be tedious and dry. MznLnx's instructional design includes moderate humor within the exam questions on occassion, to break the tedium and revitalize the brain

Chapter 1. Introduction

1. In statistics, _____ has two related meanings:

   - the arithmetic _____.
   - the expected value of a random variable, which is also called the population _____.

   It is sometimes stated that the '_____' _____s average. This is incorrect if '_____' is taken in the specific sense of 'arithmetic _____' as there are different types of averages: the _____, median, and mode. For instance, average house prices almost always use the median value for the average.

   For a real-valued random variable X, the _____ is the expectation of X.

   a. Probability
   b. Proportional hazards model
   c. Statistical population
   d. Mean

2. In calculus, the _____ states, roughly, that given a section of a smooth curve, there is at least one point on that section at which the derivative of the curve is equal to the 'average' derivative of the section. It is used to prove theorems that make global conclusions about a function on an interval starting from local hypotheses about derivatives at points of the interval.

   This theorem can be understood concretely by applying it to motion: if a car travels one hundred miles in one hour, so that its average speed during that time was 100 miles per hour, then at some time its instantaneous speed must have been exactly 100 miles per hour.

   a. Mean Value Theorem
   b. Fundamental Theorem of Calculus
   c. Functional integration
   d. Calculus controversy

3. In mathematics, a _____ is a statement that can be proved on the basis of explicitly stated or previously agreed assumptions.
   a. Logical value
   b. Disjunction introduction
   c. Boolean function
   d. Theorem

4. The mathematical concept of a _____ expresses the intuitive idea of deterministic dependence between two quantities, one of which is viewed as primary and the other as secondary. A _____ then is a way to associate a unique output for each input of a specified type, for example, a real number or an element of a given set.
   a. Coherent
   b. Grill
   c. Going up
   d. Function

5. In economics, the _____ functional form of production functions is widely used to represent the relationship of an output to inputs. It was proposed by Knut Wicksell, and tested against statistical evidence by Paul Douglas and Charles Cobb in 1928.
   a. State price
   b. Burden of proof
   c. State price vector
   d. Cobb-Douglas

6. _____s is the social science that studies the production, distribution, and consumption of goods and services.

Chapter 1. Introduction

The term _____s comes from the Ancient Greek οá¼°κονομί α (oikonomia, 'management of a household, administration') from οá¼¶κος (oikos, 'house') + νÏŒμος (nomos, 'custom' or 'law'), hence 'rules of the house(hold)'.

Current _____ models developed out of the broader field of political economy in the late 19th century, owing to a desire to use an empirical approach more akin to the physical sciences.

    a. Economic   b. Experimental economics
    c. A chemical equation   d. A Mathematical Theory of Communication

7. In calculus, a branch of mathematics, _____ essentially states that a differentiable function, which attains equal values at two points, must have a point somewhere between them where the slope is zero.

If a real-valued function f is continuous on a closed interval [a,b], differentiable on the open interval, and f

$$f'(c) = 0.$$

This version of _____ is used to prove the mean value theorem, _____ is indeed a special case of it.

A version of the theorem was first stated by the Indian astronomer BhÄ skara II in the 12th century.

    a. Continuous wave   b. Rolle's Theorem
    c. Convex polygon   d. Contingency table

8. There are two _____. The first states that any competitive equilibrium or Walrasian equilibrium leads to an efficient allocation of resources. The second states the converse, that any efficient allocation can be sustainable by a competitive equilibrium. Despite the apparent symmetry of the two theorems, in fact the first theorem is much more general than the second, requiring far weaker assumptions.

    a. 1-center problem   b. Fundamental Theorems of Welfare Economics
    c. 2-3 heap   d. 120-cell

9. In mathematics, an _____ is a generalization for the concept of a function in which the dependent variable has not been given 'explicitly' in terms of the independent variable. To give a function f explicitly is to provide a prescription for determining the value of the function y in terms of the input value x:

        y = f

    a. Ordinary differential equation   b. Inflection point
    c. Implicit differentiation   d. Implicit Function

10. In the branch of mathematics called multivariable calculus, the _____ is a tool which allows relations to be converted to functions. It does this by representing the relation as the graph of a function. There may not be a single function whose graph is the entire relation, but there may be such a function on a restriction of the domain of the relation.

a. Inverse function theorem   b. A Mathematical Theory of Communication
c. Implicit Function Theorem   d. A chemical equation

11. This article will state and prove the _____ for differentiation, and then use it to prove these two formulas.

The _____ for differentiation states that for every natural number n, the derivative of $f(x) = x^n$ is $f'(x) = nx^{n-1}$, that is,

$$(x^n)' = nx^{n-1}.$$

The _____ for integration

$$\int x^n \, dx = \frac{x^{n+1}}{n+1} + C$$

for natural n is then an easy consequence. One just needs to take the derivative of this equality and use the _____ and linearity of differentiation on the right-hand side.

a. Periodic function   b. Power Rule
c. Standard part function   d. Functional integration

12. The term market basket or _____ refers to a fixed list of items used specifically to track the progress of inflation in an economy or specific market.

The most common type of market basket is the basket of consumer goods, used to define the Consumer Price Index (CPI.) Other types of baskets are used to define

- Producer Price Index (PPI), previously known as Wholesale Price Index (WPI)
- various commodity price indices

The term market basket analysis in the retail business refers to research that provides the retailer with information to understand the purchase behaviour of a buyer. This information will enable the retailer to understand the buyer's needs and rewrite the store's layout accordingly, develop cross-promotional programs, or even capture new buyers (much like the cross-selling concept.)

a. Commodity bundle   b. 1-center problem
c. Pareto index   d. Robin Hood index

13. In mathematics, the concept of a _____ tries to capture the intuitive idea of a geometrical one-dimensional and continuous object. A simple example is the circle. In everyday use of the term '_____', a straight line is not curved, but in mathematical parlance _____s include straight lines and line segments.

a. Curve
b. Kappa curve
c. Negative pedal curve
d. Quadrifolium

14. In microeconomic theory, an _____ is a graph showing different bundles of goods, each measured as to quantity, between which a consumer is indifferent. That is, at each point on the curve, the consumer has no preference for one bundle over another. In other words, they are all equally preferred. One can equivalently refer to each point on the _____ as rendering the same level of utility for the consumer.
   a. Utility maximization problem
   b. Indifference curve
   c. Expenditure minimization problem
   d. Expenditure function

15. The _____ is a single-winner election method in which voters rank candidates in order of preference. The _____ determines the winner of an election by giving each candidate a certain number of points corresponding to the position in which he or she is ranked by each voter. Once all votes have been counted the candidate with the most points is the winner.
   a. 1-center problem
   b. 2-3 heap
   c. 120-cell
   d. Borda count

16. A _____ includes all possible consumption bundles that someone can afford given the prices of goods and the person's income level. The _____ is bounded above by the budget line.
   a. Budget set
   b. 1-center problem
   c. 2-3 heap
   d. 120-cell

17. In economics, _____ is the comparison of two different equilibrium states, before and after a change in some underlying exogenous parameter. As a study of statics it compares two different unchanging points, after they have changed. It does not study the motion towards equilibrium, nor the process of the change itself.
   a. Consumer surplus
   b. Marginal rate of technical substitution
   c. Producer surplus
   d. Comparative statics

Chapter 2. One-Variable Calculus: Foundations

1. In mathematics, a _____ is a set of real numbers with the property that any number that lies between two numbers in the set is also included in the set. For example, the set of all numbers x satisfying $0 \leq x \leq 1$ is an _____ which contains 0 and 1, as well as all numbers between them. Other examples of _____s are the set of all real numbers $\mathbb{R}$, the set of all positive real numbers, and the empty set.
   a. Order
   b. Ideal
   c. Annihilator
   d. Interval

2. The Condorcet candidate or _____ of an election is the candidate who, when compared with every other candidate, is preferred by more voters. Informally, the _____ is the person who would win a two-candidate election against each of the other candidates. A _____ will not always exist in a given set of votes, which is known as Condorcet's voting paradox.
   a. Psephology
   b. 120-cell
   c. 1-center problem
   d. Condorcet winner

3. In economics, business, retail, and accounting, a _____ is the value of money that has been used up to produce something, and hence is not available for use anymore. In business, the _____ may be one of acquisition, in which case the amount of money expended to acquire it is counted as _____. In this case, money is the input that is gone in order to acquire the thing.
   a. 120-cell
   b. 1-center problem
   c. 2-3 heap
   d. Cost

4. In economics, the cross elasticity of demand and _____ measures the responsiveness of the quantity demanded of a good to a change in the price of another good.

   It is measured as the percentage change in quantity demanded for the first good that occurs in response to a percentage change in price of the second good. For example, if, in response to a 10% increase in the price of fuel, the quantity of new cars that are fuel inefficient demanded decreased by 20%, the cross elasticity of demand would be -20%/10% = -2.

   a. Supply and demand
   b. Cross price elasticity of demand
   c. Marginal rate of substitution
   d. 1-center problem

5. In mathematics, the concept of a _____ tries to capture the intuitive idea of a geometrical one-dimensional and continuous object. A simple example is the circle. In everyday use of the term '_____', a straight line is not curved, but in mathematical parlance _____s include straight lines and line segments.
   a. Negative pedal curve
   b. Kappa curve
   c. Curve
   d. Quadrifolium

6. The mathematical concept of a _____ expresses the intuitive idea of deterministic dependence between two quantities, one of which is viewed as primary and the other as secondary. A _____ then is a way to associate a unique output for each input of a specified type, for example, a real number or an element of a given set.
   a. Going up
   b. Grill
   c. Coherent
   d. Function

7. In mathematics, the _____ or Pythagoras' theorem is a relation in Euclidean geometry among the three sides of a right triangle. The theorem is named after the Greek mathematician Pythagoras, who by tradition is credited with its discovery and proof, although it is often argued that knowledge of the theory predates him.. The theorem is as follows:

In any right triangle, the area of the square whose side is the hypotenuse is equal to the sum of the areas of the squares whose sides are the two legs.

   a. 120-cell   b. 2-3 heap
   c. 1-center problem   d. Pythagorean Theorem

8. In mathematics, a _____ is a statement that can be proved on the basis of explicitly stated or previously agreed assumptions.
   a. Boolean function   b. Logical value
   c. Disjunction introduction   d. Theorem

9. In mathematics, a _____ is the end result of a division problem. It can also be expressed as the number of times the divisor divides into the dividend.
   a. Limiting   b. Notation
   c. Marginal cost   d. Quotient

Chapter 3. One-Variable Calculus: Applications

1. In mathematics, a _____ is a point on the domain of a function where:

   - one dimension: the derivative is equal to zero or a point where the function ceases to be differentiable.
   - in general: there are two distinct concepts: either the derivative vanishes, or it is not of full rank; these agree in one dimension.

   Note that in one dimension, a critical value or critical number x of function f is the domain element at which the derivative is zero or undefined, whereas the associated ordered pair is the _____. In higher dimensions a critical value is in the range whereas a _____ is in the domain.

   There are two situations in which a point becomes a _____ of a function of one variable. The first of which is that the value of the derivative is equal to zero.

   a. Going up
   b. Critical point
   c. Decimal system
   d. Derivative algebra

2. In economics, the _____ functional form of production functions is widely used to represent the relationship of an output to inputs. It was proposed by Knut Wicksell, and tested against statistical evidence by Paul Douglas and Charles Cobb in 1928.
   a. State price
   b. State price vector
   c. Cobb-Douglas
   d. Burden of proof

3. The _____ governs the differentiation of products of differentiable functions.
   a. 120-cell
   b. Reciprocal Rule
   c. 1-center problem
   d. Product Rule

4. In mathematics, a concave function is the negative of a convex function. A concave function is also synonymously called concave downwards, _____, convex cap or upper convex.

   Formally, a real-valued function f defined on an interval is called concave, if for any two points x and y in its domain C and any t in [0,1], we have

   $$f(tx + (1-t)y) \geq tf(x) + (1-t)f(y).$$

   Also, f–f

   a. Polylogarithmic
   b. Smooth infinitesimal analysis
   c. Negligible set
   d. Concave down

5. In mathematics, a real-valued function f defined on an interval is called convex, concave upwards, _____ or convex cup, if for any two points x and y in its domain C and any t in [0,1], we have

   $$f(tx + (1-t)y) \leq tf(x) + (1-t)f(y).$$

   Convex function on an interval.

In other words, a function is convex if and only if its epigraph is a convex set.

Pictorially, a function is called 'convex' if the function lies below the straight line segment connecting two points, for any two points in the interval.

A function is called strictly convex if

$$f(tx + (1-t)y) < tf(x) + (1-t)f(y)$$

for any t in and $x \neq y$.

A function f is said to be concave if − f is convex.

    a. Mountain pass theorem   b. Total variation
    c. Concave down   d. Concave up

6. In mathematics, the concept of a _____ tries to capture the intuitive idea of a geometrical one-dimensional and continuous object. A simple example is the circle. In everyday use of the term '_____', a straight line is not curved, but in mathematical parlance _____s include straight lines and line segments.
    a. Kappa curve   b. Negative pedal curve
    c. Quadrifolium   d. Curve

7. The mathematical concept of a _____ expresses the intuitive idea of deterministic dependence between two quantities, one of which is viewed as primary and the other as secondary. A _____ then is a way to associate a unique output for each input of a specified type, for example, a real number or an element of a given set.
    a. Grill   b. Function
    c. Going up   d. Coherent

8. In economics, a _____ is a function that specifies the output of a firm, an industry, or an entire economy for all combinations of inputs. A meta-_____ compares the practice of the existing entities converting inputs X into output y to determine the most efficient practice _____ of the existing entities, whether the most efficient feasible practice production or the most efficient actual practice production. In either case, the maximum output of a technologically-determined production process is a mathematical function of input factors of production.
    a. Short-run   b. 1-center problem
    c. Long-run   d. Production function

9. The Condorcet candidate or _____ of an election is the candidate who, when compared with every other candidate, is preferred by more voters. Informally, the _____ is the person who would win a two-candidate election against each of the other candidates. A _____ will not always exist in a given set of votes, which is known as Condorcet's voting paradox.
    a. Condorcet winner   b. 1-center problem
    c. Psephology   d. 120-cell

Chapter 3. One-Variable Calculus: Applications

10. In mathematics, an _____ is a generalization for the concept of a function in which the dependent variable has not been given 'explicitly' in terms of the independent variable. To give a function f explicitly is to provide a prescription for determining the value of the function y in terms of the input value x:

   y = f

   a. Inflection point
   c. Implicit Function
   b. Ordinary differential equation
   d. Implicit differentiation

11. In the branch of mathematics called multivariable calculus, the _____ is a tool which allows relations to be converted to functions. It does this by representing the relation as the graph of a function. There may not be a single function whose graph is the entire relation, but there may be such a function on a restriction of the domain of the relation.
   a. A chemical equation
   c. Inverse function theorem
   b. A Mathematical Theory of Communication
   d. Implicit Function Theorem

12. In mathematics, a _____ is a statement that can be proved on the basis of explicitly stated or previously agreed assumptions.
   a. Boolean function
   c. Logical value
   b. Theorem
   d. Disjunction introduction

13. In mathematics, a _____ is the negative of a convex function. A _____ is also synonymously called concave downwards, concave down or convex cap.

   Formally, a real-valued function f defined on an interval is called concave, if for any two points x and y in its domain C and any t in [0,1], we have

   $$f(tx + (1-t)y) \geq tf(x) + (1-t)f(y).$$

   Also, f−f

   a. Weight function
   c. Dirichlet kernel
   b. Concave function
   d. Darboux function

14. In mathematics, a real-valued function f defined on an interval is called _____, concave upwards, concave up or _____ cup, if for any two points x and y in its domain C and any t in [0,1], we have

   $$f(tx + (1-t)y) \leq tf(x) + (1-t)f(y).$$

   _____ function on an interval.

   In other words, a function is _____ if and only if its epigraph is a _____ set.

   Pictorially, a function is called '_____' if the function lies below the straight line segment connecting two points, for any two points in the interval.

A function is called strictly _____ if

$$f(tx + (1-t)y) < tf(x) + (1-t)f(y)$$

for any t in and $x \neq y$.

A function f is said to be concave if − f is _____.

  a. Continuous wavelet   b. Continuum
  c. Contrapositive   d. Convex

15. In differential calculus, an _____, or point of inflection is a point on a curve at which the curvature changes sign. The curve changes from being concave upwards to concave downwards, or vice versa. If one imagines driving a vehicle along the curve, it is a point at which the steering-wheel is momentarily 'straight', being turned from left to right or vice versa.
  a. Implicit function   b. Implicit differentiation
  c. Ordinary differential equation   d. Inflection point

16. In mathematics, an _____ in the sense of ring theory is a subring $\mathcal{O}$ of a ring R that satisfies the conditions

  1. R is a ring which is a finite-dimensional algebra over the rational number field $\mathbb{Q}$
  2. $\mathcal{O}$ spans R over $\mathbb{Q}$, so that $\mathbb{Q}\mathcal{O} = R$, and
  3. $\mathcal{O}$ is a lattice in R.

The third condition can be stated more accurately, in terms of the extension of scalars of R to the real numbers, embedding R in a real vector space. In less formal terms, additively $\mathcal{O}$ should be a free abelian group generated by a basis for R over $\mathbb{Q}$.

The leading example is the case where R is a number field K and $\mathcal{O}$ is its ring of integers. In algebraic number theory there are examples for any K other than the rational field of proper subrings of the ring of integers that are also _____s.

  a. Annihilator   b. Efficiency
  c. Algebraic   d. Order

17. An _____ of a real-valued function y = f(x) is a curve which describes the behavior of f as either x or y tends to infinity.

In other words, as one moves along the graph of f(x) in some direction, the distance between it and the _____ eventually becomes smaller than any distance that one may specify.

If a curve A has the curve B as an _____, one says that A is asymptotic to B. Similarly B is asymptotic to A, so A and B are called asymptotic.

a. Improper integral
b. Infinite product
c. Isoperimetric dimension
d. Asymptote

18. Suppose f is a function. Then the line y = a is a _____ for f if

$$\lim_{x \to \infty} f(x) = a \text{ or } \lim_{x \to -\infty} f(x) = a.$$

Intuitively, this means that f(x) can be made as close as desired to a by making x big enough. How big is big enough depends on how close one wishes to make f(x) to a.

a. 1-center problem
b. 2-3 heap
c. 120-cell
d. Horizontal asymptote

19. The _____ is a single-winner election method in which voters rank candidates in order of preference. The _____ determines the winner of an election by giving each candidate a certain number of points corresponding to the position in which he or she is ranked by each voter. Once all votes have been counted the candidate with the most points is the winner.

a. 120-cell
b. 2-3 heap
c. 1-center problem
d. Borda count

20. In economics and consumer theory, a _____ is that which people consume more of as price rises, violating the law of demand. In normal situations, as the price of such a good rises, the substitution effect causes people to purchase less of it and more of substitute goods. In the _____ situation, cheaper close substitutes are not available.

a. 1-center problem
b. Giffen good
c. 2-3 heap
d. 120-cell

21. In topology, the _____ of a subset S of a topological space X is the set of points which can be approached both from S and from the outside of S. More formally, it is the set of points in the closure of S, not belonging to the interior of S. An element of the _____ of S is called a _____ point of S.

a. Heap
b. Character
c. Bertrand paradox
d. Boundary

22. In mathematics, an _____, or central tendency of a data set refers to a measure of the 'middle' or 'expected' value of the data set. There are many different descriptive statistics that can be chosen as a measurement of the central tendency of the data items.

An _____ is a single value that is meant to typify a list of values.

a. A Mathematical Theory of Communication
b. Average
c. A chemical equation
d. A posteriori

23. In economics, _____ is equal to total cost divided by the number of goods produced Quantity-Q. It is also equal to the sum of average variable costs total variable costs divided by Q plus average fixed costs total fixed costs divided by Q. _____s may be dependent on the time period considered increasing production may be expensive or impossible in the short term, for example. _____s affect the supply curve and are a fundamental component of supply and demand.

a. Equity
b. Average cost
c. Extreme value theorem
d. Uncertainty quantification

24. In economics, business, retail, and accounting, a _____ is the value of money that has been used up to produce something, and hence is not available for use anymore. In business, the _____ may be one of acquisition, in which case the amount of money expended to acquire it is counted as _____. In this case, money is the input that is gone in order to acquire the thing.
   a. 120-cell
   b. 2-3 heap
   c. Cost
   d. 1-center problem

25. In economics, the cross elasticity of demand and _____ measures the responsiveness of the quantity demanded of a good to a change in the price of another good.

It is measured as the percentage change in quantity demanded for the first good that occurs in response to a percentage change in price of the second good. For example, if, in response to a 10% increase in the price of fuel, the quantity of new cars that are fuel inefficient demanded decreased by 20%, the cross elasticity of demand would be -20%/10% = -2.

   a. 1-center problem
   b. Supply and demand
   c. Cross price elasticity of demand
   d. Marginal rate of substitution

26. _____ is the change in total cost that arises when the quantity produced changes by one unit.
   a. Marginal cost
   b. Notation
   c. Limiting
   d. Differential Algebra

27. In mathematics the concept of a _____ generalizes notions such as 'length', 'area', and 'volume'. Informally, given some base set, a '_____' is any consistent assignment of 'sizes' to the subsets of the base set. Depending on the application, the 'size' of a subset may be interpreted as its physical size, the amount of something that lies within the subset, or the probability that some random process will yield a result within the subset.
   a. Cusp
   b. Congruent
   c. Lattice
   d. Measure

28. In statistics and mathematical epidemiology, _____ is the risk of an event relative to exposure. _____ is a ratio of the probability of the event occurring in the exposed group versus a non-exposed group.

$$RR = \frac{p_{\text{exposed}}}{p_{\text{non-exposed}}}$$

For example, if the probability of developing lung cancer among smokers was 20% and among non-smokers 1%, then the _____ of cancer associated with smoking would be 20.

   a. 1-center problem
   b. Mendelian randomization
   c. Statistical epidemiology
   d. Relative risk

Chapter 3. One-Variable Calculus: Applications

29. _____ is a concept in economics, finance, and psychology related to the behaviour of consumers and investors under uncertainty. _____ is the reluctance of a person to accept a bargain with an uncertain payoff rather than another bargain with a more certain, but possibly lower, expected payoff.

The inverse of a person's _____ is sometimes called their risk tolerance.

a. Stochastic modelling
c. Risk aversion
b. Ruin theory
d. Life table

30. In economics, a _____ is a graph of the costs of production as a function of total quantity produced. In a free market economy, productively efficient firms use these curves to find the optimal point of production, where they make the most profits. There are a few different types of _____s, each relevant to a different area of economics.

a. Cost curve
c. 1-center problem
b. Phillips curve
d. Demand curve

31. _____ is an important concept in economics with broad applications in game theory, engineering and the social sciences. The term is named after Vilfredo Pareto, an Italian economist who used the concept in his studies of economic efficiency and income distribution.

Given a set of alternative allocations of, say, goods or income for a set of individuals, a change from one allocation to another that can make at least one individual better off without making any other individual worse off is called a Pareto improvement.

a. Multiunit auction
c. Quasi-perfect equilibrium
b. Pareto efficiency
d. Pursuit-evasion

32. In mathematics, in the realm of group theory, a group is said to be _____ if it equals its own commutator subgroup if the group has no nontrivial abelian quotients.

The smallest _____ group is the alternating group A_5. More generally, any non-abelian simple group is _____ since the commutator subgroup is a normal subgroup with abelian quotient.

a. Quaternion group
c. Group of Lie type
b. Free product
d. Perfect

33. In neoclassical economics and microeconomics, _____ describes a market in which no buyer or seller has market power. In the short term, such markets are productively inefficient and allocatively efficient. However, In the long term, such markets both allocatively and productively efficient.

a. 2-3 heap
c. 1-center problem
b. Perfect competition
d. 120-cell

34. In mathematics, the _____ of a number n is the number that, when added to n, yields zero. The _____ of n is denoted −n. For example, 7 is −7, because 7 + (−7) = 0, and the _____ of −0.3 is 0.3, because −0.3 + 0.3 = 0.

a. Associativity
c. Additive inverse
b. Arity
d. Algebraic structure

Chapter 3. One-Variable Calculus: Applications

35. In economics, an _____ is a function that maps the quantity of output supplied to the market price for that output.

In mathematical terms, if the demand function is , then the _____ is f $^{-1}$

   a. Arrow-Debreu model
   b. Enterprise value
   c. Internal rate of return
   d. Inverse demand function

36. This article will state and prove the _____ for differentiation, and then use it to prove these two formulas.

The _____ for differentiation states that for every natural number n, the derivative of $f(x) = x^n$ is $f'(x) = nx^{n-1}$, that is,

$$(x^n)' = nx^{n-1}.$$

The _____ for integration

$$\int x^n \, dx = \frac{x^{n+1}}{n+1} + C$$

for natural n is then an easy consequence. One just needs to take the derivative of this equality and use the _____ and linearity of differentiation on the right-hand side.

   a. Functional integration
   b. Power Rule
   c. Standard part function
   d. Periodic function

37. Price _____ is defined as the measure of responsivenesses in the quantity demanded for a commodity as a result of change in price of the same commodity. In other words, it is percentage change in quantity demanded as per the percentage change in price of the same commodity. In economics and business studies, the price _____ is a measure of the sensitivity of quantity demanded to changes in price. It is measured as elasticity, that is it measures the relationship as the ratio of percentage changes between quantity demanded of a good and changes in its price.
   a. A Mathematical Theory of Communication
   b. A chemical equation
   c. A posteriori
   d. Elasticity of demand

38. _____ is defined as the measure of responsiveness in the quantity demanded for a commodity as a result of change in price of the same commodity. In other words, it is percentage change in quantity demanded as per the percentage change in price of the same commodity. In economics and business studies, the _____ (PED) is a measure of the sensitivity of quantity demanded to changes in price.
   a. 120-cell
   b. 2-3 heap
   c. 1-center problem
   d. Price elasticity of demand

39. In graph theory, a _____ is an edge that connects a vertex to itself. A simple graph contains no _____s.

Chapter 3. One-Variable Calculus: Applications

Depending on the context, a graph or a multigraph may be defined so as to either allow or disallow the presence of _____s:

- Where graphs are defined so as to allow _____s and multiple edges, a graph without _____s is often called a multigraph.
- Where graphs are defined so as to disallow _____s and multiple edges, a multigraph or a pseudograph is often defined to mean a 'graph' which can have _____s and multiple edges.

For an undirected graph, the degree of a vertex is equal to the number of adjacent vertices.

A special case is a _____, which adds two to the degree.

a. Commensurable
c. FISH
b. Duality
d. Loop

40. In mathematics, a _____ is a rectangular table of elements, which may be numbers or, more generally, any abstract quantities that can be added and multiplied. Matrices are used to describe linear equations, keep track of the coefficients of linear transformations and to record data that depend on multiple parameters. Matrices are described by the field of _____ theory.

a. Double counting
c. Compression
b. Coherent
d. Matrix

41. In several fields of mathematics the term _____ is used with different but closely related meanings. They all relate to the notion of mapping the elements of a set to other elements of the same set, i.e., exchanging elements of a set.

The general concept of _____ can be defined more formally in different contexts:

In combinatorics, a _____ is usually understood to be a sequence containing each element from a finite set once, and only once.

a. Permutation
c. Tensor product
b. Linearly independent
d. Cyclic permutation

42. In mathematics, in matrix theory, a _____ is a square-matrix that has exactly one entry 1 in each row and each column and 0's elsewhere. Each such matrix represents a specific permutation of m elements and, when used to multiply another matrix, can produce that permutation in the rows or columns of the other matrix.

Given a permutation π of m elements,

$$\pi : \{1, \ldots, m\} \to \{1, \ldots, m\}$$

given in two-line form by

$$\begin{pmatrix} 1 & 2 & \cdots & m \\ \pi(1) & \pi(2) & \cdots & \pi(m) \end{pmatrix},$$

its _____ is the m × m matrix P_π whose entries are all 0 except that in row i, the entry equals 1.

    a. Cartan matrix   b. Permutation Matrix
    c. Partitioned matrix   d. Hessenberg matrix

43. _____ is the elasticity of one variable with respect to another between two given points.

The y _____ of x is defined as:

$$E_{x,y} = \frac{\% \text{ change in } x}{\% \text{ change in } y}$$

where the percentage change is calculated relative to the midpoint

$$\% \text{ change in } x = \frac{x_2 - x_1}{(x_2 + x_1)/2}$$

$$\% \text{ change in } y = \frac{y_2 - y_1}{(y_2 + y_1)/2}$$

The midpoint _____ formula was advocated by R. G. D. Allen due to the following properties: symmetric with respect to the two prices and two quantities, independent of the units of measurement, and yield a value of unity if the total revenues at two points are equal.

    a. Arc elasticity   b. Uniform algebra
    c. Equilibrium point   d. Operator theory

44. In mathematics, the interior of a set S consists of all points of S that are intuitively 'not on the edge of S'. A point that is in the interior of S is an _____ of S.

The exterior of a set is the interior of its complement; it consists of the points that are not in the set or its boundary.

    a. A Mathematical Theory of Communication   b. A posteriori
    c. A chemical equation   d. Interior point

45. _____ is a branch of mathematics which focuses on the study of matrices. Initially a sub-branch of linear algebra, it has grown to cover subjects related to graph theory, algebra, combinatorics, and statistics as well.

Chapter 3. One-Variable Calculus: Applications 17

The term matrix was first coined in 1848 by J.J. Sylvester as a name of an array of numbers.

a. Segre classification
c. Semi-simple operators
b. Matrix theory
d. Pairing

46. In mathematics, elasticity of a positive differentiable function f at point x is defined as

$$Ef(x) = \frac{x}{f(x)} f'(x) = \frac{d \log f(x)}{d \log x}$$

It is the ratio of the incremental change of the logarithm of a function with respect to an incremental change of the logarithm of the argument. This definition of elasticity is also called _____, and is the limit of arc elasticity between two points.

The term elasticity is widely used in economics; see elasticity for details.

a. Harmonic analysis
c. Concave down
b. Total variation
d. Point elasticity

47. In mathematics, _____ are functions which can be used to prove the stability of a certain fixed point in a dynamical system or autonomous differential equation. Named after the Russian mathematician Aleksandr Mikhailovich Lyapunov, _____ are important to stability theory and control theory.

Functions which might prove the stability of some equilibrium are called Lyapunov-candidate-functions.

a. Butterfly effect
c. 120-cell
b. Lyapunov functions
d. 1-center problem

48. In statistics, _____ has two related meanings:

- the arithmetic _____.
- the expected value of a random variable, which is also called the population _____.

It is sometimes stated that the '_____' _____s average. This is incorrect if '_____' is taken in the specific sense of 'arithmetic _____' as there are different types of averages: the _____, median, and mode. For instance, average house prices almost always use the median value for the average.

For a real-valued random variable X, the _____ is the expectation of X.

a. Mean
c. Probability
b. Statistical population
d. Proportional hazards model

49. In calculus, the _____ states, roughly, that given a section of a smooth curve, there is at least one point on that section at which the derivative of the curve is equal to the 'average' derivative of the section. It is used to prove theorems that make global conclusions about a function on an interval starting from local hypotheses about derivatives at points of the interval.

This theorem can be understood concretely by applying it to motion: if a car travels one hundred miles in one hour, so that its average speed during that time was 100 miles per hour, then at some time its instantaneous speed must have been exactly 100 miles per hour.

   a. Functional integration
   b. Calculus controversy
   c. Fundamental Theorem of Calculus
   d. Mean Value Theorem

50. In economics, a _____ exists when a specific individual or enterprise has sufficient control over a particular product or service to determine significantly the terms on which other individuals shall have access to it. Monopolies are thus characterized by a lack of economic competition for the good or service that they provide and a lack of viable substitute goods. The verb 'monopolize' refers to the process by which a firm gains persistently greater market share than what is expected under perfect competition.

   a. 2-3 heap
   b. 1-center problem
   c. Monopoly
   d. 120-cell

Chapter 4. One-Variable Calculus: Chain Rule

1. In calculus, the _____ is a formula for the derivative of the composite of two functions.

In intuitive terms, if a variable, y, depends on a second variable, u, which in turn depends on a third variable, x, then the rate of change of y with respect to x can be computed as the rate of change of y with respect to u multiplied by the rate of change of u with respect to x. Schematically,

$$\frac{dy}{dx} = \frac{dy}{du} \cdot \frac{du}{dx}.$$

For an explanation of notation used in this section, see Function composition.

The _____ states that, under appropriate conditions,

$$(f \circ g)'(x) = f'(g(x))g'(x),$$

which in short form is written as

$$(f \circ g)' = f' \circ g \cdot g'.$$

Alternatively, in the Leibniz notation, the _____ is

$$\frac{dy}{dx} = \frac{dy}{du} \cdot \frac{du}{dx}.$$

In integration, the counterpart to the _____ is the substitution rule.

a. 120-cell
b. Chain Rule
c. Product rule
d. 1-center problem

2. In economics, the _____ functional form of production functions is widely used to represent the relationship of an output to inputs. It was proposed by Knut Wicksell, and tested against statistical evidence by Paul Douglas and Charles Cobb in 1928.
a. State price vector
b. Burden of proof
c. State price
d. Cobb-Douglas

3. A _____ number is a positive integer which has a positive divisor other than one or itself. By definition, every integer greater than one is either a prime number or a _____ number.zero and one are considered to be neither prime nor _____. For example, the integer 14 is a _____ number because it can be factored as 2 × 7.
a. Composite
b. Key server
c. Discontinuity
d. Basis

4. The mathematical concept of a _____ expresses the intuitive idea of deterministic dependence between two quantities, one of which is viewed as primary and the other as secondary. A _____ then is a way to associate a unique output for each input of a specified type, for example, a real number or an element of a given set.

a. Going up
b. Coherent
c. Grill
d. Function

5. In mathematics, the _____ of a number to a given base is the power or exponent to which the base must be raised in order to produce the number.

For example, the _____ of 1000 to the base 10 is 3, because 3 is how many 10s one must multiply to get 1000: thus 10 × 10 × 10 = 1000; the base-2 _____ of 32 is 5 because 5 is how many 2s one must multiply to get 32: thus 2 × 2 × 2 × 2 × 2 = 32. In the language of exponents: $10^3 = 1000$, so $\log_{10} 1000 = 3$, and $2^5 = 32$, so $\log_2 32 = 5$.

a. 2-3 heap
b. Logarithm
c. 1-center problem
d. 120-cell

6. The function $\log_b(x)$ depends on both b and x, but the term _____ (or logarithmic function) in standard usage refers to a function of the form $\log_b(x)$ in which the base b is fixed and so the only argument is x. Thus there is one _____ for each value of the base b (which must be positive and must differ from 1.) Viewed in this way, the base-b _____ is the inverse function of the exponential function b^x.

a. 1-center problem
b. 120-cell
c. 2-3 heap
d. Logarithm function

7. In ecology, predation describes a biological interaction where a _____ (an organism that is hunting) feeds on its prey, the organism that is attacked. _____s may or may not kill their prey prior to feeding on them, but the act of predation always results in the death of the prey. The other main category of consumption is detritivory, the consumption of dead organic material (detritus.)

a. 120-cell
b. 1-center problem
c. Prey
d. Predator

8. In mathematics, an _____ is a generalization for the concept of a function in which the dependent variable has not been given 'explicitly' in terms of the independent variable. To give a function f explicitly is to provide a prescription for determining the value of the function y in terms of the input value x:

$$y = f$$

a. Ordinary differential equation
b. Inflection point
c. Implicit differentiation
d. Implicit Function

9. In the branch of mathematics called multivariable calculus, the _____ is a tool which allows relations to be converted to functions. It does this by representing the relation as the graph of a function. There may not be a single function whose graph is the entire relation, but there may be such a function on a restriction of the domain of the relation.

a. Inverse function theorem
b. Implicit Function Theorem
c. A Mathematical Theory of Communication
d. A chemical equation

10. This article will state and prove the _____ for differentiation, and then use it to prove these two formulas.

The _____ for differentiation states that for every natural number n, the derivative of $f(x) = x^n$ is $f'(x) = nx^{n-1}$, that is,

$$(x^n)' = nx^{n-1}.$$

The _____ for integration

$$\int x^n \, dx = \frac{x^{n+1}}{n+1} + C$$

for natural n is then an easy consequence. One just needs to take the derivative of this equality and use the _____ and linearity of differentiation on the right-hand side.

a. Standard part function
b. Functional integration
c. Periodic function
d. Power Rule

11. In mathematics, a _____ is a statement that can be proved on the basis of explicitly stated or previously agreed assumptions.
a. Boolean function
b. Disjunction introduction
c. Theorem
d. Logical value

12. In mathematics, the _____ of a number n is the number that, when added to n, yields zero. The _____ of n is denoted −n. For example, 7 is −7, because 7 + (−7) = 0, and the _____ of −0.3 is 0.3, because −0.3 + 0.3 = 0.
a. Additive inverse
b. Associativity
c. Arity
d. Algebraic structure

13. In economics, an _____ is a function that maps the quantity of output supplied to the market price for that output.

In mathematical terms, if the demand function is , then the _____ is f $^{-1}$

a. Arrow-Debreu model
b. Internal rate of return
c. Enterprise value
d. Inverse demand function

14. In mathematics, an _____ is a function which associates distinct arguments with distinct values.

An _____ is called an injection, and is also said to be an information-preserving or one-to-one function.

A function f that is not injective is sometimes called many-to-one.

a. A chemical equation
b. Injective function
c. Unary function
d. A Mathematical Theory of Communication

15. An _____ is a function which does the reverse of a given function.
    a. Empty function
    b. Empty set
    c. A Mathematical Theory of Communication
    d. Inverse Function

16. In mathematics, the _____ gives sufficient conditions for a vector-valued function to be invertible on an open region containing a point in its domain. Further, the theorem shows the total derivative of the inverse function exists and gives a formula for it. The theorem can be generalized to maps defined on manifolds, and on infinite dimensional Banach spaces.
    a. Isoperimetric inequality
    b. A chemical equation
    c. A Mathematical Theory of Communication
    d. Inverse Function Theorem

Chapter 5. Exponents and Logarithms

1. In mathematics and computer science, _____ (also base-16, hexa or base, of 16. It uses sixteen distinct symbols, most often the symbols 0-9 to represent values zero to nine, and A, B, C, D, E, F (or a through f) to represent values ten to fifteen.

Its primary use is as a human friendly representation of binary coded values, so it is often used in digital electronics and computer engineering.

   a. Tetradecimal
   b. Factoradic
   c. Radix
   d. Hexadecimal

2. Exponentiation is a mathematical operation, written a^n, involving two numbers, the base a and the _____ n. When n is a positive integer, exponentiation corresponds to repeated multiplication:

$$a^n = \underbrace{a \times \cdots \times a}_{n},$$

just as multiplication by a positive integer corresponds to repeated addition:

$$a \times n = \underbrace{a + \cdots + a}_{n}.$$

The _____ is usually shown as a superscript to the right of the base. The exponentiation a^n can be read as: a raised to the n-th power, a raised to the power [of] n or possibly a raised to the _____ [of] n, or more briefly: a to the n-th power or a to the power [of] n, or even more briefly: a to the n.

   a. Exponent
   b. Exponential tree
   c. Exponential sum
   d. Exponentiating by squaring

3. The _____ is a function in mathematics. The application of this function to a value x is written as ex. Equivalently, this can be written in the form e^x, where e is a mathematical constant, the base of the natural logarithm, which equals approximately 2.718281828, and is also known as Euler's number.
   a. A chemical equation
   b. A Mathematical Theory of Communication
   c. Area hyperbolic functions
   d. Exponential function

4. The mathematical concept of a _____ expresses the intuitive idea of deterministic dependence between two quantities, one of which is viewed as primary and the other as secondary. A _____ then is a way to associate a unique output for each input of a specified type, for example, a real number or an element of a given set.
   a. Coherent
   b. Grill
   c. Going up
   d. Function

5. In mathematics, a _____ is a statement that can be proved on the basis of explicitly stated or previously agreed assumptions.
   a. Disjunction introduction
   b. Boolean function
   c. Logical value
   d. Theorem

Chapter 5. Exponents and Logarithms

6. In mathematics, the _____ of a number to a given base is the power or exponent to which the base must be raised in order to produce the number.

For example, the _____ of 1000 to the base 10 is 3, because 3 is how many 10s one must multiply to get 1000: thus 10 × 10 × 10 = 1000; the base-2 _____ of 32 is 5 because 5 is how many 2s one must multiply to get 32: thus 2 × 2 × 2 × 2 × 2 = 32. In the language of exponents: 10^3 = 1000, so $\log_{10} 1000 = 3$, and $2^5 = 32$, so $\log_2 32 = 5$.

   a. 1-center problem   b. 120-cell
   c. 2-3 heap   d. Logarithm

7. The _____, formerly known as the hyperbolic logarithm, is the logarithm to the base e, where e is an irrational constant approximately equal to 2.718 281 828. It is also sometimes referred to as the Napierian logarithm, although the original meaning of this term is slightly different. In simple terms, the _____ of a number x is the power to which e would have to be raised to equal x -- for example the natural log of e itself is 1 because $e^1 = e$, while the _____ of 1 would be 0, since $e^0 = 1$.

   a. Natural logarithm   b. Logarithmic growth
   c. Logarithmic identities   d. 1-center problem

8. The Condorcet candidate or _____ of an election is the candidate who, when compared with every other candidate, is preferred by more voters. Informally, the _____ is the person who would win a two-candidate election against each of the other candidates. A _____ will not always exist in a given set of votes, which is known as Condorcet's voting paradox.

   a. Condorcet winner   b. 120-cell
   c. Psephology   d. 1-center problem

9. In differential geometry, a discipline within mathematics, a _____ is a subset of the tangent bundle of a manifold satisfying certain properties. _____s are used to build up notions of integrability, and specifically of a foliation of a manifold.

   a. Discontinuity   b. Distribution
   c. Constraint   d. Coherence

10. In mathematics, specifically in combinatorial commutative algebra, a convex lattice polytope P is called _____ if it has the following property: given any positive integer n, every lattice point of the dilation nP, obtained from P by scaling its vertices by the factor n and taking the convex hull of the resulting points, can be written as the sum of exactly n lattice points in P. This property plays an important role in the theory of toric varieties, where it corresponds to projective normality of the toric variety determined by P.

The simplex in R^k with the vertices at the origin and along the unit coordinate vectors is _____.

   a. Demihypercubes   b. Polytetrahedron
   c. Hypercube   d. Normal

Chapter 5. Exponents and Logarithms

11. The _____ is an important family of continuous probability distributions, applicable in many fields. Each member of the family may be defined by two parameters, location and scale: the mean and variance respectively. The standard _____ is the _____ with a mean of zero and a variance of one.

   a. Coefficient of variation
   b. Percentile rank
   c. Null hypothesis
   d. Normal distribution

12. _____ is the likelihood or chance that something is the case or will happen. Theoretical _____ is used extensively in areas such as statistics, mathematics, science and philosophy to draw conclusions about the likelihood of potential events and the underlying mechanics of complex systems.

   The word _____ does not have a consistent direct definition.

   a. Statistical significance
   b. Standardized moment
   c. Probability
   d. Discrete random variable

13. In probability theory and statistics, a _____ identifies either the probability of each value of an unidentified random variable, or the probability of the value falling within a particular interval. The probability function describes the range of possible values that a random variable can attain and the probability that the value of the random variable is within any subset of that range.

   When the random variable takes values in the set of real numbers, the _____ is completely described by the cumulative distribution function, whose value at each real x is the probability that the random variable is smaller than or equal to x.

   a. Normal distribution
   b. Z-test
   c. Statistical graphics
   d. Probability distribution

14. This article will state and prove the _____ for differentiation, and then use it to prove these two formulas.

The _____ for differentiation states that for every natural number n, the derivative of $f(x) = x^n$ is $f'(x) = nx^{n-1}$, that is,

$$(x^n)' = nx^{n-1}.$$

The _____ for integration

$$\int x^n \, dx = \frac{x^{n+1}}{n+1} + C$$

for natural n is then an easy consequence. One just needs to take the derivative of this equality and use the _____ and linearity of differentiation on the right-hand side.

a. Periodic function
b. Functional integration
c. Standard part function
d. Power Rule

15. _____ is an important concept in economics with broad applications in game theory, engineering and the social sciences. The term is named after Vilfredo Pareto, an Italian economist who used the concept in his studies of economic efficiency and income distribution.

Given a set of alternative allocations of, say, goods or income for a set of individuals, a change from one allocation to another that can make at least one individual better off without making any other individual worse off is called a Pareto improvement.

a. Multiunit auction
b. Pursuit-evasion
c. Quasi-perfect equilibrium
d. Pareto efficiency

16. In computational complexity theory, an algorithm is said to take _____ if the asymptotic upper bound for the time it requires is proportional to the size of the input, which is usually denoted n.

Informally spoken, the running time increases linearly with the size of the input. For example, a procedure that adds up all elements of a list requires time proportional to the length of the list.

a. Truth table reduction
b. Time-constructible function
c. Linear time
d. Constructible function

Chapter 6. Introduction to Linear Algebra

1. In mathematics, _____ are functions which can be used to prove the stability of a certain fixed point in a dynamical system or autonomous differential equation. Named after the Russian mathematician Aleksandr Mikhailovich Lyapunov, _____ are important to stability theory and control theory.

Functions which might prove the stability of some equilibrium are called Lyapunov-candidate-functions.

   a. 1-center problem
   b. Butterfly effect
   c. 120-cell
   d. Lyapunov functions

2. The mathematical concept of a _____ expresses the intuitive idea of deterministic dependence between two quantities, one of which is viewed as primary and the other as secondary. A _____ then is a way to associate a unique output for each input of a specified type, for example, a real number or an element of a given set.
   a. Going up
   b. Grill
   c. Coherent
   d. Function

3. A _____ is an algebraic equation in which each term is either a constant or the product of a constant and a single variable. _____s can have one, two, three or more variables.

   _____s occur with great regularity in applied mathematics.

   a. Quadratic equation
   b. Quartic equation
   c. Difference of two squares
   d. Linear equation

4. A _____ is a mathematical model of a system based on the use of a linear operator. _____s typically exhibit features and properties that are much simpler than the general, nonlinear case. As a mathematical abstraction or idealization, _____s find important applications in automatic control theory, signal processing, and telecommunications.
   a. Hybrid system
   b. Linear system
   c. Percolation
   d. Predispositioning Theory

5. The Condorcet candidate or _____ of an election is the candidate who, when compared with every other candidate, is preferred by more voters. Informally, the _____ is the person who would win a two-candidate election against each of the other candidates. A _____ will not always exist in a given set of votes, which is known as Condorcet's voting paradox.
   a. Psephology
   b. Condorcet winner
   c. 120-cell
   d. 1-center problem

6. The _____ governs the differentiation of products of differentiable functions.
   a. Reciprocal Rule
   b. Product Rule
   c. 120-cell
   d. 1-center problem

7. In Boolean algebra, any Boolean function can be expressed in a _____ using the dual concepts of minterms and maxterms. All logical functions are expressible in _____, both as a 'sum of minterms' and as a 'product of maxterms'. This allows for greater analysis into the simplification of these functions, which is of great importance in the minimization of digital circuits.

Chapter 6. Introduction to Linear Algebra

    a. Reduct
    c. Topological module
    b. Multiplicative digital root
    d. Canonical form

8. In economics, _____ and economies of scale are related terms that describe what happens as the scale of production increases. They are different terms and are not to be used interchangeably.

_____ refers to a technical property of production that examines changes in output subsequent to a proportional change in all inputs (where all inputs increase by a constant factor.)

    a. Producer surplus
    c. Consumer surplus
    b. Marginal rate of technical substitution
    d. Returns to scale

9. In mathematics, an _____ is a generalization for the concept of a function in which the dependent variable has not been given 'explicitly' in terms of the independent variable. To give a function f explicitly is to provide a prescription for determining the value of the function y in terms of the input value x:

    y = f

    a. Implicit differentiation
    c. Ordinary differential equation
    b. Inflection point
    d. Implicit Function

10. In the branch of mathematics called multivariable calculus, the _____ is a tool which allows relations to be converted to functions. It does this by representing the relation as the graph of a function. There may not be a single function whose graph is the entire relation, but there may be such a function on a restriction of the domain of the relation.

    a. Inverse function theorem
    c. A chemical equation
    b. A Mathematical Theory of Communication
    d. Implicit Function Theorem

11. In mathematics, a _____ is a statement that can be proved on the basis of explicitly stated or previously agreed assumptions.

    a. Disjunction introduction
    c. Boolean function
    b. Logical value
    d. Theorem

12. In mathematics, a _____ is a constant multiplicative factor of a certain object. For example, in the expression $9x^2$, the _____ of x^2 is 9.

The object can be such things as a variable, a vector, a function, etc.

    a. Stability radius
    c. Coefficient
    b. Multivariate division algorithm
    d. Fibonacci polynomials

Chapter 6. Introduction to Linear Algebra

13. _____ refers to an action or object coming from outside a system. It is the opposite of endogenous, something generated from within the system.

- In an economic model, an _____ change is one that comes from outside the model and is unexplained by the model. For example, in the simple supply and demand model, a change in consumer tastes or preferences is unexplained by the model and also leads to endogenous changes in demand that lead to changes in the equilibrium price. Put another way, an _____ change involves an alteration of a variable that is autonomous.

- In linear regression, it means that the variable is independent of all other response values.

- In biology, '_____' refers to an action or object coming from the outside of a system. For example, an _____ contrast agent in medical imaging refers to a liquid injected into the patient intravenously that enhances visibility of a pathology, such as a tumor.

a. A chemical equation
b. A posteriori
c. A Mathematical Theory of Communication
d. Exogenous

14. A _____, named after the Russian mathematician Andrey Markov, is a mathematical model for the random evolution of a memoryless system, that is, one for which the likelihood of a given future state, at any given moment, depends only on its present state, and not on any past states.

In a common description, a stochastic process with the Markov property, or memorylessness, is one for which conditional on the present state of the system, its future and past are independent.

Often, the term Markov chain is used to mean a discrete-time _____.

a. Random measure
b. Polar distribution
c. Hellinger distance
d. Markov process

15. In mathematics, the _____ is a representation of a function as an infinite sum of terms calculated from the values of its derivatives at a single point. It may be regarded as the limit of the Taylor polynomials. _____ are named after English mathematician Brook Taylor.

a. Taylor series
b. C^r topology
c. 1-center problem
d. Local linearity

16. In mathematics, a _____ is often represented as the sum of a sequence of terms. That is, a _____ is represented as a list of numbers with addition operations between them, for example this arithmetic sequence:

1 + 2 + 3 + 4 + 5 + ... + 99 + 100

In most cases of interest the terms of the sequence are produced according to a certain rule, such as by a formula, by an algorithm, by a sequence of measurements, or even by a random number generator.

a. Blind
b. Contact
c. Series
d. Concavity

Chapter 6. Introduction to Linear Algebra

17. In mathematics, a _____, named after Andrey Markov, is a stochastic process with the Markov property. Having the Markov property means that, given the present state, future states are independent of the past states. In other words, the description of the present state fully captures all the information that could influence the future evolution of the process. Future states will be reached through a probabilistic process instead of a deterministic one.
    a. Markov chain
    b. Possibility theory
    c. Variance-to-mean ratio
    d. Law of Truly Large Numbers

18. _____ County lies just north of the Mexican border--sharing a border with Tijuana--and lies south of Orange County. It is home to miles of beaches, a mild Mediterranean climate and 16 military facilities hosting the United States Navy, the United States Coast Guard and the United States Marine Corps.

    _____'s economy is largely composed of agriculture, biotechnology/biosciences, computer sciences, electronics manufacturing, defense-related manufacturing, financial and business services, ship-repair and construction, software development, telecommunications, and tourism.

    a. 2-3 heap
    b. 120-cell
    c. 1-center problem
    d. San Diego

19. In mathematics, a recurrence relation is an equation that defines a sequence recursively: each term of the sequence is defined as a function of the preceding terms.

    A _____ is a specific type of recurrence relation.

    An example of a recurrence relation is the logistic map:

    $$x_{n+1} = rx_n(1 - x_n).$$

    Some simply defined recurrence relations can have very complex behaviours and are sometimes studied by physicists and mathematicians in a field of mathematics known as nonlinear analysis.

    a. Continuant
    b. Laws of Form
    c. Digital root
    d. Difference equation

20. In differential geometry, a discipline within mathematics, a _____ is a subset of the tangent bundle of a manifold satisfying certain properties. _____s are used to build up notions of integrability, and specifically of a foliation of a manifold
    a. Discontinuity
    b. Coherence
    c. Distribution
    d. Constraint

21. In mathematics and in the sciences, a _____ (plural: _____e, formulæ or _____s) is a concise way of expressing information symbolically (as in a mathematical or chemical _____), or a general relationship between quantities. One of many famous _____e is Albert Einstein's E = mc² (see special relativity

    In mathematics, a _____ is a key to solve an equation with variables. For example, the problem of determining the volume of a sphere is one that requires a significant amount of integral calculus to solve.

a. 2-3 heap
b. 120-cell
c. 1-center problem
d. Formula

22. In economics and consumer theory, a _____ is that which people consume more of as price rises, violating the law of demand. In normal situations, as the price of such a good rises, the substitution effect causes people to purchase less of it and more of substitute goods. In the _____ situation, cheaper close substitutes are not available.
   a. 120-cell
   b. Giffen good
   c. 2-3 heap
   d. 1-center problem

23. In mathematics, the _____ of a number n is the number that, when added to n, yields zero. The _____ of n is denoted −n. For example, 7 is −7, because 7 + (−7) = 0, and the _____ of −0.3 is 0.3, because −0.3 + 0.3 = 0.
   a. Algebraic structure
   b. Associativity
   c. Arity
   d. Additive inverse

24. An _____ is a function which does the reverse of a given function.
   a. A Mathematical Theory of Communication
   b. Empty function
   c. Inverse Function
   d. Empty set

25. In mathematics, the _____ gives sufficient conditions for a vector-valued function to be invertible on an open region containing a point in its domain. Further, the theorem shows the total derivative of the inverse function exists and gives a formula for it. The theorem can be generalized to maps defined on manifolds, and on infinite dimensional Banach spaces.
   a. Isoperimetric inequality
   b. A chemical equation
   c. A Mathematical Theory of Communication
   d. Inverse Function Theorem

26. In model theory, a complete theory is called _____ if it does not have too many types. One goal of classification theory is to divide all complete theories into those whose models can be classified and those whose models are too complicated to classify, and to classify all models in the cases where this can be done. Roughly speaking, if a theory is not _____ then its models are too complicated and numerous to classify, while if a theory is _____ there might be some hope of classifying its models, especially if the theory is superstable or totally transcendental.
   a. Spectrum of a theory
   b. Stable
   c. Non-standard calculus
   d. Transfer principle

27. This article will state and prove the _____ for differentiation, and then use it to prove these two formulas.

The _____ for differentiation states that for every natural number n, the derivative of $f(x) = x^n$ is $f'(x) = nx^{n-1}$, that is,

$$(x^n)' = nx^{n-1}.$$

The _____ for integration

$$\int x^n \, dx = \frac{x^{n+1}}{n+1} + C$$

for natural n is then an easy consequence. One just needs to take the derivative of this equality and use the _____ and linearity of differentiation on the right-hand side.

a. Standard part function
b. Functional integration
c. Periodic function
d. Power Rule

28. Georg Friedrich Bernhard _____ was a German mathematician who made important contributions to analysis and differential geometry, some of them paving the way for the later development of general relativity.

_____ was born in Breselenz, a village near Dannenberg in the Kingdom of Hanover in what is today Germany. His father, Friedrich Bernhard _____, was a poor Lutheran pastor in Breselenz who fought in the Napoleonic Wars.

a. Brook Taylor
b. Paul C. van Oorschot
c. Gustave Bertrand
d. Riemann

29. In mathematics, a _____ is a method for approximating the total area underneath a curve on a graph, otherwise known as an integral. It may also be used to define the integration operation. The sums are named after the German mathematician Bernhard Riemann.

a. Riemann sum
b. Multiple integral
c. Solid of revolution
d. Singular measure

30. In statistics, _____ is one measure of desirability of an estimator. The _____ of an unbiased statistic T is defined as

$$e(T) = \frac{1/\mathcal{I}(\theta)}{\mathrm{var}(T)}$$

where $\mathcal{I}(\theta)$ is the Fisher information of the sample. Thus e is the minimum possible variance for an unbiased estimator divided by its actual variance.

a. Efficiency
b. ISAAC
c. Anomaly
d. Advice

31. The _____ is an observable concept in economics that measures the increase in personal consumer spending that occurs with an increase in disposable income. For example, if a household earns one extra dollar of disposable income, and the _____ is 0.65, then of that dollar, the household will spend 65 cents and save 35 cents.

Mathematically, the _____ function is expressed as the derivative of the consumption function with respect to disposable income.

a. 120-cell
b. 2-3 heap
c. 1-center problem
d. Marginal propensity to consume

Chapter 6. Introduction to Linear Algebra

32. The _____ refers to the increase in saving that results from an increase in income. For example, if a household earns one extra dollar, and the _____ is 0.35, then of that dollar, the household will spend 65 cents and save 35 cents. It can also go the other way, referring to the decrease in saving that results from a decrease in income.

   a. 2-3 heap
   b. 1-center problem
   c. Marginal propensity to save
   d. 120-cell

33. _____ is the demand for financial assets, such as securities, money or foreign currency; it is money people want in case of emergency.

In economic theory, specifically Keynesian economics, _____ is one of the determinants of demand for money, the others being transactions demand and Speculative demand.

   a. Marshallian demand function
   b. Hicksian demand function
   c. 1-center problem
   d. Precautionary demand

34. _____ is the demand for financial assets, such as securities, money or foreign currency that is not dictated by real transactions such as trade, or financing.

The need for cash to take advantage of investment opportunities that may arise.

In economic theory, specifically Keynesian economics, _____ is one of the determinants of demand for money (and credit), the others being transactions demand and precautionary demand.

   a. 2-3 heap
   b. 1-center problem
   c. Speculative demand
   d. 120-cell

35. _____ is an important concept in economics with broad applications in game theory, engineering and the social sciences. The term is named after Vilfredo Pareto, an Italian economist who used the concept in his studies of economic efficiency and income distribution.

Given a set of alternative allocations of, say, goods or income for a set of individuals, a change from one allocation to another that can make at least one individual better off without making any other individual worse off is called a Pareto improvement.

   a. Pursuit-evasion
   b. Multiunit auction
   c. Pareto efficiency
   d. Quasi-perfect equilibrium

36. In mathematics, the _____ or Pythagoras' theorem is a relation in Euclidean geometry among the three sides of a right triangle. The theorem is named after the Greek mathematician Pythagoras, who by tradition is credited with its discovery and proof, although it is often argued that knowledge of the theory predates him.. The theorem is as follows:

In any right triangle, the area of the square whose side is the hypotenuse is equal to the sum of the areas of the squares whose sides are the two legs.

Chapter 6. Introduction to Linear Algebra

a. 1-center problem
c. Pythagorean Theorem
b. 2-3 heap
d. 120-cell

37. In finance, _____ rate of profit or sometimes just return, is the ratio of money gained or lost on an investment relative to the amount of money invested. The amount of money gained or lost may be referred to as interest, profit/loss, gain/loss, or net income/loss. The money invested may be referred to as the asset, capital, principal, or the cost basis of the investment.
    a. Return on equity
    b. 1-center problem
    c. P/E ratio
    d. Rate of return

38. In finance, _____ or 'shorting' is the practice of selling a financial instrument that the seller does not own at the time of the sale. _____ is done with intent of later purchasing the financial instrument at a lower price. Short-sellers attempt to profit from an expected decline in the price of a financial instrument.
    a. 1-center problem
    b. 2-3 heap
    c. 120-cell
    d. Short selling

39. In mathematics, the term _____ has several different important meanings:

    - An _____ is an equality that remains true regardless of the values of any variables that appear within it, to distinguish it from an equality which is true under more particular conditions. For this, the 'triple bar' symbol ≡ is sometimes used.
    - In algebra, an _____ or _____ element of a set S with a binary operation Â· is an element e that, when combined with any element x of S, produces that same x. That is, eÂ·x = xÂ·e = x for all x in S.
        - The _____ function from a set S to itself, often denoted id or id$_S$, s the function such that i = x for all x in S. This function serves as the _____ element in the set of all functions from S to itself with respect to function composition.
        - In linear algebra, the _____ matrix of size n is the n-by-n square matrix with ones on the main diagonal and zeros elsewhere. This matrix serves as the _____ with respect to matrix multiplication.

A common example of the first meaning is the trigonometric _____

$$\sin^2 \theta + \cos^2 \theta = 1$$

which is true for all real values of θ, as opposed to

$$\cos \theta = 1,$$

which is true only for some values of θ, not all. For example, the latter equation is true when $\theta = 0$, false when $\theta = 2$

Chapter 6. Introduction to Linear Algebra 35

The concepts of 'additive _____' and 'multiplicative _____' are central to the Peano axioms. The number 0 is the 'additive _____' for integers, real numbers, and complex numbers. For the real numbers, for all $a \in \mathbb{R}$,

$$0 + a = a,$$

$a + 0 = a$, and

$$0 + 0 = 0.$$

Similarly, The number 1 is the 'multiplicative _____' for integers, real numbers, and complex numbers.

   a. Action
   c. Identity
   b. Intersection
   d. ARIA

40. _____ is a branch of mathematics which focuses on the study of matrices. Initially a sub-branch of linear algebra, it has grown to cover subjects related to graph theory, algebra, combinatorics, and statistics as well.

The term matrix was first coined in 1848 by J.J. Sylvester as a name of an array of numbers.

   a. Semi-simple operators
   c. Segre classification
   b. Matrix theory
   d. Pairing

41. In financial economics, a _____ security is a contract that agrees to pay one unit of a numeraire if a particular state occurs at a particular time in the future and pay zero numeraire in all other states. The price of this security is the _____ of this particular state of the world, which may be represented by a vector. The _____ vector is the vector of _____s for all states.

   a. Beyond the shadow of a doubt
   c. State price vector
   b. State price
   d. Howland will forgery trial

42. In financial economics, a state-price security is a contract that agrees to pay one unit of a numeraire if a particular state occurs at a particular time in the future and pay zero numeraire in all other states. The price of this security is the state price of this particular state of the world, which may be represented by a vector. The _____ is the vector of state prices for all states.

   a. Radar gun
   c. Law of excluded middle
   b. Pareto principle
   d. State price vector

43. In physics and in _____ calculus, a _____ is a concept characterized by a magnitude and a direction. A _____ can be thought of as an arrow in Euclidean space, drawn from an initial point A pointing to a terminal point B.

   a. Deviation
   c. Dominance
   b. Constraint
   d. Vector

44. In mathematics, a _____ is a rectangular table of elements, which may be numbers or, more generally, any abstract quantities that can be added and multiplied. Matrices are used to describe linear equations, keep track of the coefficients of linear transformations and to record data that depend on multiple parameters. Matrices are described by the field of _____ theory.

    a. Coherent
    b. Compression
    c. Matrix
    d. Double counting

45. In linear algebra, a row vector or _____ is a 1 × n matrix, that is, a matrix consisting of a single row:

$$\mathbf{x} = \begin{bmatrix} x_1 & x_2 & \ldots & x_m \end{bmatrix}.$$

The transpose of a row vector is a column vector:

$$\begin{bmatrix} x_1 \\ x_2 \\ \vdots \\ x_m \end{bmatrix} = \begin{bmatrix} x_1 & x_2 & \ldots & x_m \end{bmatrix}^\mathrm{T}.$$

The set of all row vectors forms a vector space which is the dual space to the set of all column vectors.

Row vectors are sometimes written using the following non-standard notation:

$$\mathbf{x} = \begin{bmatrix} x_1, x_2, \ldots, x_m \end{bmatrix}.$$

- Matrix multiplication involves the action of multiplying each row vector of one matrix by each column vector of another matrix.

- The dot product of two vectors a and b is equivalent to multiplying the row vector representation of a by the column vector representation of b:

$$\mathbf{a} \cdot \mathbf{b} = \begin{bmatrix} a_1 & a_2 & a_3 \end{bmatrix} \begin{bmatrix} b_1 \\ b_2 \\ b_3 \end{bmatrix}.$$

    a. Dual vector space
    b. Row Matrix
    c. Gram-Schmidt process
    d. Woodbury matrix identity

Chapter 7. Systems of Linear Equations

1. In economics, the _____ functional form of production functions is widely used to represent the relationship of an output to inputs. It was proposed by Knut Wicksell, and tested against statistical evidence by Paul Douglas and Charles Cobb in 1928.
   a. State price
   b. State price vector
   c. Burden of proof
   d. Cobb-Douglas

2. The mathematical concept of a _____ expresses the intuitive idea of deterministic dependence between two quantities, one of which is viewed as primary and the other as secondary. A _____ then is a way to associate a unique output for each input of a specified type, for example, a real number or an element of a given set.
   a. Function
   b. Coherent
   c. Grill
   d. Going up

3. In mathematics, an _____ is a generalization for the concept of a function in which the dependent variable has not been given 'explicitly' in terms of the independent variable. To give a function f explicitly is to provide a prescription for determining the value of the function y in terms of the input value x:

   y = f

   a. Implicit differentiation
   b. Implicit Function
   c. Ordinary differential equation
   d. Inflection point

4. In the branch of mathematics called multivariable calculus, the _____ is a tool which allows relations to be converted to functions. It does this by representing the relation as the graph of a function. There may not be a single function whose graph is the entire relation, but there may be such a function on a restriction of the domain of the relation.
   a. Implicit Function Theorem
   b. Inverse function theorem
   c. A chemical equation
   d. A Mathematical Theory of Communication

5. Georg Friedrich Bernhard _____ was a German mathematician who made important contributions to analysis and differential geometry, some of them paving the way for the later development of general relativity.

   _____ was born in Breselenz, a village near Dannenberg in the Kingdom of Hanover in what is today Germany. His father, Friedrich Bernhard _____, was a poor Lutheran pastor in Breselenz who fought in the Napoleonic Wars.

   a. Brook Taylor
   b. Paul C. van Oorschot
   c. Gustave Bertrand
   d. Riemann

6. In mathematics, a _____ is a method for approximating the total area underneath a curve on a graph, otherwise known as an integral. It may also be used to define the integration operation. The sums are named after the German mathematician Bernhard Riemann.
   a. Singular measure
   b. Solid of revolution
   c. Multiple integral
   d. Riemann sum

7. In mathematics, a _____ is a statement that can be proved on the basis of explicitly stated or previously agreed assumptions.

Chapter 7. Systems of Linear Equations

a. Theorem
c. Boolean function
b. Logical value
d. Disjunction introduction

8. In mathematics, a _____ is a constant multiplicative factor of a certain object. For example, in the expression $9x^2$, the _____ of x^2 is 9.

The object can be such things as a variable, a vector, a function, etc.

a. Multivariate division algorithm
c. Coefficient
b. Fibonacci polynomials
d. Stability radius

9. The _____ is a basic theorem used to solve maximization problems in microeconomics. It may be used to prove Hotelling's lemma, Shephard's lemma, and Roy's identity. The statement of the theorem is:

Consider an arbitrary maximization problem where the objective function (f) depends on some parameter (a):

$$M(a) = \max_x f(x, a)$$

where the function M(a) gives the maximized value of the objective function (f) as a function of the parameter (a.)

a. Envelope Theorem
c. A posteriori
b. A Mathematical Theory of Communication
d. A chemical equation

10. In computational complexity theory, the complexity class _____ is the union of the classes in the exponential hierarchy.

$$\text{ELEMENTARY} = \text{EXP} \cup \text{2EXP} \cup \text{3EXP} \cup \cdots$$
$$= \text{DTIME}(2^n) \cup \text{DTIME}(2^{2^n}) \cup \text{DTIME}(2^{2^{2^n}}) \cup \cdots$$

The name was coined by Laszlo Kalmar, in the context of recursive functions and undecidability; most problems in it are far from _____. Some natural recursive problems lie outside _____, and are thus NONELEMENTARY.

a. Elementary
c. A Mathematical Theory of Communication
b. A posteriori
d. A chemical equation

11. In the study of metric spaces in mathematics, there are various notions of two metrics on the same underlying space being 'the same', or _____.

In the following, M will denote a non-empty set and d_1 and d_2 will denote two metrics on M.

The two metrics d_1 and d_2 are said to be topologically _____ if they generate the same topology on M.

a. A Mathematical Theory of Communication
b. A posteriori
c. Equivalent
d. A chemical equation

12. In linear algebra, _____ is a version of Gaussian elimination that puts zeros both above and below each pivot element as it goes from the top row of the given matrix to the bottom. In other words, _____ brings a matrix to reduced row echelon form, whereas Gaussian elimination takes it only as far as row echelon form. Every matrix has a reduced row echelon form, and this algorithm is guaranteed to produce it.
   a. Gauss-Jordan elimination
   b. Lax equivalence theorem
   c. Spheroidal wave functions
   d. Conservation form

13. In linear algebra, _____ is an efficient algorithm for solving systems of linear equations, finding the rank of a matrix, and calculating the inverse of an invertible square matrix. _____ is named after German mathematician and scientist Carl Friedrich Gauss.

Elementary row operations are used to reduce a matrix to row echelon form.

   a. Crout matrix decomposition
   b. Cholesky decomposition
   c. Gaussian elimination
   d. Conjugate gradient method

14. In mathematics, a _____ is a rectangular table of elements, which may be numbers or, more generally, any abstract quantities that can be added and multiplied. Matrices are used to describe linear equations, keep track of the coefficients of linear transformations and to record data that depend on multiple parameters. Matrices are described by the field of _____ theory.
   a. Coherent
   b. Double counting
   c. Compression
   d. Matrix

15. In several fields of mathematics the term _____ is used with different but closely related meanings. They all relate to the notion of mapping the elements of a set to other elements of the same set, i.e., exchanging elements of a set.

The general concept of _____ can be defined more formally in different contexts:

In combinatorics, a _____ is usually understood to be a sequence containing each element from a finite set once, and only once.

   a. Tensor product
   b. Cyclic permutation
   c. Linearly independent
   d. Permutation

16. In mathematics, in matrix theory, a _____ is a square-matrix that has exactly one entry 1 in each row and each column and 0's elsewhere. Each such matrix represents a specific permutation of m elements and, when used to multiply another matrix, can produce that permutation in the rows or columns of the other matrix.

Given a permutation π of m elements,

$$\pi : \{1, \ldots, m\} \to \{1, \ldots, m\}$$

given in two-line form by

$$\begin{pmatrix} 1 & 2 & \cdots & m \\ \pi(1) & \pi(2) & \cdots & \pi(m) \end{pmatrix},$$

its _____ is the m × m matrix P_π whose entries are all 0 except that in row i, the entry equals 1.

    a. Cartan matrix   b. Partitioned matrix
    c. Permutation Matrix   d. Hessenberg matrix

17. The process of solving a linear system of equations that has been transformed into row-echelon form or reduced row-echelon form is _____. The last equation is solved first, then the next-to-last, and so.
    a. LU decomposition   b. Back substitution
    c. Crout matrix decomposition   d. Jacobi rotation

18. In microeconomics, a consumer's _____ specifies what the consumer would buy in each price and wealth situation, assuming it perfectly solves the utility maximization problem. Marshallian demand is sometimes called Walrasian demand or uncompensated demand function instead, because the original Marshallian analysis ignored wealth effects.

According to the utility maximization problem, there are L commodities with prices p.

    a. 1-center problem   b. Precautionary demand
    c. Marshallian demand function   d. Hicksian demand function

19. In linear algebra, the _____ of a matrix is obtained by changing a matrix in some way.

Given the matrices A and B, where:

$$A = \begin{bmatrix} 1 & 3 & 2 \\ 2 & 0 & 1 \\ 5 & 2 & 2 \end{bmatrix}, \quad B = \begin{bmatrix} 4 \\ 3 \\ 1 \end{bmatrix}$$

Then, the _____ is written as:

$$(A|B) = \begin{bmatrix} 1 & 3 & 2 & 4 \\ 2 & 0 & 1 & 3 \\ 5 & 2 & 2 & 1 \end{bmatrix}$$

This is useful when solving systems of linear equations or the _____ may also be used to find the inverse of a matrix by combining it with the identity matrix.

$$C = \begin{bmatrix} 1 & 3 \\ -5 & 0 \end{bmatrix}$$

Let C be a square 2×2 matrix where

To find the inverse of C we create where I is the 2×2 identity matrix.

- a. Unimodular polynomial matrix
- b. Eigendecomposition
- c. Alternating sign matrix
- d. Augmented matrix

20. In mathematics the concept of a _____ generalizes notions such as 'length', 'area', and 'volume'. Informally, given some base set, a '_____' is any consistent assignment of 'sizes' to the subsets of the base set. Depending on the application, the 'size' of a subset may be interpreted as its physical size, the amount of something that lies within the subset, or the probability that some random process will yield a result within the subset.
- a. Cusp
- b. Congruent
- c. Lattice
- d. Measure

21. In statistics and mathematical epidemiology, _____ is the risk of an event relative to exposure. _____ is a ratio of the probability of the event occurring in the exposed group versus a non-exposed group.

$$RR = \frac{p_{\text{exposed}}}{p_{\text{non-exposed}}}$$

For example, if the probability of developing lung cancer among smokers was 20% and among non-smokers 1%, then the _____ of cancer associated with smoking would be 20.

- a. Statistical epidemiology
- b. 1-center problem
- c. Mendelian randomization
- d. Relative risk

22. _____ is a concept in economics, finance, and psychology related to the behaviour of consumers and investors under uncertainty. _____ is the reluctance of a person to accept a bargain with an uncertain payoff rather than another bargain with a more certain, but possibly lower, expected payoff.

The inverse of a person's _____ is sometimes called their risk tolerance.

- a. Stochastic modelling
- b. Ruin theory
- c. Life table
- d. Risk aversion

23. In linear algebra a matrix is in _____ if

- All nonzero rows are above any rows of all zeroes, and
- The leading coefficient of a row is always strictly to the right of the leading coefficient of the row above it.

This is the definition used in this article, but some texts add a third condition:

- The leading coefficient of each nonzero row is one.

A matrix is in reduced _____ if it satisfies the above three conditions, and if, in addition

- Every leading coefficient is the only nonzero entry in its column.

The first non-zero entry in each row is called a pivot.

This matrix is in reduced _____:

$$\begin{bmatrix} 0 & 1 & 4 & 0 & 0 \\ 0 & 0 & 0 & 1 & 0 \\ 0 & 0 & 0 & 0 & 1 \\ 0 & 0 & 0 & 0 & 0 \end{bmatrix}.$$

The following matrix is also in _____, but not in reduced row form:

$$\begin{bmatrix} 1 & 1 & 1 & 1 \\ 0 & 9 & 0 & 2 \\ 0 & 0 & 0 & 3 \end{bmatrix}.$$

However, this matrix is not in _____, as the leading coefficient of row 3 is not strictly to the right of the leading coefficient of row 2.

$$\begin{bmatrix} 1 & 2 & 3 & 4 \\ 0 & 3 & 7 & 2 \\ 0 & 2 & 0 & 0 \end{bmatrix}$$

Every non-zero matrix can be reduced to an infinite number of echelon forms via elementary matrix transformations.

a. Portable, Extensible Toolkit for Scientific Computation
b. Reduced row echelon form
c. Gaussian elimination
d. Row echelon form

24. A _____ is any zero that leads a number string with a non-zero value. For example, James Bond's famous identifier, 007, has two _____s. Often, _____s are found on non-electronic and LED digital displays that contain fixed sets of digits, such as the manual counter, the stopwatch, the odometer, and the digital clock.
a. Scientific notation
b. Radix point
c. 1-center problem
d. Leading zero

Chapter 7. Systems of Linear Equations 43

25. _____ describes the property of operations in mathematics and computer science which means that multiple applications of the operation does not change the result. The concept of _____ arises in a number of places in abstract algebra.

There are several meanings of _____, depending on what the concept is applied to:

- A unary operation is called idempotent if, whenever it is applied twice to any value, it gives the same result as if it were applied once. For example, the absolute value function is idempotent as a function from the set of real numbers to the set of real numbers: ab = ab.
- A binary operation is called idempotent if, whenever it is applied to two equal values, it gives that value as the result. For example, the operation giving the maximum value of two values is idempotent: ma = x.
- Given a binary operation, an idempotent element for the operation is a value for which the operation, when given that value for both of its operands, gives the value as the result. For example, the number 1 is an idempotent of multiplication: 1 × 1 = 1.

A unary operation f that is a map from some set S into itself is called idempotent if, for all x in S,

f

In particular, the identity function id_S, defined by
id_S, is idempotent, as is the constant function K_c, where c is an element of S, defined by $K_c(x) = c$.

- a. Idempotence
- b. Ordered exponential
- c. Antiisomorphism
- d. Absorption law

26. In mathematics, an _____ or member of a set is any one of the distinct objects that make up that set.

Writing A = {1,2,3,4}, means that the _____s of the set A are the numbers 1, 2, 3 and 4. Groups of _____s of A, for example {1,2}, are subsets of A.

- a. Order
- b. Ideal
- c. Universal code
- d. Element

27. In mathematics and in the sciences, a _____ (plural: _____e, formulæ or _____s) is a concise way of expressing information symbolically (as in a mathematical or chemical _____), or a general relationship between quantities. One of many famous _____e is Albert Einstein's $E = mc^2$ (see special relativity

In mathematics, a _____ is a key to solve an equation with variables. For example, the problem of determining the volume of a sphere is one that requires a significant amount of integral calculus to solve.

- a. Formula
- b. 1-center problem
- c. 2-3 heap
- d. 120-cell

28. In mathematics, the term _____ has several different important meanings:

- An _____ is an equality that remains true regardless of the values of any variables that appear within it, to distinguish it from an equality which is true under more particular conditions. For this, the 'triple bar' symbol ≡ is sometimes used.
- In algebra, an _____ or _____ element of a set S with a binary operation Â· is an element e that, when combined with any element x of S, produces that same x. That is, eÂ·x = xÂ·e = x for all x in S.
  - The _____ function from a set S to itself, often denoted id or id$_S$, s the function such that i = x for all x in S. This function serves as the _____ element in the set of all functions from S to itself with respect to function composition.
  - In linear algebra, the _____ matrix of size n is the n-by-n square matrix with ones on the main diagonal and zeros elsewhere. This matrix serves as the _____ with respect to matrix multiplication.

A common example of the first meaning is the trigonometric _____

$$\sin^2\theta + \cos^2\theta = 1$$

which is true for all real values of θ, as opposed to

$$\cos\theta = 1,$$

which is true only for some values of θ, not all. For example, the latter equation is true when $\theta = 0$, false when $\theta = 2$

The concepts of 'additive _____' and 'multiplicative _____' are central to the Peano axioms. The number 0 is the 'additive _____' for integers, real numbers, and complex numbers. For the real numbers, for all $a \in \mathbb{R}$,

$$0 + a = a,$$

$$a + 0 = a, \text{ and}$$

$$0 + 0 = 0.$$

Similarly, The number 1 is the 'multiplicative _____' for integers, real numbers, and complex numbers.

a. Action
c. Intersection
b. Identity
d. ARIA

29. In linear algebra, the _____ or unit matrix of size n is the n-by-n square matrix with ones on the main diagonal and zeros elsewhere. It is denoted by I_n, or simply by I if the size is immaterial or can be trivially determined by the context. (In some fields, such as quantum mechanics, the _____ is denoted by a boldface one, 1; otherwise it is identical to I.)

a. Associativity
c. Arity

b. Unital
d. Identity matrix

30. In mathematics, the _____ or Pythagoras' theorem is a relation in Euclidean geometry among the three sides of a right triangle. The theorem is named after the Greek mathematician Pythagoras, who by tradition is credited with its discovery and proof, although it is often argued that knowledge of the theory predates him.. The theorem is as follows:

In any right triangle, the area of the square whose side is the hypotenuse is equal to the sum of the areas of the squares whose sides are the two legs.

a. 120-cell
c. 1-center problem

b. Pythagorean Theorem
d. 2-3 heap

31. In linear algebra a matrix is in row echelon form if

- All nonzero rows are above any rows of all zeroes, and
- The leading coefficient of a row is always strictly to the right of the leading coefficient of the row above it.

This is the definition used in this article, but some texts add a third condition:

- The leading coefficient of each nonzero row is one.

A matrix is in _____ (also called row canonical form) if it satisfies the above three conditions, and if, in addition

- Every leading coefficient is the only nonzero entry in its column.

The first non-zero entry in each row is called a pivot.

This matrix is in _____:

$$\begin{bmatrix} 0 & 1 & 4 & 0 & 0 \\ 0 & 0 & 0 & 1 & 0 \\ 0 & 0 & 0 & 0 & 1 \\ 0 & 0 & 0 & 0 & 0 \end{bmatrix}.$$

The following matrix is also in row echelon form, but not in reduced row form:

$$\begin{bmatrix} 1 & 1 & 1 & 1 \\ 0 & 9 & 0 & 2 \\ 0 & 0 & 0 & 3 \end{bmatrix}.$$

However, this matrix is not in row echelon form, as the leading coefficient of row 3 is not strictly to the right of the leading coefficient of row 2.

$$\begin{bmatrix} 1 & 2 & 3 & 4 \\ 0 & 3 & 7 & 2 \\ 0 & 2 & 0 & 0 \end{bmatrix}$$

Every non-zero matrix can be reduced to an infinite number of echelon forms (they can all be multiples of each other, for example) via elementary matrix transformations.

a. Basic Linear Algebra Subprograms
b. Folded spectrum method
c. Pseudospectrum
d. Reduced row echelon form

32. In mathematics, the _____ of a number n is the number that, when added to n, yields zero. The _____ of n is denoted −n. For example, 7 is −7, because 7 + (−7) = 0, and the _____ of −0.3 is 0.3, because −0.3 + 0.3 = 0.
a. Associativity
b. Arity
c. Algebraic structure
d. Additive inverse

33. An _____ is a function which does the reverse of a given function.
a. Inverse Function
b. A Mathematical Theory of Communication
c. Empty set
d. Empty function

34. In mathematics, the _____ gives sufficient conditions for a vector-valued function to be invertible on an open region containing a point in its domain. Further, the theorem shows the total derivative of the inverse function exists and gives a formula for it. The theorem can be generalized to maps defined on manifolds, and on infinite dimensional Banach spaces.
a. A chemical equation
b. Isoperimetric inequality
c. A Mathematical Theory of Communication
d. Inverse Function Theorem

35. In linear algebra, a row vector or _____ is a 1 × n matrix, that is, a matrix consisting of a single row:

$$\mathbf{x} = \begin{bmatrix} x_1 & x_2 & \ldots & x_m \end{bmatrix}.$$

The transpose of a row vector is a column vector:

$$\begin{bmatrix} x_1 \\ x_2 \\ \vdots \\ x_m \end{bmatrix} = \begin{bmatrix} x_1 & x_2 & \ldots & x_m \end{bmatrix}^T.$$

The set of all row vectors forms a vector space which is the dual space to the set of all column vectors.

Chapter 7. Systems of Linear Equations

Row vectors are sometimes written using the following non-standard notation:

$$\mathbf{x} = \begin{bmatrix} x_1, x_2, \ldots, x_m \end{bmatrix}.$$

- Matrix multiplication involves the action of multiplying each row vector of one matrix by each column vector of another matrix.

- The dot product of two vectors a and b is equivalent to multiplying the row vector representation of a by the column vector representation of b:

$$\mathbf{a} \cdot \mathbf{b} = \begin{bmatrix} a_1 & a_2 & a_3 \end{bmatrix} \begin{bmatrix} b_1 \\ b_2 \\ b_3 \end{bmatrix}.$$

a. Woodbury matrix identity
c. Row Matrix

b. Gram-Schmidt process
d. Dual vector space

36. In financial economics, a _____ security is a contract that agrees to pay one unit of a numeraire if a particular state occurs at a particular time in the future and pay zero numeraire in all other states. The price of this security is the _____ of this particular state of the world, which may be represented by a vector. The _____ vector is the vector of _____s for all states.

a. Howland will forgery trial
c. State price vector

b. Beyond the shadow of a doubt
d. State price

37. In mathematics, a group G is called _____ if there is a subset S of G such that any element of G can be written in one and only one way as a product of finitely many elements of S and their inverses.

A related but different notion is a _____ abelian group.

_____ groups first arose in the study of hyperbolic geometry, as examples of Fuchsian groups.

a. Boolean algebra
c. Free

b. Leibniz formula
d. Barycentric coordinates

38. In mathematics, and in other disciplines involving formal languages, including mathematical logic and computer science, a _____ is a notation that specifies places in an expression where substitution may take place. The idea is related to a placeholder, or a wildcard character that stands for an unspecified symbol.

The variable x becomes a bound variable, for example, when we write

'For all x,² = x² + 2x + 1.'

or

'There exists x such that x² = 2.'

In either of these propositions, it does not matter logically whether we use x or some other letter.

a. 120-cell
c. Free variable
b. 1-center problem
d. 2-3 heap

39. In mathematics, the _____ of an abelian group measures how large a group is in terms of how large a vector space over the rational numbers one would need to 'contain' it; or alternatively how large a free abelian group it can contain as a subgroup.

The _____ of a finite abelian group has a different definition.

An abelian group is often thought of as composed of its torsion subgroup T, and its torsion-free part A/T.

a. Coherence
c. Chord
b. Discontinuity
d. Rank

40. In microeconomics, a consumer's _____ function is the demand of a consumer over a bundle of goods that minimizes their expenditure while delivering a fixed level of utility. The function is named after John Hicks.

Mathematically,

$$h(p, \bar{u}) = \arg\min_x \sum_i p_i x_i$$
$$\text{such that } u(x) > \bar{u}$$

where h is the _____ function, or commodity bundle demanded, at price level p and utility level $\bar{u}$.

a. Precautionary demand
c. 1-center problem
b. Marshallian demand function
d. Hicksian demand

41. If $A_1, A_2, ..., A_n$ are _____ square matrices over a field, then

$$(A_1 A_2 \cdots A_n)^{-1} = A_n^{-1} A_{n-1}^{-1} \cdots A_1^{-1}.$$

Chapter 7. Systems of Linear Equations

It becomes evident why this is the case if one attempts to find an inverse for the product of the A_is from first principles, that is, that we wish to determine B such that

$$(A_1 A_2 \cdots A_n) B = I$$

where B is the inverse matrix of the product. To remove A_1 from the product, we can then write

$$A_1^{-1}(A_1 A_2 \cdots A_n) B = A_1^{-1} I$$

which would reduce the equation to

$$(A_2 A_3 \cdots A_n) B = A_1^{-1} I.$$

Likewise, then, from

$$A_2^{-1}(A_2 A_3 \cdots A_n) B = A_2^{-1} A_1^{-1} I$$

which simplifies to

$$(A_3 A_4 \cdots A_n) B = A_2^{-1} A_1^{-1} I.$$

If one repeat the process up to A_n, the equation becomes

$$B = A_n^{-1} A_{n-1}^{-1} \cdots A_2^{-1} A_1^{-1} I$$

$$B = A_n^{-1} A_{n-1}^{-1} \cdots A_2^{-1} A_1^{-1}$$

but B is the inverse matrix, i.e. $B = (A_1 A_2 \cdots A_n)^{-1}$ so the property is established.

Over the field of real numbers, the set of singular n-by-n matrices, considered as a subset of $R^{n \times n}$, is a null set, i.e., has Lebesgue measure zero.

a. Jordan normal form
c. Nonsingular
b. Projection-valued measure
d. Matrix pencil

42. In algebra, a _____ is a function depending on n that associates a scalar, de, to every n×n square matrix A. The fundamental geometric meaning of a _____ is as the scale factor for measure when A is regarded as a linear transformation. _____s are important both in calculus, where they enter the substitution rule for several variables, and in multilinear algebra.

a. Pfaffian
c. Determinant
b. 1-center problem
d. Functional determinant

43. _____ and independent variables refer to values that change in relationship to each other. The _____ are those that are observed to change in response to the independent variables. The independent variables are those that are deliberately manipulated to invoke a change in the _____.
   a. Round robin test
   b. Steiner system
   c. Yates analysis
   d. Dependent variables

44. In an economic model, parameters or variables are said to be _____ when they are predicted by other variables in the model.

For example, in a simple supply and demand model, when predicting the quantity demanded, the price is _____ because consumers change their demand in response to the price. In contrast, a change in consumer tastes or preferences would be an exogenous change on the demand curve.

   a. A Mathematical Theory of Communication
   b. A chemical equation
   c. A posteriori
   d. Endogenous

45. _____ refers to an action or object coming from outside a system. It is the opposite of endogenous, something generated from within the system.

   - In an economic model, an _____ change is one that comes from outside the model and is unexplained by the model. For example, in the simple supply and demand model, a change in consumer tastes or preferences is unexplained by the model and also leads to endogenous changes in demand that lead to changes in the equilibrium price. Put another way, an _____ change involves an alteration of a variable that is autonomous.

   - In linear regression, it means that the variable is independent of all other response values.

   - In biology, '_____' refers to an action or object coming from the outside of a system. For example, an _____ contrast agent in medical imaging refers to a liquid injected into the patient intravenously that enhances visibility of a pathology, such as a tumor.

   a. A posteriori
   b. A chemical equation
   c. A Mathematical Theory of Communication
   d. Exogenous

46. Dependent variables and _____ refer to values that change in relationship to each other. The dependent variables are those that are observed to change in response to the _____. The _____ are those that are deliberately manipulated to invoke a change in the dependent variables.
   a. Independent variables
   b. One-factor-at-a-time method
   c. Operational confound
   d. Experimental design diagram

Chapter 8. Matrix Algebra

1. The _____ is a single-winner election method in which voters rank candidates in order of preference. The _____ determines the winner of an election by giving each candidate a certain number of points corresponding to the position in which he or she is ranked by each voter. Once all votes have been counted the candidate with the most points is the winner.
   a. 1-center problem
   b. 2-3 heap
   c. 120-cell
   d. Borda count

2. In economics, the _____ functional form of production functions is widely used to represent the relationship of an output to inputs. It was proposed by Knut Wicksell, and tested against statistical evidence by Paul Douglas and Charles Cobb in 1928.
   a. State price vector
   b. State price
   c. Burden of proof
   d. Cobb-Douglas

3. The Condorcet candidate or _____ of an election is the candidate who, when compared with every other candidate, is preferred by more voters. Informally, the _____ is the person who would win a two-candidate election against each of the other candidates. A _____ will not always exist in a given set of votes, which is known as Condorcet's voting paradox.
   a. 120-cell
   b. Psephology
   c. 1-center problem
   d. Condorcet winner

4. The mathematical concept of a _____ expresses the intuitive idea of deterministic dependence between two quantities, one of which is viewed as primary and the other as secondary. A _____ then is a way to associate a unique output for each input of a specified type, for example, a real number or an element of a given set.
   a. Grill
   b. Going up
   c. Coherent
   d. Function

5. In mathematics, the _____ is the square matrix of second-order partial derivatives of a function; that is, it describes the local curvature of a function of many variables. The _____ was developed in the 19th century by the German mathematician Ludwig Otto Hesse and later named after him. Hesse himself had used the term 'functional determinants'.
   a. Multivariable calculus
   b. Jacobian
   c. Hessian matrix
   d. Partial derivative

6. In mathematics, an _____ is a generalization for the concept of a function in which the dependent variable has not been given 'explicitly' in terms of the independent variable. To give a function f explicitly is to provide a prescription for determining the value of the function y in terms of the input value x:

   $y = f$

   a. Implicit differentiation
   b. Implicit Function
   c. Inflection point
   d. Ordinary differential equation

7. In the branch of mathematics called multivariable calculus, the _____ is a tool which allows relations to be converted to functions. It does this by representing the relation as the graph of a function. There may not be a single function whose graph is the entire relation, but there may be such a function on a restriction of the domain of the relation.
   a. A chemical equation
   b. Inverse function theorem
   c. A Mathematical Theory of Communication
   d. Implicit Function Theorem

8. In microeconomics, a consumer's _____ specifies what the consumer would buy in each price and wealth situation, assuming it perfectly solves the utility maximization problem. Marshallian demand is sometimes called Walrasian demand or uncompensated demand function instead, because the original Marshallian analysis ignored wealth effects.

According to the utility maximization problem, there are L commodities with prices p.

   a. 1-center problem
   b. Precautionary demand
   c. Hicksian demand function
   d. Marshallian demand function

9. _____ is an important concept in economics with broad applications in game theory, engineering and the social sciences. The term is named after Vilfredo Pareto, an Italian economist who used the concept in his studies of economic efficiency and income distribution.

Given a set of alternative allocations of, say, goods or income for a set of individuals, a change from one allocation to another that can make at least one individual better off without making any other individual worse off is called a Pareto improvement.

   a. Pursuit-evasion
   b. Multiunit auction
   c. Quasi-perfect equilibrium
   d. Pareto efficiency

10. In mathematics, the _____ is a representation of a function as an infinite sum of terms calculated from the values of its derivatives at a single point. It may be regarded as the limit of the Taylor polynomials. _____ are named after English mathematician Brook Taylor.

   a. 1-center problem
   b. C^r topology
   c. Local linearity
   d. Taylor series

11. In mathematics, a _____ is a statement that can be proved on the basis of explicitly stated or previously agreed assumptions.

   a. Disjunction introduction
   b. Boolean function
   c. Logical value
   d. Theorem

12. In mathematics, a _____ is a constant multiplicative factor of a certain object. For example, in the expression $9x^2$, the _____ of x^2 is 9.

The object can be such things as a variable, a vector, a function, etc.

   a. Multivariate division algorithm
   b. Coefficient
   c. Fibonacci polynomials
   d. Stability radius

13. _____ is a theory of microeconomics that relates preferences to consumer demand curves. The link between personal preferences, consumption, and the demand curve is one of the most complex relations in economics. Implicitly, economists assume that anything purchased will be consumed, unless the purchase is for a productive activity.

   a. Computational economic
   b. Consumer theory
   c. Tobit model
   d. Mathematical economics

Chapter 8. Matrix Algebra

14. In probability theory and statistics, _____ indicates the strength and direction of a linear relationship between two random variables. That is in contrast with the usage of the term in colloquial speech, denoting any relationship, not necessarily linear. In general statistical usage, _____ or co-relation refers to the departure of two random variables from independence.
    a. Correlation
    b. Sample size
    c. Summary statistics
    d. Random variables

15. _____s is concerned with the tasks of developing and applying quantitative or statistical methods to the study and elucidation of economic principles. _____s combines economic theory with statistics to analyze and test economic relationships. Theoretical _____s considers questions about the statistical properties of estimators and tests, while applied _____s is concerned with the application of _____ methods to assess economic theories.
    a. Econometric
    b. A Mathematical Theory of Communication
    c. Economic
    d. A chemical equation

16. A _____ is a structured activity, usually undertaken for enjoyment and sometimes also used as an educational tool. _____s are distinct from work, which is usually carried out for remuneration, and from art, which is more concerned with the expression of ideas. However, the distinction is not clear-cut, and many _____s are also considered to be work (such as professional players of spectator sports/_____s) or art (such as jigsaw puzzles or _____s involving an artistic layout such as Mah-jongg solitaire.)
    a. 2-3 heap
    b. 1-center problem
    c. Game
    d. 120-cell

17. _____ is a branch of mathematics which focuses on the study of matrices. Initially a sub-branch of linear algebra, it has grown to cover subjects related to graph theory, algebra, combinatorics, and statistics as well.

The term matrix was first coined in 1848 by J.J. Sylvester as a name of an array of numbers.

    a. Pairing
    b. Segre classification
    c. Semi-simple operators
    d. Matrix theory

18. In mathematics, a _____ is a rectangular table of elements, which may be numbers or, more generally, any abstract quantities that can be added and multiplied. Matrices are used to describe linear equations, keep track of the coefficients of linear transformations and to record data that depend on multiple parameters. Matrices are described by the field of _____ theory.
    a. Coherent
    b. Compression
    c. Double counting
    d. Matrix

19. In mathematics, a _____ is often represented as the sum of a sequence of terms. That is, a _____ is represented as a list of numbers with addition operations between them, for example this arithmetic sequence:

$$1 + 2 + 3 + 4 + 5 + ... + 99 + 100$$

In most cases of interest the terms of the sequence are produced according to a certain rule, such as by a formula, by an algorithm, by a sequence of measurements, or even by a random number generator.

a. Blind
b. Concavity
c. Contact
d. Series

20. The word _____ has many distinct meanings in different fields of knowledge, depending on their methodologies and the context of discussion. Broadly speaking we can say that a _____ is some kind of belief or claim that (supposedly) explains, asserts, or consolidates some class of claims. Additionally, in contrast with a theorem the statement of the _____ is generally accepted only in some tentative fashion as opposed to regarding it as having been conclusively established.
   a. Per mil
   b. Transport of structure
   c. Defined
   d. Theory

21. _____ is a branch of applied mathematics that is used in the social sciences, biology, engineering, political science, international relations, computer science, and philosophy. _____ attempts to mathematically capture behavior in strategic situations, in which an individual's success in making choices depends on the choices of others. While initially developed to analyze competitions in which one individual does better at another's expense, it has been expanded to treat a wide class of interactions, which are classified according to several criteria.
   a. Game theory
   b. Mathematical economics
   c. Computational economic
   d. Consumer theory

22. In mathematics the _____ of a set which is equipped with the operation of addition is an element which, when added to any element x in the set, yields x. One of the most familiar additive identities is the number 0 from elementary mathematics, but additive identities occur in other mathematical structures where addition is defined, such as in groups and rings.

   - The _____ familiar from elementary mathematics is zero, denoted 0. For example,

   $5 + 0 = 5 = 0 + 5.$

   - In the natural numbers N and all of its supersets, the _____ is 0. Thus for any one of these numbers n,

   $n + 0 = n = 0 + n.$

Let N be a set which is closed under the operation of addition, denoted +. An _____ for N is any element e such that for any element n in N,

   $e + n = n = n + e.$

   a. Unique factorization domain
   b. Unit ring
   c. Algebraically independent
   d. Additive identity

Chapter 8. Matrix Algebra

23. In mathematics, the term _____ has several different important meanings:

- An _____ is an equality that remains true regardless of the values of any variables that appear within it, to distinguish it from an equality which is true under more particular conditions. For this, the 'triple bar' symbol ≡ is sometimes used.
- In algebra, an _____ or _____ element of a set S with a binary operation Â· is an element e that, when combined with any element x of S, produces that same x. That is, eÂ·x = xÂ·e = x for all x in S.
    - The _____ function from a set S to itself, often denoted id or id_S, s the function such that i = x for all x in S. This function serves as the _____ element in the set of all functions from S to itself with respect to function composition.
    - In linear algebra, the _____ matrix of size n is the n-by-n square matrix with ones on the main diagonal and zeros elsewhere. This matrix serves as the _____ with respect to matrix multiplication.

A common example of the first meaning is the trigonometric _____

$$\sin^2 \theta + \cos^2 \theta = 1$$

which is true for all real values of θ, as opposed to

$$\cos \theta = 1,$$

which is true only for some values of θ, not all. For example, the latter equation is true when $\theta = 0$, false when $\theta = 2$

The concepts of 'additive _____' and 'multiplicative _____' are central to the Peano axioms. The number 0 is the 'additive _____' for integers, real numbers, and complex numbers. For the real numbers, for all $a \in \mathbb{R}$,

$$0 + a = a,$$

$$a + 0 = a,$$ and

$$0 + 0 = 0.$$

Similarly, The number 1 is the 'multiplicative _____' for integers, real numbers, and complex numbers.

a. Intersection
c. Action
b. ARIA
d. Identity

24. In mathematics, _____ is the operation of multiplying a matrix with either a scalar or another matrix

This is the most often used and most important way to multiply matrices.

a. Matrix multiplication　　　　　　　　　　b. Matrix calculus
c. Logarithmic norm　　　　　　　　　　　　d. Jordan matrix

25. _____ is the mathematical operation of scaling one number by another. It is one of the four basic operations in elementary arithmetic.

_____ is defined for whole numbers in terms of repeated addition; for example, 4 multiplied by 3 can be calculated by adding 3 copies of 4 together:

$$4 + 4 + 4 = 12.$$

_____ of rational numbers and real numbers is defined by systematic generalization of this basic idea.

a. Multiplication　　　　　　　　　　　　b. Highest common factor
c. Least common multiple　　　　　　　　d. The number 0 is even.

26. In mathematics, _____ is one of the basic operations defining a vector space in linear algebra. Note that _____ is different from scalar product which is an inner product between two vectors.

More specifically, if K is a field and V is a vector space over K, then _____ is a function from K × V to V.

a. Scalar multiplication　　　　　　　　b. Non-negative matrix factorization
c. Jordan normal form　　　　　　　　　d. Frobenius normal form

27. _____ describes the property of operations in mathematics and computer science which means that multiple applications of the operation does not change the result. The concept of _____ arises in a number of places in abstract algebra.

There are several meanings of _____, depending on what the concept is applied to:

- A unary operation is called idempotent if, whenever it is applied twice to any value, it gives the same result as if it were applied once. For example, the absolute value function is idempotent as a function from the set of real numbers to the set of real numbers: ab = ab.
- A binary operation is called idempotent if, whenever it is applied to two equal values, it gives that value as the result. For example, the operation giving the maximum value of two values is idempotent: ma = x.
- Given a binary operation, an idempotent element for the operation is a value for which the operation, when given that value for both of its operands, gives the value as the result. For example, the number 1 is an idempotent of multiplication: 1 × 1 = 1.

A unary operation f that is a map from some set S into itself is called idempotent if, for all x in S,

f

In particular, the identity function id_S, defined by
id_S, is idempotent, as is the constant function K_c, where c is an element of S, defined by $K_c(x) = c$.

   a. Antiisomorphism   b. Absorption law
   c. Ordered exponential   d. Idempotence

28. In mathematics, _____ is a property that a binary operation can have. It means that, within an expression containing two or more of the same associative operators in a row, the order that the operations are performed does not matter as long as the sequence of the operands is not changed. That is, rearranging the parentheses in such an expression will not change its value.
   a. Idempotence   b. Unital
   c. Associativity   d. Algebraically closed

29. The _____ is a rule which states that when you add or multiply numbers, changing the order doesn't change the result.
   a. Coimage   b. Commutative law
   c. Conditional event algebra   d. Semigroupoid

30. In mathematics, and in particular in abstract algebra, distributivity is a property of binary operations that generalises the _____ law from elementary algebra.
   a. Permutation   b. General linear group
   c. Closure with a twist   d. Distributive

31. In mathematics and in the sciences, a _____ (plural: _____e, formulæ or _____s) is a concise way of expressing information symbolically (as in a mathematical or chemical _____), or a general relationship between quantities. One of many famous _____e is Albert Einstein's $E = mc^2$ (see special relativity

In mathematics, a _____ is a key to solve an equation with variables. For example, the problem of determining the volume of a sphere is one that requires a significant amount of integral calculus to solve.

   a. Formula   b. 2-3 heap
   c. 1-center problem   d. 120-cell

32. In linear algebra, the _____ or unit matrix of size n is the n-by-n square matrix with ones on the main diagonal and zeros elsewhere. It is denoted by I_n, or simply by I if the size is immaterial or can be trivially determined by the context. (In some fields, such as quantum mechanics, the _____ is denoted by a boldface one, 1; otherwise it is identical to I.)
   a. Arity   b. Identity matrix
   c. Unital   d. Associativity

33. In mathematics the concept of a _____ generalizes notions such as 'length', 'area', and 'volume'. Informally, given some base set, a '_____' is any consistent assignment of 'sizes' to the subsets of the base set. Depending on the application, the 'size' of a subset may be interpreted as its physical size, the amount of something that lies within the subset, or the probability that some random process will yield a result within the subset.

a. Cusp
b. Measure
c. Lattice
d. Congruent

34. In statistics and mathematical epidemiology, _____ is the risk of an event relative to exposure. _____ is a ratio of the probability of the event occurring in the exposed group versus a non-exposed group.

$$RR = \frac{p_{\text{exposed}}}{p_{\text{non-exposed}}}$$

For example, if the probability of developing lung cancer among smokers was 20% and among non-smokers 1%, then the _____ of cancer associated with smoking would be 20.

a. Mendelian randomization
b. Statistical epidemiology
c. 1-center problem
d. Relative risk

35. _____ is a concept in economics, finance, and psychology related to the behaviour of consumers and investors under uncertainty. _____ is the reluctance of a person to accept a bargain with an uncertain payoff rather than another bargain with a more certain, but possibly lower, expected payoff.

The inverse of a person's _____ is sometimes called their risk tolerance.

a. Life table
b. Risk aversion
c. Stochastic modelling
d. Ruin theory

36. In linear algebra, the _____ of a matrix A is another matrix A^T created by any one of the following equivalent actions:

- write the rows of A as the columns of A^T
- write the columns of A as the rows of A^T
- reflect A by its main diagonal to obtain A^T

Formally, the _____ of an m × n matrix A is the n × m matrix

$$A^T_{ij} = A_{ji} \text{ for } 1 \leq i \leq n, 1 \leq j \leq m.$$

- $\begin{bmatrix} 1 & 2 \\ 3 & 4 \end{bmatrix}^T = \begin{bmatrix} 1 & 3 \\ 2 & 4 \end{bmatrix}.$

- $\begin{bmatrix} 1 & 2 \\ 3 & 4 \\ 5 & 6 \end{bmatrix}^T = \begin{bmatrix} 1 & 3 & 5 \\ 2 & 4 & 6 \end{bmatrix}.$

Chapter 8. Matrix Algebra

For matrices A, B and scalar c we have the following properties of _____:

1. $\left(\mathbf{A}^T\right)^T = \mathbf{A}$

   Taking the _____ is an involution.

- $(\mathbf{A}+\mathbf{B})^T = \mathbf{A}^T + \mathbf{B}^T$

   The _____ respects addition.

- $(\mathbf{AB})^T = \mathbf{B}^T\mathbf{A}^T$

   Note that the order of the factors reverses. From this one can deduce that a square matrix A is invertible if and only if A^T is invertible, and in this case we have^T =$^{-1}$. It is relatively easy to extend this result to the general case of multiple matrices, where we find that^T = $Z^T Y^T X^T ... C^T B^T A^T$.

- $(c\mathbf{A})^T = c\mathbf{A}^T$

   The _____ of a scalar is the same scalar. Together with, this states that the _____ is a linear map from the space of m × n matrices to the space of all n × m matrices.

- $\det(\mathbf{A}^T) = \det(\mathbf{A})$

   The determinant of a matrix is the same as that of its _____.

- The dot product of two column vectors a and b can be computed as

   $$\mathbf{a} \cdot \mathbf{b} = \mathbf{a}^T \mathbf{b},$$

   which is written as $a_i b^i$ in Einstein notation.
- If A has only real entries, then $A^T A$ is a positive-semidefinite matrix.
- $\left(\mathbf{A}^T\right)^{-1} = \left(\mathbf{A}^{-1}\right)^T$

   The _____ of an invertible matrix is also invertible, and its inverse is the _____ of the inverse of the original matrix.

- If A is a square matrix, then its eigenvalues are equal to the eigenvalues of its _____.

A square matrix whose _____ is equal to itself is called a symmetric matrix; that is, A is symmetric if

$$\mathbf{A}^T = \mathbf{A}.$$

A square matrix whose _____ is also its inverse is called an orthogonal matrix; that is, G is orthogonal if

$$\mathbf{GG}^T = \mathbf{G}^T\mathbf{G} = \mathbf{I}_n,$$ the identity matrix.

A square matrix whose _____ is equal to its negative is called skew-symmetric matrix; that is, A is skew-symmetric if

$$\mathbf{A}^T = -\mathbf{A}.$$

The conjugate _____ of the complex matrix A, written as A*, is obtained by taking the _____ of A and the complex conjugate of each entry:

$$\mathbf{A}^* = (\overline{\mathbf{A}})^T = \overline{(\mathbf{A}^T)}.$$

If f: V→W is a linear map between vector spaces V and W with nondegenerate bilinear forms, we define the _____ of f to be the linear map $^t f$: W→V, determined by

$$B_V(v, {}^t f(w)) = B_W(f(v), w) \quad \forall\ v \in V, w \in W.$$

Here, B_V and B_W are the bilinear forms on V and W respectively. The matrix of the _____ of a map is the transposed matrix only if the bases are orthonormal with respect to their bilinear forms.

Over a complex vector space, one often works with sesquilinear forms instead of bilinear.

- a. Polynomial matrix
- b. Tridiagonal matrix
- c. Transpose
- d. Cartan matrix

37. The _____ is a basic theorem used to solve maximization problems in microeconomics. It may be used to prove Hotelling's lemma, Shephard's lemma, and Roy's identity. The statement of the theorem is:

Consider an arbitrary maximization problem where the objective function (f) depends on some parameter (a):

$$M(a) = \max_x f(x, a)$$

where the function M(a) gives the maximized value of the objective function (f) as a function of the parameter (a.)

Chapter 8. Matrix Algebra

a. A posteriori
c. A Mathematical Theory of Communication
b. A chemical equation
d. Envelope Theorem

38. In linear algebra, a column vector or _____ is an m × 1 matrix, i.e. a matrix consisting of a single column of m elements.

$$\mathbf{x} = \begin{bmatrix} x_1 \\ x_2 \\ \vdots \\ x_m \end{bmatrix}$$

The transpose of a column vector is a row vector and vice versa.

The set of all column vectors forms a vector space which is the dual space to the set of all row vectors.

a. Spread of a matrix
c. Column matrix
b. Cayley-Hamilton theorem
d. Split-complex number

39. In several fields of mathematics the term _____ is used with different but closely related meanings. They all relate to the notion of mapping the elements of a set to other elements of the same set, i.e., exchanging elements of a set.

The general concept of _____ can be defined more formally in different contexts:

In combinatorics, a _____ is usually understood to be a sequence containing each element from a finite set once, and only once.

a. Linearly independent
c. Tensor product
b. Cyclic permutation
d. Permutation

40. In mathematics, in matrix theory, a _____ is a square-matrix that has exactly one entry 1 in each row and each column and 0's elsewhere. Each such matrix represents a specific permutation of m elements and, when used to multiply another matrix, can produce that permutation in the rows or columns of the other matrix.

Given a permutation π of m elements,

$$\pi : \{1, \ldots, m\} \to \{1, \ldots, m\}$$

given in two-line form by

$$\begin{pmatrix} 1 & 2 & \cdots & m \\ \pi(1) & \pi(2) & \cdots & \pi(m) \end{pmatrix},$$

its _____ is the m × m matrix P_π whose entries are all 0 except that in row i, the entry equals 1.

a. Cartan matrix
b. Hessenberg matrix
c. Partitioned matrix
d. Permutation Matrix

41. In linear algebra, a row vector or _____ is a 1 × n matrix, that is, a matrix consisting of a single row:

$$\mathbf{x} = \begin{bmatrix} x_1 & x_2 & \ldots & x_m \end{bmatrix}.$$

The transpose of a row vector is a column vector:

$$\begin{bmatrix} x_1 \\ x_2 \\ \vdots \\ x_m \end{bmatrix} = \begin{bmatrix} x_1 & x_2 & \ldots & x_m \end{bmatrix}^T.$$

The set of all row vectors forms a vector space which is the dual space to the set of all column vectors.

Row vectors are sometimes written using the following non-standard notation:

$$\mathbf{x} = \begin{bmatrix} x_1, x_2, \ldots, x_m \end{bmatrix}.$$

- Matrix multiplication involves the action of multiplying each row vector of one matrix by each column vector of another matrix.

- The dot product of two vectors a and b is equivalent to multiplying the row vector representation of a by the column vector representation of b:

$$\mathbf{a} \cdot \mathbf{b} = \begin{bmatrix} a_1 & a_2 & a_3 \end{bmatrix} \begin{bmatrix} b_1 \\ b_2 \\ b_3 \end{bmatrix}.$$

a. Woodbury matrix identity
b. Dual vector space
c. Gram-Schmidt process
d. Row Matrix

42. In mathematics, the concept of a _____ tries to capture the intuitive idea of a geometrical one-dimensional and continuous object. A simple example is the circle. In everyday use of the term '_____', a straight line is not curved, but in mathematical parlance _____s include straight lines and line segments.

a. Quadrifolium
c. Curve

b. Negative pedal curve
d. Kappa curve

43. In linear algebra, a _____ is a square matrix in which the entries outside the main diagonal are all zero. The diagonal entries themselves may or may not be zero. Thus, the matrix D = with n columns and n rows is diagonal if:

$$d_{i,j} = 0 \text{ if } i \neq j \quad \forall i,j \in \{1,2,\ldots,n\}$$

For example, the following matrix is diagonal:

$$\begin{bmatrix} 1 & 0 & 0 \\ 0 & 4 & 0 \\ 0 & 0 & -3 \end{bmatrix}.$$

The term _____ may sometimes refer to a rectangular _____, which is an m-by-n matrix with only the entries of the form $d_{i,i}$ possibly non-zero; for example,

$$\begin{bmatrix} 1 & 0 & 0 \\ 0 & 4 & 0 \\ 0 & 0 & -3 \\ 0 & 0 & 0 \end{bmatrix} \text{ or } \begin{bmatrix} 1 & 0 & 0 & 0 & 0 \\ 0 & 4 & 0 & 0 & 0 \\ 0 & 0 & -3 & 0 & 0 \end{bmatrix}.$$

a. Design matrix
c. Hankel matrix

b. Transition matrix
d. Diagonal matrix

44. If $A_1, A_2, \ldots, A_n$ are _____ square matrices over a field, then

$$(\mathbf{A}_1 \mathbf{A}_2 \cdots \mathbf{A}_n)^{-1} = \mathbf{A}_n^{-1} \mathbf{A}_{n-1}^{-1} \cdots \mathbf{A}_1^{-1}.$$

It becomes evident why this is the case if one attempts to find an inverse for the product of the A_is from first principles, that is, that we wish to determine B such that

$$(\mathbf{A}_1 \mathbf{A}_2 \cdots \mathbf{A}_n)\mathbf{B} = \mathbf{I}$$

where B is the inverse matrix of the product. To remove A_1 from the product, we can then write

$$\mathbf{A}_1^{-1}(\mathbf{A}_1 \mathbf{A}_2 \cdots \mathbf{A}_n)\mathbf{B} = \mathbf{A}_1^{-1}\mathbf{I}$$

which would reduce the equation to

$$(A_2 A_3 \cdots A_n)B = A_1^{-1} I.$$

Likewise, then, from

$$A_2^{-1}(A_2 A_3 \cdots A_n)B = A_2^{-1} A_1^{-1} I$$

which simplifies to

$$(A_3 A_4 \cdots A_n)B = A_2^{-1} A_1^{-1} I.$$

If one repeat the process up to A_n, the equation becomes

$$B = A_n^{-1} A_{n-1}^{-1} \cdots A_2^{-1} A_1^{-1} I$$

$$B = A_n^{-1} A_{n-1}^{-1} \cdots A_2^{-1} A_1^{-1}$$

but B is the inverse matrix, i.e. $B = (A_1 A_2 \cdots A_n)^{-1}$ so the property is established.

Over the field of real numbers, the set of singular n-by-n matrices, considered as a subset of $R^{n \times n}$, is a null set, i.e., has Lebesgue measure zero.

a. Matrix pencil
b. Jordan normal form
c. Projection-valued measure
d. Nonsingular

45. In linear algebra, a _____ is a square matrix, A, that is equal to its transpose

$$A = A^T.$$

The entries of a _____ are symmetric with respect to the main diagonal. So if the entries are written as A =, then

$$a_{ij} = a_{ji}$$

for all indices i and j. The following 3×3 matrix is symmetric:

$$\begin{bmatrix} 1 & 2 & 3 \\ 2 & 4 & -5 \\ 3 & -5 & 6 \end{bmatrix}.$$

A matrix is called skew-symmetric or antisymmetric if its transpose is the same as its negative.

a. Contour integration
b. Conway triangle notation
c. Broken-line graph
d. Symmetric matrix

46. In computational complexity theory, the complexity class _____ is the union of the classes in the exponential hierarchy.

$$\begin{aligned} \text{ELEMENTARY} &= \text{EXP} \cup \text{2EXP} \cup \text{3EXP} \cup \cdots \\ &= \text{DTIME}(2^n) \cup \text{DTIME}(2^{2^n}) \cup \text{DTIME}(2^{2^{2^n}}) \cup \cdots \end{aligned}$$

The name was coined by Laszlo Kalmar, in the context of recursive functions and undecidability; most problems in it are far from _____. Some natural recursive problems lie outside _____, and are thus NONELEMENTARY.

a. A Mathematical Theory of Communication
b. A chemical equation
c. A posteriori
d. Elementary

47. In mathematics, an elementary matrix is a simple matrix which differs from the identity matrix in a minimal way. The _____ generate the general linear group of invertible matrices, and left multiplication by an elementary matrix represent elementary row operations.

In algebraic K-theory, '_____' refers only to the row-addition matrices.

a. Antiunitary
b. Euclidean subspace
c. Elementary matrices
d. Orthogonal Procrustes problem

48. In mathematics, the _____ of a number n is the number that, when added to n, yields zero. The _____ of n is denoted −n. For example, 7 is −7, because 7 + (−7) = 0, and the _____ of −0.3 is 0.3, because −0.3 + 0.3 = 0.
a. Additive inverse
b. Algebraic structure
c. Arity
d. Associativity

49. An _____ is a function which does the reverse of a given function.
a. A Mathematical Theory of Communication
b. Inverse Function
c. Empty set
d. Empty function

50. In mathematics, the _____ gives sufficient conditions for a vector-valued function to be invertible on an open region containing a point in its domain. Further, the theorem shows the total derivative of the inverse function exists and gives a formula for it. The theorem can be generalized to maps defined on manifolds, and on infinite dimensional Banach spaces.
   a. A Mathematical Theory of Communication
   b. A chemical equation
   c. Isoperimetric inequality
   d. Inverse Function Theorem

51. Georg Friedrich Bernhard _____ was a German mathematician who made important contributions to analysis and differential geometry, some of them paving the way for the later development of general relativity.

   _____ was born in Breselenz, a village near Dannenberg in the Kingdom of Hanover in what is today Germany. His father, Friedrich Bernhard _____, was a poor Lutheran pastor in Breselenz who fought in the Napoleonic Wars.

   a. Gustave Bertrand
   b. Brook Taylor
   c. Paul C. van Oorschot
   d. Riemann

52. In mathematics, a _____ is a method for approximating the total area underneath a curve on a graph, otherwise known as an integral. It may also be used to define the integration operation. The sums are named after the German mathematician Bernhard Riemann.
   a. Riemann sum
   b. Solid of revolution
   c. Multiple integral
   d. Singular measure

53. This article will state and prove the _____ for differentiation, and then use it to prove these two formulas.

The _____ for differentiation states that for every natural number n, the derivative of $f(x) = x^n$ is $f'(x) = nx^{n-1}$, that is,

$$(x^n)' = nx^{n-1}.$$

The _____ for integration

$$\int x^n \, dx = \frac{x^{n+1}}{n+1} + C$$

for natural n is then an easy consequence. One just needs to take the derivative of this equality and use the _____ and linearity of differentiation on the right-hand side.

   a. Standard part function
   b. Functional integration
   c. Periodic function
   d. Power Rule

54. In the mathematical discipline of matrix theory, a block matrix or a _____ is a partition of a matrix into rectangular smaller matrices called blocks. Looking at it another way, the matrix is written in terms of smaller matrices written side-by-side. A block matrix must conform to a consistent way of splitting up the rows, and the columns: we group the rows into some adjacent 'bunches', and the columns likewise.

a. Polynomial matrix
b. Bidiagonal matrix
c. Binary matrix
d. Partitioned matrix

55. In mathematics, a _____ is a matrix formed by selecting certain rows and columns from a bigger matrix. That is, as an array, it is cut down to those entries constrained by row and column.

For example

$$\mathbf{A} = \begin{bmatrix} a_{11} & a_{12} & a_{13} & a_{14} \\ a_{21} & a_{22} & a_{23} & a_{24} \\ a_{31} & a_{32} & a_{33} & a_{34} \end{bmatrix}.$$

Then

$$\mathbf{A}[1,2;1,3,4] = \begin{bmatrix} a_{11} & a_{13} & a_{14} \\ a_{21} & a_{23} & a_{24} \end{bmatrix}$$

is a _____ of A formed by rows 1,2 and columns 1,3,4.

a. Jordan matrix
b. Matrix unit
c. Matrix decomposition
d. Submatrix

56. In linear algebra, the _____ is a matrix decomposition which writes a matrix as the product of a lower and upper triangular matrix. The product sometimes includes a permutation matrix as well. This decomposition is used in numerical analysis to solve systems of linear equations or calculate the determinant.

a. Stone's method
b. Row-echelon form
c. LU decomposition
d. Block matrix pseudoinverse

Chapter 9. Determinants: An Overview

1. In economics, the _____ functional form of production functions is widely used to represent the relationship of an output to inputs. It was proposed by Knut Wicksell, and tested against statistical evidence by Paul Douglas and Charles Cobb in 1928.
    a. State price vector
    b. State price
    c. Cobb-Douglas
    d. Burden of proof

2. In statistics, _____ has two related meanings:

    • the arithmetic _____.
    • the expected value of a random variable, which is also called the population _____.

It is sometimes stated that the '_____' _____s average. This is incorrect if '_____' is taken in the specific sense of 'arithmetic _____' as there are different types of averages: the _____, median, and mode. For instance, average house prices almost always use the median value for the average.

For a real-valued random variable X, the _____ is the expectation of X.

    a. Probability
    b. Mean
    c. Statistical population
    d. Proportional hazards model

3. In calculus, the _____ states, roughly, that given a section of a smooth curve, there is at least one point on that section at which the derivative of the curve is equal to the 'average' derivative of the section. It is used to prove theorems that make global conclusions about a function on an interval starting from local hypotheses about derivatives at points of the interval.

This theorem can be understood concretely by applying it to motion: if a car travels one hundred miles in one hour, so that its average speed during that time was 100 miles per hour, then at some time its instantaneous speed must have been exactly 100 miles per hour.

    a. Fundamental Theorem of Calculus
    b. Functional integration
    c. Calculus controversy
    d. Mean Value Theorem

4. In mathematics, a _____ is a statement that can be proved on the basis of explicitly stated or previously agreed assumptions.
    a. Logical value
    b. Boolean function
    c. Disjunction introduction
    d. Theorem

5. In algebra, a _____ is a function depending on n that associates a scalar, de, to every n×n square matrix A. The fundamental geometric meaning of a _____ is as the scale factor for measure when A is regarded as a linear transformation. _____s are important both in calculus, where they enter the substitution rule for several variables, and in multilinear algebra.
    a. Functional determinant
    b. Pfaffian
    c. 1-center problem
    d. Determinant

6. In mathematics and in the sciences, a _____ (plural: _____e, formulæ or _____s) is a concise way of expressing information symbolically (as in a mathematical or chemical _____), or a general relationship between quantities. One of many famous _____e is Albert Einstein's E = mc^2 (see special relativity

In mathematics, a _____ is a key to solve an equation with variables. For example, the problem of determining the volume of a sphere is one that requires a significant amount of integral calculus to solve.

- a. 1-center problem
- b. 2-3 heap
- c. Formula
- d. 120-cell

7. The mathematical concept of a _____ expresses the intuitive idea of deterministic dependence between two quantities, one of which is viewed as primary and the other as secondary. A _____ then is a way to associate a unique output for each input of a specified type, for example, a real number or an element of a given set.
- a. Grill
- b. Going up
- c. Coherent
- d. Function

8. In linear algebra, a _____ of a matrix A is the determinant of some smaller square matrix, cut down from A by removing one or more of its rows or columns.

_____s obtained by removing just one row and one column from square matrices are required for calculating matrix cofactors, which in turn are useful for computing both the determinant and inverse of square matrices.

Let A be an m × n matrix and k an integer with 0 < k ≤ m, and k ≤ n.

- a. Homogeneity
- b. Block size
- c. Minor
- d. Chiral

9. In linear algebra a matrix is in _____ if

- All nonzero rows are above any rows of all zeroes, and
- The leading coefficient of a row is always strictly to the right of the leading coefficient of the row above it.

This is the definition used in this article, but some texts add a third condition:

- The leading coefficient of each nonzero row is one.

A matrix is in reduced _____ if it satisfies the above three conditions, and if, in addition

- Every leading coefficient is the only nonzero entry in its column.

The first non-zero entry in each row is called a pivot.

This matrix is in reduced _____:

$$\begin{bmatrix} 0 & 1 & 4 & 0 & 0 \\ 0 & 0 & 0 & 1 & 0 \\ 0 & 0 & 0 & 0 & 1 \\ 0 & 0 & 0 & 0 & 0 \end{bmatrix}.$$

The following matrix is also in _____, but not in reduced row form:

$$\begin{bmatrix} 1 & 1 & 1 & 1 \\ 0 & 9 & 0 & 2 \\ 0 & 0 & 0 & 3 \end{bmatrix}.$$

However, this matrix is not in _____, as the leading coefficient of row 3 is not strictly to the right of the leading coefficient of row 2.

$$\begin{bmatrix} 1 & 2 & 3 & 4 \\ 0 & 3 & 7 & 2 \\ 0 & 2 & 0 & 0 \end{bmatrix}$$

Every non-zero matrix can be reduced to an infinite number of echelon forms via elementary matrix transformations.

   a. Reduced row echelon form   b. Gaussian elimination
   c. Portable, Extensible Toolkit for Scientific Computation   d. Row echelon form

10. In mathematics, a _____ is a rectangular table of elements, which may be numbers or, more generally, any abstract quantities that can be added and multiplied. Matrices are used to describe linear equations, keep track of the coefficients of linear transformations and to record data that depend on multiple parameters. Matrices are described by the field of _____ theory.
   a. Coherent   b. Compression
   c. Double counting   d. Matrix

11. If $A_1, A_2, ..., A_n$ are _____ square matrices over a field, then

$$(\mathbf{A}_1 \mathbf{A}_2 \cdots \mathbf{A}_n)^{-1} = \mathbf{A}_n^{-1} \mathbf{A}_{n-1}^{-1} \cdots \mathbf{A}_1^{-1}.$$

Chapter 9. Determinants: An Overview

It becomes evident why this is the case if one attempts to find an inverse for the product of the A_is from first principles, that is, that we wish to determine B such that

$$(A_1 A_2 \cdots A_n) B = I$$

where B is the inverse matrix of the product. To remove A_1 from the product, we can then write

$$A_1^{-1}(A_1 A_2 \cdots A_n) B = A_1^{-1} I$$

which would reduce the equation to

$$(A_2 A_3 \cdots A_n) B = A_1^{-1} I.$$

Likewise, then, from

$$A_2^{-1}(A_2 A_3 \cdots A_n) B = A_2^{-1} A_1^{-1} I$$

which simplifies to

$$(A_3 A_4 \cdots A_n) B = A_2^{-1} A_1^{-1} I.$$

If one repeat the process up to A_n, the equation becomes

$$B = A_n^{-1} A_{n-1}^{-1} \cdots A_2^{-1} A_1^{-1} I$$

$$B = A_n^{-1} A_{n-1}^{-1} \cdots A_2^{-1} A_1^{-1}$$

but B is the inverse matrix, i.e. $B = (A_1 A_2 \cdots A_n)^{-1}$ so the property is established.

Over the field of real numbers, the set of singular n-by-n matrices, considered as a subset of $R^{n \times n}$, is a null set, i.e., has Lebesgue measure zero.

a. Projection-valued measure
c. Jordan normal form
b. Nonsingular
d. Matrix pencil

12. In mathematics, the conjugate transpose, Hermitian transpose, or _____ of an m-by-n matrix A with complex entries is the n-by-m matrix A* obtained from A by taking the transpose and then taking the complex conjugate of each entry. The conjugate transpose is formally defined by

$$(A^*)_{ij} = \overline{A_{ji}}$$

where the subscripts denote the i,j-th entry, for 1 ≤ i ≤ n and 1 ≤ j ≤ m, and the overbar denotes a scalar complex conjugate.

This definition can also be written as

$$A^* = (\overline{A})^{\mathrm{T}} = \overline{A^{\mathrm{T}}}$$

where A^{T} denotes the transpose and $\overline{A}$ denotes the matrix with complex conjugated entries.

    a. Adjoint matrix
    c. Orthogonal Procrustes problem
    b. Invariant subspace
    d. Independent equation

13. In microeconomics, a consumer's _____ specifies what the consumer would buy in each price and wealth situation, assuming it perfectly solves the utility maximization problem. Marshallian demand is sometimes called Walrasian demand or uncompensated demand function instead, because the original Marshallian analysis ignored wealth effects.

According to the utility maximization problem, there are L commodities with prices p.

    a. Marshallian demand function
    c. Precautionary demand
    b. 1-center problem
    d. Hicksian demand function

14. In mathematics, the _____ of a number n is the number that, when added to n, yields zero. The _____ of n is denoted −n. For example, 7 is −7, because 7 + (−7) = 0, and the _____ of −0.3 is 0.3, because −0.3 + 0.3 = 0.
    a. Algebraic structure
    c. Arity
    b. Associativity
    d. Additive inverse

15. The _____, first developed by Sir John Hicks and Alvin Hansen, has been used from 1937 onwards to summarize a major part of Keynesian macroeconomics. IS/LM stands for Investment Saving / Liquidity preference Money supply.

The _____ was born at the Econometric Conference held in Oxford during September, 1936.

    a. A posteriori
    c. IS/LM model
    b. A chemical equation
    d. A Mathematical Theory of Communication

Chapter 10. Euclidean Spaces

1. In mathematics, a _____ is, informally, an infinitely vast and infinitely thin sheet. _____s may be thought of as objects in some higher dimensional space, or they may be considered without any outside space, as in the setting of Euclidean geometry
    a. Group
    b. Blocking
    c. Bandwidth
    d. Plane

2. The Condorcet candidate or _____ of an election is the candidate who, when compared with every other candidate, is preferred by more voters. Informally, the _____ is the person who would win a two-candidate election against each of the other candidates. A _____ will not always exist in a given set of votes, which is known as Condorcet's voting paradox.
    a. Condorcet winner
    b. 120-cell
    c. Psephology
    d. 1-center problem

3. In mathematics, the _____ of a Euclidean space is a special point, usually denoted by the letter O, used as a fixed point of reference for the geometry of the surrounding space. In a Cartesian coordinate system, the _____ is the point where the axes of the system intersect. In Euclidean geometry, the _____ may be chosen freely as any convenient point of reference.
    a. Interval
    b. OMAC
    c. Origin
    d. Autonomous system

4. _____s is concerned with the tasks of developing and applying quantitative or statistical methods to the study and elucidation of economic principles. _____s combines economic theory with statistics to analyze and test economic relationships. Theoretical _____s considers questions about the statistical properties of estimators and tests, while applied _____s is concerned with the application of _____ methods to assess economic theories.
    a. A Mathematical Theory of Communication
    b. A chemical equation
    c. Economic
    d. Econometric

5. In mathematics and in the sciences, a _____ (plural: _____e, formulæ or _____s) is a concise way of expressing information symbolically (as in a mathematical or chemical _____), or a general relationship between quantities. One of many famous _____e is Albert Einstein's $E = mc^2$ (see special relativity

In mathematics, a _____ is a key to solve an equation with variables. For example, the problem of determining the volume of a sphere is one that requires a significant amount of integral calculus to solve.

    a. 1-center problem
    b. 2-3 heap
    c. Formula
    d. 120-cell

6. In quantum field theory and statistical mechanics in the thermodynamic limit, a system with a global symmetry can have more than one phase. For parameters where the symmetry is spontaneously broken, the system is said to be _____. When the global symmetry is unbroken the system is disordered.
    a. Ursell function
    b. Ordered
    c. Einstein relation
    d. Isoenthalpic-isobaric ensemble

7. In mathematics, an _____ is a collection of objects having two coordinates (or entries or projections), such that one can always uniquely determine the object, which is the first coordinate (or first entry or left projection) of the pair as well as the second coordinate (or second entry or right projection.) If the first coordinate is a and the second is b, the usual notation for an _____ is (a, b.) The pair is 'ordered' in that (a, b) differs from (b, a) unless a = b.

Chapter 10. Euclidean Spaces

a. A chemical equation
c. A Mathematical Theory of Communication
b. A posteriori
d. Ordered pair

8. In physics and in _____ calculus, a _____ is a concept characterized by a magnitude and a direction. A _____ can be thought of as an arrow in Euclidean space, drawn from an initial point A pointing to a terminal point B.
   a. Vector
   c. Constraint
   b. Dominance
   d. Deviation

9. In mathematics, _____ is one of the basic operations defining a vector space in linear algebra. Note that _____ is different from scalar product which is an inner product between two vectors.

More specifically, if K is a field and V is a vector space over K, then _____ is a function from K × V to V.

   a. Scalar multiplication
   c. Frobenius normal form
   b. Non-negative matrix factorization
   d. Jordan normal form

10. In mathematics the _____ of a set which is equipped with the operation of addition is an element which, when added to any element x in the set, yields x. One of the most familiar additive identities is the number 0 from elementary mathematics, but additive identities occur in other mathematical structures where addition is defined, such as in groups and rings.

- The _____ familiar from elementary mathematics is zero, denoted 0. For example,

  5 + 0 = 5 = 0 + 5.

- In the natural numbers N and all of its supersets, the _____ is 0. Thus for any one of these numbers n,

  n + 0 = n = 0 + n.

Let N be a set which is closed under the operation of addition, denoted +. An _____ for N is any element e such that for any element n in N,

  e + n = n = n + e.

   a. Unit ring
   c. Unique factorization domain
   b. Algebraically independent
   d. Additive identity

11. In mathematics, the _____ of a number n is the number that, when added to n, yields zero. The _____ of n is denoted −n. For example, 7 is −7, because 7 + (−7) = 0, and the _____ of −0.3 is 0.3, because −0.3 + 0.3 = 0.
   a. Additive inverse
   c. Algebraic structure
   b. Arity
   d. Associativity

12. In mathematics, _____ is a property that a binary operation can have. It means that, within an expression containing two or more of the same associative operators in a row, the order that the operations are performed does not matter as long as the sequence of the operands is not changed. That is, rearranging the parentheses in such an expression will not change its value.

Chapter 10. Euclidean Spaces

a. Idempotence
c. Associativity
b. Unital
d. Algebraically closed

13. In mathematics, the term _____ has several different important meanings:

- An _____ is an equality that remains true regardless of the values of any variables that appear within it, to distinguish it from an equality which is true under more particular conditions. For this, the 'triple bar' symbol ≡ is sometimes used.
- In algebra, an _____ or _____ element of a set S with a binary operation Â· is an element e that, when combined with any element x of S, produces that same x. That is, eÂ·x = xÂ·e = x for all x in S.
  - The _____ function from a set S to itself, often denoted id or id_S, s the function such that i = x for all x in S. This function serves as the _____ element in the set of all functions from S to itself with respect to function composition.
  - In linear algebra, the _____ matrix of size n is the n-by-n square matrix with ones on the main diagonal and zeros elsewhere. This matrix serves as the _____ with respect to matrix multiplication.

A common example of the first meaning is the trigonometric _____

$$\sin^2 \theta + \cos^2 \theta = 1$$

which is true for all real values of θ, as opposed to

$$\cos \theta = 1,$$

which is true only for some values of θ, not all. For example, the latter equation is true when $\theta = 0$, false when $\theta = 2$

The concepts of 'additive _____' and 'multiplicative _____' are central to the Peano axioms. The number 0 is the 'additive _____' for integers, real numbers, and complex numbers. For the real numbers, for all $a \in \mathbb{R}$,

$$0 + a = a,$$

$$a + 0 = a, \text{ and}$$

$$0 + 0 = 0.$$

Similarly, The number 1 is the 'multiplicative _____' for integers, real numbers, and complex numbers.

a. ARIA
c. Intersection
b. Identity
d. Action

14. In mathematics the concept of a _____ generalizes notions such as 'length', 'area', and 'volume'. Informally, given some base set, a '_____' is any consistent assignment of 'sizes' to the subsets of the base set. Depending on the application, the 'size' of a subset may be interpreted as its physical size, the amount of something that lies within the subset, or the probability that some random process will yield a result within the subset.
   a. Congruent
   b. Cusp
   c. Lattice
   d. Measure

15. In statistics and mathematical epidemiology, _____ is the risk of an event relative to exposure. _____ is a ratio of the probability of the event occurring in the exposed group versus a non-exposed group.

$$RR = \frac{p_{\text{exposed}}}{p_{\text{non-exposed}}}$$

For example, if the probability of developing lung cancer among smokers was 20% and among non-smokers 1%, then the _____ of cancer associated with smoking would be 20.

   a. Mendelian randomization
   b. Statistical epidemiology
   c. 1-center problem
   d. Relative risk

16. _____ is a concept in economics, finance, and psychology related to the behaviour of consumers and investors under uncertainty. _____ is the reluctance of a person to accept a bargain with an uncertain payoff rather than another bargain with a more certain, but possibly lower, expected payoff.

The inverse of a person's _____ is sometimes called their risk tolerance.

   a. Life table
   b. Stochastic modelling
   c. Ruin theory
   d. Risk aversion

17. In mathematics, and in particular in abstract algebra, distributivity is a property of binary operations that generalises the _____ law from elementary algebra.
   a. Closure with a twist
   b. Permutation
   c. General linear group
   d. Distributive

18. _____ is the mathematical operation of scaling one number by another. It is one of the four basic operations in elementary arithmetic.

_____ is defined for whole numbers in terms of repeated addition; for example, 4 multiplied by 3 can be calculated by adding 3 copies of 4 together:

$$4 + 4 + 4 = 12.$$

_____ of rational numbers and real numbers is defined by systematic generalization of this basic idea.

Chapter 10. Euclidean Spaces

a. Multiplication
c. Highest common factor

b. The number 0 is even.
d. Least common multiple

19. In mathematics, the _____ or Pythagoras' theorem is a relation in Euclidean geometry among the three sides of a right triangle. The theorem is named after the Greek mathematician Pythagoras, who by tradition is credited with its discovery and proof, although it is often argued that knowledge of the theory predates him.. The theorem is as follows:

In any right triangle, the area of the square whose side is the hypotenuse is equal to the sum of the areas of the squares whose sides are the two legs.

a. Pythagorean Theorem
c. 2-3 heap

b. 1-center problem
d. 120-cell

20. In mathematics, a _____ is a statement that can be proved on the basis of explicitly stated or previously agreed assumptions.
a. Logical value
c. Boolean function

b. Theorem
d. Disjunction introduction

21. The mathematical concept of a _____ expresses the intuitive idea of deterministic dependence between two quantities, one of which is viewed as primary and the other as secondary. A _____ then is a way to associate a unique output for each input of a specified type, for example, a real number or an element of a given set.
a. Grill
c. Going up

b. Coherent
d. Function

22. In mathematics, an _____ is a generalization for the concept of a function in which the dependent variable has not been given 'explicitly' in terms of the independent variable. To give a function f explicitly is to provide a prescription for determining the value of the function y in terms of the input value x:

$$y = f$$

a. Inflection point
c. Ordinary differential equation

b. Implicit Function
d. Implicit differentiation

23. In the branch of mathematics called multivariable calculus, the _____ is a tool which allows relations to be converted to functions. It does this by representing the relation as the graph of a function. There may not be a single function whose graph is the entire relation, but there may be such a function on a restriction of the domain of the relation.
a. A chemical equation
c. A Mathematical Theory of Communication

b. Inverse function theorem
d. Implicit Function Theorem

24. In mathematics, the concept of a _____ tries to capture the intuitive idea of a geometrical one-dimensional and continuous object. A simple example is the circle. In everyday use of the term '_____', a straight line is not curved, but in mathematical parlance _____s include straight lines and line segments.
a. Negative pedal curve
c. Quadrifolium

b. Kappa curve
d. Curve

25. In mathematics, an _____ is a vector space with the additional structure of inner product. This additional structure associates each pair of vectors in the space with a scalar quantity known as the inner product of the vectors. Inner products allow the rigorous introduction of intuitive geometrical notions such as the length of a vector or the angle between two vectors.
   a. A chemical equation
   b. A Mathematical Theory of Communication
   c. A posteriori
   d. Inner product space

26. In geometry and trigonometry, an _____ is the figure formed by two rays sharing a common endpoint, called the vertex of the _____. The magnitude of the _____ is the 'amount of rotation' that separates the two rays, and can be measured by considering the length of circular arc swept out when one ray is rotated about the vertex to coincide with the other. Where there is no possibility of confusion, the term '_____' is used interchangeably for both the geometric configuration itself and for its angular magnitude.
   a. A Mathematical Theory of Communication
   b. Angle
   c. A posteriori
   d. A chemical equation

27. In mathematics, the _____ is an operation which takes two vectors over the real numbers R and returns a real-valued scalar quantity. It is the standard inner product of the orthonormal Euclidean space.

The _____ of two vectors a = [a_1, a_2, …, a_n] and b = [b_1, b_2, …, b_n] is defined as:

$$\mathbf{a} \cdot \mathbf{b} = \sum_{i=1}^{n} a_i b_i = a_1 b_1 + a_2 b_2 + \cdots + a_n b_n$$

where Σ denotes summation notation and n is the dimension of the vectors.

   a. Conjugate transpose
   b. Matrix determinant lemma
   c. Principal axis theorem
   d. Dot product

28. In mathematics, the _____ is a representation of a function as an infinite sum of terms calculated from the values of its derivatives at a single point. It may be regarded as the limit of the Taylor polynomials. _____ are named after English mathematician Brook Taylor.
   a. Local linearity
   b. 1-center problem
   c. C^r topology
   d. Taylor series

29. In mathematics, an _____ is a statement about the relative size or order of two objects, or about whether they are the same or not

   - The notation a < b means that a is less than b.
   - The notation a > b means that a is greater than b.
   - The notation a ≠ b means that a is not equal to b, but does not say that one is bigger than the other or even that they can be compared in size.

In all these cases, a is not equal to b, hence, '_____'.

Chapter 10. Euclidean Spaces 79

These relations are known as strict _____

- The notation a ≤ b means that a is less than or equal to b;
- The notation a ≥ b means that a is greater than or equal to b;

An additional use of the notation is to show that one quantity is much greater than another, normally by several orders of magnitude.

- The notation a << b means that a is much less than b.
- The notation a >> b means that a is much greater than b.

If the sense of the _____ is the same for all values of the variables for which its members are defined, then the _____ is called an 'absolute' or 'unconditional' _____. If the sense of an _____ holds only for certain values of the variables involved, but is reversed or destroyed for other values of the variables, it is called a conditional _____.

An _____ may appear unsolvable because it only states whether a number is larger or smaller than another number; but it is possible to apply the same operations for equalities to inequalities. For example, to find x for the _____ 10x > 23 one would divide 23 by 10.

   a. A chemical equation
   b. A posteriori
   c. A Mathematical Theory of Communication
   d. Inequality

   30.   In mathematics, a _____ is often represented as the sum of a sequence of terms. That is, a _____ is represented as a list of numbers with addition operations between them, for example this arithmetic sequence:

   1 + 2 + 3 + 4 + 5 + ... + 99 + 100

In most cases of interest the terms of the sequence are produced according to a certain rule, such as by a formula, by an algorithm, by a sequence of measurements, or even by a random number generator.

   a. Concavity
   b. Blind
   c. Contact
   d. Series

   31.   A _____ is one of the basic shapes of geometry: a polygon with three corners or vertices and three sides or edges which are line segments. A _____ with vertices A, B, and C is denoted ABC.

In Euclidean geometry any three non-collinear points determine a unique _____ and a unique plane.

   a. Triangle
   b. 1-center problem
   c. Fuhrmann circle
   d. Kepler triangle

   32.   In mathematics, the _____ states that for any triangle, the length of a given side must be less than the sum of the other two sides but greater than the difference between the two sides.

In Euclidean geometry and some other geometries this is a theorem. In the Euclidean case, in both the less than or equal to and greater than or equal to statements, equality occurs only if the triangle has a 180° angle and two 0° angles, as shown in the bottom example in the image to the right.

a. Rearrangement inequality
b. Triangle inequality
c. Minkowski inequality
d. Greater than

33. In mathematics, _____ are functions which can be used to prove the stability of a certain fixed point in a dynamical system or autonomous differential equation. Named after the Russian mathematician Aleksandr Mikhailovich Lyapunov, _____ are important to stability theory and control theory.

Functions which might prove the stability of some equilibrium are called Lyapunov-candidate-functions.

a. 120-cell
b. 1-center problem
c. Butterfly effect
d. Lyapunov functions

34. In mathematics, a _____ is a rectangular table of elements, which may be numbers or, more generally, any abstract quantities that can be added and multiplied. Matrices are used to describe linear equations, keep track of the coefficients of linear transformations and to record data that depend on multiple parameters. Matrices are described by the field of _____ theory.

a. Double counting
b. Matrix
c. Compression
d. Coherent

35. In several fields of mathematics the term _____ is used with different but closely related meanings. They all relate to the notion of mapping the elements of a set to other elements of the same set, i.e., exchanging elements of a set.

The general concept of _____ can be defined more formally in different contexts:

In combinatorics, a _____ is usually understood to be a sequence containing each element from a finite set once, and only once.

a. Cyclic permutation
b. Tensor product
c. Linearly independent
d. Permutation

36. In mathematics, in matrix theory, a _____ is a square-matrix that has exactly one entry 1 in each row and each column and 0's elsewhere. Each such matrix represents a specific permutation of m elements and, when used to multiply another matrix, can produce that permutation in the rows or columns of the other matrix.

Given a permutation π of m elements,

$$\pi : \{1, \ldots, m\} \to \{1, \ldots, m\}$$

given in two-line form by

$$\begin{pmatrix} 1 & 2 & \cdots & m \\ \pi(1) & \pi(2) & \cdots & \pi(m) \end{pmatrix},$$

its _____ is the m × m matrix P_π whose entries are all 0 except that in row i, the entry equals 1.

- a. Hessenberg matrix
- b. Partitioned matrix
- c. Cartan matrix
- d. Permutation Matrix

37. In mathematics, the _____ is an approach to finding a particular solution to certain inhomogeneous ordinary differential equations and recurrence relations. It is closely related to the annihilator method, but instead of using a particular kind of differential operator in order to find the best possible form of the particular solution, a 'guess' is made as to the appropriate form, which is then tested by differentiating the resulting equation. In this sense, the _____ is less formal but more intuitive than the annihilator method.

- a. Method of undetermined coefficients
- b. Differential algebraic equations
- c. Linear differential equation
- d. Phase line

38. In mathematics, _____ are two-dimensional manifolds or surfaces that are perfectly flat.
- a. 2-3 heap
- b. Planes
- c. 120-cell
- d. 1-center problem

39. In mathematics, _____ are a method of defining a curve. A simple kinematical example is when one uses a time parameter to determine the position, velocity, and other information about a body in motion.

Abstractly, a relation is given in the form of an equation, and it is shown also to be the image of functions from items such as R^n.

- a. Differential operator
- b. Multipole moment
- c. Laplace operator
- d. Parametric equations

40. In geometry, a _____ is a part of a line that is bounded by two distinct end points, and contains every point on the line between its end points. Examples of _____s include the sides of a triangle or square. More generally, when the end points are both vertices of a polygon, the _____ is either an edge if they are adjacent vertices, or otherwise a diagonal.
- a. Transversal line
- b. Cuboid
- c. Golden angle
- d. Line segment

41. In combinatorial mathematics, a _____ is an un-ordered collection of distinct elements, usually of a prescribed size and taken from a given set. Given such a set S, a _____ of elements of S is just a subset of S, where as always forsets the order of the elements is not taken into account. Also, as always forsets, no elements can be repeated more than once in a _____; this is often referred to as a 'collection without repetition'.
- a. Sparsity
- b. Combination
- c. Fill-in
- d. Heawood number

Chapter 10. Euclidean Spaces

42. In mathematics, _____ are a concept central to linear algebra and related fields of mathematics

Suppose that K is a field and V is a vector space over K.

   a. Polarization
   c. Setoid
   b. Linear span
   d. Linear combinations

43. In linear algebra, a family of vectors is _____ if none of them can be written as a linear combination of finitely many other vectors in the collection. A family of vectors which is not _____ is called linearly dependent. For instance, in the three-dimensional real vector space R^3 we have the following example.

   a. Linearly independent
   c. Binary function
   b. Direct product
   d. Linear combinations

44. In mathematics, a _____, named after Augustin Cauchy, is a sequence whose elements become arbitrarily close to each other as the sequence progresses. To be more precise, by dropping enough terms from the start of the sequence, it is possible to make the maximum of the distances from any of the remaining elements to any other such element smaller than any preassigned positive value.

In other words, suppose a pre-assigned positive real value ε is chosen.

   a. Systolic inequalities for curves on surfaces
   c. Cauchy sequence
   b. Contraction mapping
   d. Hausdorff distance

45. In mathematics, _____ are coordinates defined by the vertices of a simplex. _____ are a form of homogeneous coordinates.

Let $x_1, ..., x_n$ be the vertices of a simplex in a vector space A.

   a. Conchoid
   c. Barycentric coordinates
   b. Field
   d. Functional

46. In geometry, the _____, geometric center, or barycenter of a plane figure X is the intersection of all straight lines that divide X into two parts of equal moment about the line. Informally, it is the 'average' of all points of X. The definition extends to any object X in n-dimensional space: its _____ is the intersection of all hyperplanes that divide X into two parts of equal moment about the hyperplane.

   a. Line element
   c. 120-cell
   b. Centroid
   d. 1-center problem

47. In mathematics, specifically in combinatorial commutative algebra, a convex lattice polytope P is called _____ if it has the following property: given any positive integer n, every lattice point of the dilation nP, obtained from P by scaling its vertices by the factor n and taking the convex hull of the resulting points, can be written as the sum of exactly n lattice points in P. This property plays an important role in the theory of toric varieties, where it corresponds to projective normality of the toric variety determined by P.

The simplex in R^k with the vertices at the origin and along the unit coordinate vectors is _____.

a. Hypercube
b. Demihypercubes
c. Normal
d. Polytetrahedron

48. A surface normal to a flat surface is a vector which is perpendicular to that surface. A normal to a non-flat surface at a point P on the surface is a vector perpendicular to the tangent plane to that surface at P. The word 'normal' is also used as an adjective: a line normal to a plane, the normal component of a force, the _____, etc.
   a. Torus
   b. Normal vector
   c. Real projective plane
   d. Prolate spheroid

49. A _____ is a concept in geometry. It is a higher-dimensional generalization of the concepts of a line in Euclidean plane geometry and a plane in 3-dimensional Euclidean geometry. The most familiar kinds of _____ are affine and linear _____s; less familiar is the projective _____.
   a. Special affine group
   b. Hyperplane
   c. Homological mirror symmetry
   d. Great grand stellated 120-cell

50. The _____ is a single-winner election method in which voters rank candidates in order of preference. The _____ determines the winner of an election by giving each candidate a certain number of points corresponding to the position in which he or she is ranked by each voter. Once all votes have been counted the candidate with the most points is the winner.
   a. 1-center problem
   b. Borda count
   c. 120-cell
   d. 2-3 heap

51. In economics, the _____ functional form of production functions is widely used to represent the relationship of an output to inputs. It was proposed by Knut Wicksell, and tested against statistical evidence by Paul Douglas and Charles Cobb in 1928.
   a. State price vector
   b. Cobb-Douglas
   c. State price
   d. Burden of proof

52. A _____ includes all possible consumption bundles that someone can afford given the prices of goods and the person's income level. The _____ is bounded above by the budget line.
   a. Budget set
   b. 2-3 heap
   c. 1-center problem
   d. 120-cell

53. The term market basket or _____ refers to a fixed list of items used specifically to track the progress of inflation in an economy or specific market.

The most common type of market basket is the basket of consumer goods, used to define the Consumer Price Index (CPI.) Other types of baskets are used to define

- Producer Price Index (PPI), previously known as Wholesale Price Index (WPI)
- various commodity price indices

The term market basket analysis in the retail business refers to research that provides the retailer with information to understand the purchase behaviour of a buyer. This information will enable the retailer to understand the buyer's needs and rewrite the store's layout accordingly, develop cross-promotional programs, or even capture new buyers (much like the cross-selling concept.)

Chapter 10. Euclidean Spaces

a. 1-center problem
b. Commodity bundle
c. Pareto index
d. Robin Hood index

54. In geometry, a closed _____ is one of the 2^n subsets of an n-dimensional Euclidean space defined by constraining each Cartesian coordinate axis to be nonnegative or nonpositive. That is, a closed _____ is the analogue of a closed quadrant in the plane and a closed octant in three-dimensional space. A closed _____ is defined by a system of inequalities

$$\varepsilon_i x_i \geq 0 \text{ for } 1 \leq i \leq n$$

on the coordinates x_i, where each ε_i is +1 or −1.

a. Orthant
b. Ortsbogen theorem
c. Euclidean space
d. Equal incircles theorem

55. This article will state and prove the _____ for differentiation, and then use it to prove these two formulas.

The _____ for differentiation states that for every natural number n, the derivative of $f(x) = x^n$ is $f'(x) = nx^{n-1}$, that is,

$$(x^n)' = nx^{n-1}.$$

The _____ for integration

$$\int x^n \, dx = \frac{x^{n+1}}{n+1} + C$$

for natural n is then an easy consequence. One just needs to take the derivative of this equality and use the _____ and linearity of differentiation on the right-hand side.

a. Power Rule
b. Standard part function
c. Periodic function
d. Functional integration

56. _____ is the likelihood or chance that something is the case or will happen. Theoretical _____ is used extensively in areas such as statistics, mathematics, science and philosophy to draw conclusions about the likelihood of potential events and the underlying mechanics of complex systems.

The word _____ does not have a consistent direct definition.

a. Statistical significance
b. Discrete random variable
c. Standardized moment
d. Probability

Chapter 10. Euclidean Spaces

57. In geometry, a _____ or n-_____ is an n-dimensional analogue of a triangle. Specifically, a _____ is the convex hull of a set of affinely independent points in some Euclidean space of dimension n or higher.

For example, a 0-_____ is a point, a 1-_____ is a line segment, a 2-_____ is a triangle, a 3-_____ is a tetrahedron, and a 4-_____ is a pentachoron.

a. Demihypercubes
b. Hypercell
c. Polytetrahedron
d. Simplex

58. The _____, first developed by Sir John Hicks and Alvin Hansen, has been used from 1937 onwards to summarize a major part of Keynesian macroeconomics. IS/LM stands for Investment Saving / Liquidity preference Money supply.

The _____ was born at the Econometric Conference held in Oxford during September, 1936.

a. A posteriori
b. A Mathematical Theory of Communication
c. IS/LM model
d. A chemical equation

Chapter 11. Linear Independence

1. In mathematics, the _____ makes several statements regarding vector spaces. These may be stated concretely in terms of the rank r of an m×n matrix A and its LDU factorization:

   PA = LDU

wherein P is a permutation matrix, L is a lower triangular matrix, D is a diagonal matrix, and U is an upper triangular matrix. At a more abstract level there is an interpretation that reads it in terms of a linear mapping and its transpose.

   a. Linear complementarity problem
   b. Fundamental Theorem of Linear Algebra
   c. Purification
   d. Matrix determinant lemma

2. In linear algebra, _____ is an efficient algorithm for solving systems of linear equations, finding the rank of a matrix, and calculating the inverse of an invertible square matrix. _____ is named after German mathematician and scientist Carl Friedrich Gauss.

Elementary row operations are used to reduce a matrix to row echelon form.

   a. Cholesky decomposition
   b. Crout matrix decomposition
   c. Conjugate gradient method
   d. Gaussian elimination

3. _____ is the branch of mathematics concerned with the study of vectors, vector spaces, linear maps, and systems of linear equations. Vector spaces are a central theme in modern mathematics; thus, _____ is widely used in both abstract algebra and functional analysis. _____ also has a concrete representation in analytic geometry and it is generalized in operator theory.
   a. Linear Algebra
   b. Generalized eigenvector
   c. Dual basis
   d. Binomial inverse theorem

4. Georg Friedrich Bernhard _____ was a German mathematician who made important contributions to analysis and differential geometry, some of them paving the way for the later development of general relativity.

   _____ was born in Breselenz, a village near Dannenberg in the Kingdom of Hanover in what is today Germany. His father, Friedrich Bernhard _____, was a poor Lutheran pastor in Breselenz who fought in the Napoleonic Wars.

   a. Paul C. van Oorschot
   b. Brook Taylor
   c. Gustave Bertrand
   d. Riemann

5. In mathematics, a _____ is a method for approximating the total area underneath a curve on a graph, otherwise known as an integral. It may also be used to define the integration operation. The sums are named after the German mathematician Bernhard Riemann.
   a. Solid of revolution
   b. Riemann sum
   c. Singular measure
   d. Multiple integral

6. In mathematics, a _____ is a statement that can be proved on the basis of explicitly stated or previously agreed assumptions.

Chapter 11. Linear Independence

a. Boolean function
c. Logical value
b. Disjunction introduction
d. Theorem

7. In mathematics and in the sciences, a _____ (plural: _____e, formulæ or _____s) is a concise way of expressing information symbolically (as in a mathematical or chemical _____), or a general relationship between quantities. One of many famous _____e is Albert Einstein's E = mc² (see special relativity

In mathematics, a _____ is a key to solve an equation with variables. For example, the problem of determining the volume of a sphere is one that requires a significant amount of integral calculus to solve.

a. 120-cell
c. Formula
b. 2-3 heap
d. 1-center problem

8. In mathematics, _____ are functions which can be used to prove the stability of a certain fixed point in a dynamical system or autonomous differential equation. Named after the Russian mathematician Aleksandr Mikhailovich Lyapunov, _____ are important to stability theory and control theory.

Functions which might prove the stability of some equilibrium are called Lyapunov-candidate-functions.

a. 1-center problem
c. 120-cell
b. Lyapunov functions
d. Butterfly effect

9. In combinatorial mathematics, a _____ is an un-ordered collection of distinct elements, usually of a prescribed size and taken from a given set. Given such a set S, a _____ of elements of S is just a subset of S, where as always forsets the order of the elements is not taken into account. Also, as always forsets, no elements can be repeated more than once in a _____; this is often referred to as a 'collection without repetition'.

a. Sparsity
c. Combination
b. Fill-in
d. Heawood number

10. The mathematical concept of a _____ expresses the intuitive idea of deterministic dependence between two quantities, one of which is viewed as primary and the other as secondary. A _____ then is a way to associate a unique output for each input of a specified type, for example, a real number or an element of a given set.

a. Grill
c. Going up
b. Coherent
d. Function

11. In mathematics, _____ are a concept central to linear algebra and related fields of mathematics

Suppose that K is a field and V is a vector space over K.

a. Setoid
c. Polarization
b. Linear span
d. Linear combinations

12. In linear algebra, a family of vectors is linearly independent if none of them can be written as a linear combination of finitely many other vectors in the collection. A family of vectors which is not linearly independent is called _____. For instance, in the three-dimensional real vector space R^3 we have the following example.

Chapter 11. Linear Independence

a. Normal extension
c. Linearly dependent
b. Coimage
d. Restriction of scalars

13. In linear algebra, a family of vectors is _____ if none of them can be written as a linear combination of finitely many other vectors in the collection. A family of vectors which is not _____ is called linearly dependent. For instance, in the three-dimensional real vector space R^3 we have the following example.
 a. Binary function
 c. Linear combinations
 b. Direct product
 d. Linearly independent

14. In linear algebra, a _____ is a set of vectors that, in a linear combination, can represent every vector in a given vector space or free module, and such that no element of the set can be represented as a linear combination of the others. In other words, a _____ is a linearly independent spanning set. This picture illustrates the standard _____ in R^2.
 a. Dot plot
 c. Chiral
 b. Conchoid
 d. Basis

15. In mathematics, the notion of _____ refers to a basis of an algebraic structure which is canonical in a sense that depends on the precise context:

- In a coordinate space, and more generally in a free module, it refers to the standard basis defined by the Kronecker delta.
- In a polynomial ring, it refers to its standard basis given by the monomials, i.
- For finite extension fields, it means the polynomial basis.
- In representation theory, Lusztig's _____ and closely related Kashiwara's crystal basis in quantum groups and their representations.

- Canonical
- Canonical form
- Normal form
- Polynomial basis
- Normal basis
- Change of bases

a. Schmidt decomposition
c. Row space
b. Complex conjugate vector space
d. Canonical basis

Chapter 12. Limits and Open Sets

1. In mathematics, a _____ is a rectangular table of elements, which may be numbers or, more generally, any abstract quantities that can be added and multiplied. Matrices are used to describe linear equations, keep track of the coefficients of linear transformations and to record data that depend on multiple parameters. Matrices are described by the field of _____ theory.
   a. Double counting
   b. Compression
   c. Matrix
   d. Coherent

2. In several fields of mathematics the term _____ is used with different but closely related meanings. They all relate to the notion of mapping the elements of a set to other elements of the same set, i.e., exchanging elements of a set.

   The general concept of _____ can be defined more formally in different contexts:

   In combinatorics, a _____ is usually understood to be a sequence containing each element from a finite set once, and only once.

   a. Cyclic permutation
   b. Permutation
   c. Linearly independent
   d. Tensor product

3. In mathematics, in matrix theory, a _____ is a square-matrix that has exactly one entry 1 in each row and each column and 0's elsewhere. Each such matrix represents a specific permutation of m elements and, when used to multiply another matrix, can produce that permutation in the rows or columns of the other matrix.

   Given a permutation π of m elements,

   $$\pi : \{1, \ldots, m\} \to \{1, \ldots, m\}$$

   given in two-line form by

   $$\begin{pmatrix} 1 & 2 & \cdots & m \\ \pi(1) & \pi(2) & \cdots & \pi(m) \end{pmatrix},$$

   its _____ is the m × m matrix P_π whose entries are all 0 except that in row i, the entry equals 1.

   a. Hessenberg matrix
   b. Partitioned matrix
   c. Permutation Matrix
   d. Cartan matrix

4. The _____ are the set of numbers consisting of the natural numbers including 0 and their negatives. They are numbers that can be written without a fractional or decimal component, and fall within the set {... −2, −1, 0, 1, 2, ...}.
   a. A Mathematical Theory of Communication
   b. A posteriori
   c. A chemical equation
   d. Integers

5. In mathematics, a _____ can mean either an element of the set {1, 2, 3, ...} or an element of the set {0, 1, 2, 3, ...}. The latter is especially preferred in mathematical logic, set theory, and computer science.

   _____s have two main purposes: they can be used for counting, and they can be used for ordering.

a. Cardinal numbers
b. Strong partition cardinal
c. Natural number
d. Suslin cardinal

6. The _____ is a basic theorem used to solve maximization problems in microeconomics. It may be used to prove Hotelling's lemma, Shephard's lemma, and Roy's identity. The statement of the theorem is:

Consider an arbitrary maximization problem where the objective function (f) depends on some parameter (a):

$$M(a) = \max_x f(x, a)$$

where the function M(a) gives the maximized value of the objective function (f) as a function of the parameter (a.)

a. A posteriori
b. A chemical equation
c. A Mathematical Theory of Communication
d. Envelope Theorem

7. The mathematical concept of a _____ expresses the intuitive idea of deterministic dependence between two quantities, one of which is viewed as primary and the other as secondary. A _____ then is a way to associate a unique output for each input of a specified type, for example, a real number or an element of a given set.
a. Going up
b. Grill
c. Coherent
d. Function

8. In mathematics, an _____ is a generalization for the concept of a function in which the dependent variable has not been given 'explicitly' in terms of the independent variable. To give a function f explicitly is to provide a prescription for determining the value of the function y in terms of the input value x:

y = f

a. Implicit differentiation
b. Inflection point
c. Ordinary differential equation
d. Implicit Function

9. In the branch of mathematics called multivariable calculus, the _____ is a tool which allows relations to be converted to functions. It does this by representing the relation as the graph of a function. There may not be a single function whose graph is the entire relation, but there may be such a function on a restriction of the domain of the relation.
a. A chemical equation
b. A Mathematical Theory of Communication
c. Inverse function theorem
d. Implicit Function Theorem

10. In mathematics, _____ are functions which can be used to prove the stability of a certain fixed point in a dynamical system or autonomous differential equation. Named after the Russian mathematician Aleksandr Mikhailovich Lyapunov, _____ are important to stability theory and control theory.

Functions which might prove the stability of some equilibrium are called Lyapunov-candidate-functions.

a. Butterfly effect
b. 120-cell
c. 1-center problem
d. Lyapunov functions

Chapter 12. Limits and Open Sets

11. In mathematics, a _____ is a statement that can be proved on the basis of explicitly stated or previously agreed assumptions.
    a. Boolean function
    b. Disjunction introduction
    c. Logical value
    d. Theorem

12. In mathematics, a _____ is a set of real numbers with the property that any number that lies between two numbers in the set is also included in the set. For example, the set of all numbers x satisfying $0 \leq x \leq 1$ is an _____ which contains 0 and 1, as well as all numbers between them. Other examples of _____s are the set of all real numbers $\mathbb{R}$, the set of all positive real numbers, and the empty set.
    a. Interval
    b. Annihilator
    c. Order
    d. Ideal

13. In mathematics, the concept of a '_____' is used to describe the behavior of a function as its argument or input either 'gets close' to some point, or as the argument becomes arbitrarily large; or the behavior of a sequence's elements as their index increases indefinitely. _____s are used in calculus and other branches of mathematical analysis to define derivatives and continuity.

    In formulas, _____ is usually abbreviated as lim.

    a. Copula
    b. Contact
    c. Duality
    d. Limit

14. In calculus, the _____ is a formula for the derivative of the composite of two functions.

In intuitive terms, if a variable, y, depends on a second variable, u, which in turn depends on a third variable, x, then the rate of change of y with respect to x can be computed as the rate of change of y with respect to u multiplied by the rate of change of u with respect to x. Schematically,

$$\frac{dy}{dx} = \frac{dy}{du} \cdot \frac{du}{dx}.$$

For an explanation of notation used in this section, see Function composition.

The _____ states that, under appropriate conditions,

$$(f \circ g)'(x) = f'(g(x))g'(x),$$

which in short form is written as

$$(f \circ g)' = f' \circ g \cdot g'.$$

Alternatively, in the Leibniz notation, the _____ is

$$\frac{dy}{dx} = \frac{dy}{du} \cdot \frac{du}{dx}.$$

In integration, the counterpart to the _____ is the substitution rule.

   a. 120-cell   b. 1-center problem
   c. Product rule   d. Chain Rule

15. The Condorcet candidate or _____ of an election is the candidate who, when compared with every other candidate, is preferred by more voters. Informally, the _____ is the person who would win a two-candidate election against each of the other candidates. A _____ will not always exist in a given set of votes, which is known as Condorcet's voting paradox.

   a. 120-cell   b. 1-center problem
   c. Psephology   d. Condorcet winner

16. In mathematics, a _____ of some sequence is a new sequence which is formed from the original sequence by deleting some of the elements without disturbing the relative positions of the remaining elements.

Formally, suppose that X is a set and that $_{k \in K}$ is a sequence in X, where K = {1,2,3,...,n} if is a finite sequence and K = N if is an infinite sequence. Then, a _____ of is a sequence of the form (a_{n_r}) where is a strictly increasing sequence in the index set K.

   a. Subsequence   b. Cognitively Guided Instruction
   c. Point plotting   d. Nicomachus's theorem

17. In mathematics, the _____ is a representation of a function as an infinite sum of terms calculated from the values of its derivatives at a single point. It may be regarded as the limit of the Taylor polynomials. _____ are named after English mathematician Brook Taylor.

   a. Local linearity   b. C^r topology
   c. 1-center problem   d. Taylor series

18. In mathematics, an _____ is a statement about the relative size or order of two objects, or about whether they are the same or not

- The notation a < b means that a is less than b.
- The notation a > b means that a is greater than b.
- The notation a ≠ b means that a is not equal to b, but does not say that one is bigger than the other or even that they can be compared in size.

In all these cases, a is not equal to b, hence, '_____'.

Chapter 12. Limits and Open Sets 93

These relations are known as strict _____

- The notation a ≤ b means that a is less than or equal to b;
- The notation a ≥ b means that a is greater than or equal to b;

An additional use of the notation is to show that one quantity is much greater than another, normally by several orders of magnitude.

- The notation a << b means that a is much less than b.
- The notation a >> b means that a is much greater than b.

If the sense of the _____ is the same for all values of the variables for which its members are defined, then the _____ is called an 'absolute' or 'unconditional' _____. If the sense of an _____ holds only for certain values of the variables involved, but is reversed or destroyed for other values of the variables, it is called a conditional _____.

An _____ may appear unsolvable because it only states whether a number is larger or smaller than another number; but it is possible to apply the same operations for equalities to inequalities. For example, to find x for the _____ 10x > 23 one would divide 23 by 10.

a. Inequality
c. A chemical equation
b. A Mathematical Theory of Communication
d. A posteriori

19. In mathematics, a _____ is often represented as the sum of a sequence of terms. That is, a _____ is represented as a list of numbers with addition operations between them, for example this arithmetic sequence:

1 + 2 + 3 + 4 + 5 + ... + 99 + 100

In most cases of interest the terms of the sequence are produced according to a certain rule, such as by a formula, by an algorithm, by a sequence of measurements, or even by a random number generator.

a. Concavity
c. Series
b. Contact
d. Blind

20. A _____ is one of the basic shapes of geometry: a polygon with three corners or vertices and three sides or edges which are line segments. A _____ with vertices A, B, and C is denoted ABC.

In Euclidean geometry any three non-collinear points determine a unique _____ and a unique plane.

a. Triangle
c. Kepler triangle
b. 1-center problem
d. Fuhrmann circle

21. In mathematics, the _____ states that for any triangle, the length of a given side must be less than the sum of the other two sides but greater than the difference between the two sides.

Chapter 12. Limits and Open Sets

In Euclidean geometry and some other geometries this is a theorem. In the Euclidean case, in both the less than or equal to and greater than or equal to statements, equality occurs only if the triangle has a 180° angle and two 0° angles, as shown in the bottom example in the image to the right.

a. Rearrangement inequality
b. Greater than
c. Minkowski inequality
d. Triangle inequality

22. The _____ is a single-winner election method in which voters rank candidates in order of preference. The _____ determines the winner of an election by giving each candidate a certain number of points corresponding to the position in which he or she is ranked by each voter. Once all votes have been counted the candidate with the most points is the winner.

a. 1-center problem
b. 120-cell
c. 2-3 heap
d. Borda count

23. A set S of real numbers is called _____ from above if there is a real number k such that k ≥ s for all s in S. The number k is called an upper bound of S. The terms _____ from below and lower bound are similarly defined.

a. Harmonic series
b. Bounded
c. Derivative algebra
d. Descent

24. In mathematics, the Euclidean distance or _____ is the 'ordinary' distance between two points that one would measure with a ruler, which can be proven by repeated application of the Pythagorean theorem. By using this formula as distance, Euclidean space becomes a metric space. The associated norm is called the Euclidean norm.

Older literature refers to this metric as Pythagorean metric.

a. A chemical equation
b. Intrinsic metric
c. Euclidean metric
d. A Mathematical Theory of Communication

25. In topology and related areas of mathematics, a _____ is one of the basic concepts in a topological space. Intuitively speaking, a _____ of a point is a set containing the point where you can wiggle the point a bit without leaving the set.

This concept is closely related to the concepts of open set and interior.

a. Second-countable space
b. Boundary
c. Closeness
d. Neighbourhood

26. In metric topology and related fields of mathematics, a set U is called an _____ if, intuitively speaking, starting from any point x in U one can move by a small amount in any direction and still be in the set U. In other words, the distance between any point x in U and the edge of U is always greater than zero.

As an example, consider the open interval consisting of all real numbers x with 0 < x < 1. Here, the topology is the usual topology on the real line.

a. A Mathematical Theory of Communication
b. Open map
c. Upper topology
d. Open set

27. In economics, the _____ functional form of production functions is widely used to represent the relationship of an output to inputs. It was proposed by Knut Wicksell, and tested against statistical evidence by Paul Douglas and Charles Cobb in 1928.
a. State price vector
b. State price
c. Burden of proof
d. Cobb-Douglas

28. In discrete mathematics and predominantly in set theory, a _____ is a concept used in comparisons of sets to refer to the unique values of one set in relation to another. The terms 'absolute' and 'relative' _____ refer to more specific applications of the concept, with universal _____s referring to elements unique to the universal set and the latter referring to the unique elements of one set in relation to another. In this image, the universal set is represented by the border of the image, and the set A as a disc.
a. Huge
b. Kernel
c. Complement
d. Derivative algebra

29. In geometry, a closed _____ is one of the 2^n subsets of an n-dimensional Euclidean space defined by constraining each Cartesian coordinate axis to be nonnegative or nonpositive. That is, a closed _____ is the analogue of a closed quadrant in the plane and a closed octant in three-dimensional space. A closed _____ is defined by a system of inequalities

$\varepsilon_i x_i \geq 0$ for $1 \leq i \leq n$

on the coordinates x_i, where each ε_i is +1 or −1.

a. Euclidean space
b. Equal incircles theorem
c. Ortsbogen theorem
d. Orthant

30. In mathematics, a set is said to be _____ if the operation on members of the set produces a member of the set. For example, the real numbers are closed under subtraction, but the natural numbers are not: 3 and 7 are both natural numbers, but the result of 3 − 7 is not.

Similarly, a set is said to be closed under a collection of operations if it is closed under each of the operations individually.

a. Continuous linear extension
b. Closed under some operation
c. Control chart
d. Contingency table

31. In topology, the _____ of a subset S of a topological space X is the set of points which can be approached both from S and from the outside of S. More formally, it is the set of points in the closure of S, not belonging to the interior of S. An element of the _____ of S is called a _____ point of S.
a. Heap
b. Bertrand paradox
c. Character
d. Boundary

32. In real analysis, the _____ is a fundamental result about convergence in a finite-dimensional Euclidean space $\mathbb{R}^n$. The theorem states that each bounded sequence in $\mathbb{R}^n$ has a convergent subsequence. An equivalent formulation is that a subset of $\mathbb{R}^n$ is sequentially compact if and only if it is closed and bounded.

   a. Heine-Borel theorem
   b. Fundamental axiom of analysis
   c. Least upper bound axiom
   d. Bolzano-Weierstrass Theorem

33. In linear algebra, _____ is an efficient algorithm for solving systems of linear equations, finding the rank of a matrix, and calculating the inverse of an invertible square matrix. _____ is named after German mathematician and scientist Carl Friedrich Gauss.

Elementary row operations are used to reduce a matrix to row echelon form.

   a. Cholesky decomposition
   b. Conjugate gradient method
   c. Crout matrix decomposition
   d. Gaussian elimination

34. In the mathematical area of order theory, the _____ or finite elements of a partially ordered set are those elements that cannot be subsumed by a supremum of any non-empty directed set that does not already contain members above the _____ element.

Note that there are other notions of compactness in mathematics; also, the term 'finite' in its normal set theoretic meaning does not coincide with the order-theoretic notion of a 'finite element'.

In a partially ordered set an element c is called _____ if it satisfies one of the following equivalent conditions:

- For every nonempty directed subset D of P, if D has a supremum sup D and c ≤ sup D then c ≤ d for some element d of D.
- For every ideal I of P, if I has a supremum sup I and c ≤ sup I then c is an element of I.

If the poset P additionally is a join-semilattice then these conditions are equivalent to the following statement:

- For every nonempty subset S of P, if S has a supremum sup S and c ≤ sup S, then c ≤ sup T for some finite subset T of S.

In particular, if c = sup S, then c is the supremum of a finite subset of S.

   a. Locally regular space
   b. Train track
   c. Matching distance
   d. Compact

Chapter 13. Functions of Several Variables 97

1. _____ describes the property of operations in mathematics and computer science which means that multiple applications of the operation does not change the result. The concept of _____ arises in a number of places in abstract algebra.

There are several meanings of _____, depending on what the concept is applied to:

- A unary operation is called idempotent if, whenever it is applied twice to any value, it gives the same result as if it were applied once. For example, the absolute value function is idempotent as a function from the set of real numbers to the set of real numbers: ab = ab.
- A binary operation is called idempotent if, whenever it is applied to two equal values, it gives that value as the result. For example, the operation giving the maximum value of two values is idempotent: ma = x.
- Given a binary operation, an idempotent element for the operation is a value for which the operation, when given that value for both of its operands, gives the value as the result. For example, the number 1 is an idempotent of multiplication: 1 × 1 = 1.

A unary operation f that is a map from some set S into itself is called idempotent if, for all x in S,

    f

In particular, the identity function id_S, defined by
id_S, is idempotent, as is the constant function K_c, where c is an element of S, defined by $K_c(x) = c$.

a. Antiisomorphism   b. Ordered exponential
c. Idempotence   d. Absorption law

2. In graph theory, a _____ is an edge that connects a vertex to itself. A simple graph contains no _____s.

Depending on the context, a graph or a multigraph may be defined so as to either allow or disallow the presence of _____s:

- Where graphs are defined so as to allow _____s and multiple edges, a graph without _____s is often called a multigraph.
- Where graphs are defined so as to disallow _____s and multiple edges, a multigraph or a pseudograph is often defined to mean a 'graph' which can have _____s and multiple edges.

For an undirected graph, the degree of a vertex is equal to the number of adjacent vertices.

A special case is a _____, which adds two to the degree.

a. Commensurable   b. Duality
c. FISH   d. Loop

3. In mathematics, a _____ is a rectangular table of elements, which may be numbers or, more generally, any abstract quantities that can be added and multiplied. Matrices are used to describe linear equations, keep track of the coefficients of linear transformations and to record data that depend on multiple parameters. Matrices are described by the field of _____ theory.

a. Matrix
b. Double counting
c. Compression
d. Coherent

4. In mathematics, especially in the area of abstract algebra known as ring theory, a _____ is a ring with 0 ≠ 1 such that ab = 0 implies that either a = 0 or b = 0. That is, it is a nontrivial ring without left or right zero divisors. A commutative _____ is called an integral _____.

a. Simple ring
b. Left primitive ring
c. Modular representation theory
d. Domain

5. In mathematics and in the sciences, a _____ (plural: _____e, formulæ or _____s) is a concise way of expressing information symbolically (as in a mathematical or chemical _____), or a general relationship between quantities. One of many famous _____e is Albert Einstein's $E = mc^2$ (see special relativity

In mathematics, a _____ is a key to solve an equation with variables. For example, the problem of determining the volume of a sphere is one that requires a significant amount of integral calculus to solve.

a. 120-cell
b. 2-3 heap
c. 1-center problem
d. Formula

6. The mathematical concept of a _____ expresses the intuitive idea of deterministic dependence between two quantities, one of which is viewed as primary and the other as secondary. A _____ then is a way to associate a unique output for each input of a specified type, for example, a real number or an element of a given set.

a. Going up
b. Coherent
c. Grill
d. Function

7. An _____ is an artifact, usually two-dimensional (a picture), that has a similar appearance to some subject--usually a physical object or a person.

_____s may be two-dimensional, such as a photograph, screen display, and as well as a three-dimensional, such as a statue. They may be captured by optical devices--such as cameras, mirrors, lenses, telescopes, microscopes, etc.

a. A Mathematical Theory of Communication
b. Image
c. A posteriori
d. A chemical equation

8. The Condorcet candidate or _____ of an election is the candidate who, when compared with every other candidate, is preferred by more voters. Informally, the _____ is the person who would win a two-candidate election against each of the other candidates. A _____ will not always exist in a given set of votes, which is known as Condorcet's voting paradox.

a. Psephology
b. 1-center problem
c. 120-cell
d. Condorcet winner

Chapter 13. Functions of Several Variables

9. In mathematics, an _____ is a generalization for the concept of a function in which the dependent variable has not been given 'explicitly' in terms of the independent variable. To give a function f explicitly is to provide a prescription for determining the value of the function y in terms of the input value x:

    y = f

    a. Implicit differentiation
    c. Inflection point
    b. Ordinary differential equation
    d. Implicit Function

10. In the branch of mathematics called multivariable calculus, the _____ is a tool which allows relations to be converted to functions. It does this by representing the relation as the graph of a function. There may not be a single function whose graph is the entire relation, but there may be such a function on a restriction of the domain of the relation.
    a. Implicit Function Theorem
    c. A chemical equation
    b. Inverse function theorem
    d. A Mathematical Theory of Communication

11. The _____ governs the differentiation of products of differentiable functions.
    a. 120-cell
    c. Product Rule
    b. 1-center problem
    d. Reciprocal Rule

12. In mathematics, a _____ is a statement that can be proved on the basis of explicitly stated or previously agreed assumptions.
    a. Theorem
    c. Boolean function
    b. Disjunction introduction
    d. Logical value

13. In economic models, the _____ time frame assumes no fixed factors of production. Firms can enter or leave the marketplace, and the cost of land, labor, raw materials, and capital goods can be assumed to vary. In contrast, in the short-run time frame, certain factors are assumed to be fixed, because there is not sufficient time for them to change.
    a. 1-center problem
    c. Short-run
    b. Production function
    d. Long-run

14. In economics, a _____ is a function that specifies the output of a firm, an industry, or an entire economy for all combinations of inputs. A meta-_____ compares the practice of the existing entities converting inputs X into output y to determine the most efficient practice _____ of the existing entities, whether the most efficient feasible practice production or the most efficient actual practice production. In either case, the maximum output of a technologically-determined production process is a mathematical function of input factors of production.
    a. Long-run
    c. Production function
    b. Short-run
    d. 1-center problem

15. In economics, the concept of the _____ refers to the decision-making time frame of a firm in which at least one factor of production is fixed. Costs which are fixed in the _____ have no impact on a firms decisions. For example a firm can raise output by increasing the amount of labour through overtime.
    a. Short-run
    c. Long-run
    b. Production function
    d. 1-center problem

Chapter 13. Functions of Several Variables

16. In economics, the _____ functional form of production functions is widely used to represent the relationship of an output to inputs. It was proposed by Knut Wicksell, and tested against statistical evidence by Paul Douglas and Charles Cobb in 1928.

    a. State price vector   b. State price
    c. Burden of proof   d. Cobb-Douglas

17. In mathematics, _____ are functions which can be used to prove the stability of a certain fixed point in a dynamical system or autonomous differential equation. Named after the Russian mathematician Aleksandr Mikhailovich Lyapunov, _____ are important to stability theory and control theory.

Functions which might prove the stability of some equilibrium are called Lyapunov-candidate-functions.

    a. 120-cell   b. Butterfly effect
    c. Lyapunov functions   d. 1-center problem

18. The term market basket or _____ refers to a fixed list of items used specifically to track the progress of inflation in an economy or specific market.

The most common type of market basket is the basket of consumer goods, used to define the Consumer Price Index (CPI.) Other types of baskets are used to define

- Producer Price Index (PPI), previously known as Wholesale Price Index (WPI)
- various commodity price indices

The term market basket analysis in the retail business refers to research that provides the retailer with information to understand the purchase behaviour of a buyer. This information will enable the retailer to understand the buyer's needs and rewrite the store's layout accordingly, develop cross-promotional programs, or even capture new buyers (much like the cross-selling concept.)

    a. Pareto index   b. Commodity bundle
    c. 1-center problem   d. Robin Hood index

19. _____ (CES) is a property of some production functions and utility functions.

More precisely, it refers to a particular type of aggregator function which combines two or more types of consumption, or two or more types of productive inputs into an aggregate quantity. This aggregator function exhibits _____.

    a. Production function   b. Short-run
    c. 1-center problem   d. Constant elasticity of substitution

20. In mathematics, the concept of a _____ tries to capture the intuitive idea of a geometrical one-dimensional and continuous object. A simple example is the circle. In everyday use of the term '_____', a straight line is not curved, but in mathematical parlance _____s include straight lines and line segments.

Chapter 13. Functions of Several Variables

a. Kappa curve
b. Quadrifolium
c. Negative pedal curve
d. Curve

21. In mathematics, a level set of a real-valued function f of n variables is a set of the form

$$\{ [x_1,...,x_n] \mid f[x_1,...,x_n] = c \}$$

where c is a constant. That is, it is the set where the function takes on a given constant value.

When the number of variables is two, this is a _____, if it is three this is a level surface, and for higher values of n the level set is a level hypersurface.

a. Multipole moment
b. Parametric equations
c. Shift theorem
d. Level curve

22. The _____, first developed by Sir John Hicks and Alvin Hansen, has been used from 1937 onwards to summarize a major part of Keynesian macroeconomics. IS/LM stands for Investment Saving / Liquidity preference Money supply.

The _____ was born at the Econometric Conference held in Oxford during September, 1936.

a. A posteriori
b. A chemical equation
c. A Mathematical Theory of Communication
d. IS/LM model

23. A _____ of a function of two variables is a curve along which the function has a constant value. In cartography, a _____ joins points of equal elevation above a given level, such as mean sea level. A contour map is a map illustrated with _____s, for example a topographic map, which thus shows valleys and hills, and the steepness of slopes.

a. Contour line
b. Convex
c. Contrapositive
d. Cauchy-Riemann differential equations

24. In microeconomic theory, an _____ is a graph showing different bundles of goods, each measured as to quantity, between which a consumer is indifferent. That is, at each point on the curve, the consumer has no preference for one bundle over another. In other words, they are all equally preferred. One can equivalently refer to each point on the _____ as rendering the same level of utility for the consumer.

a. Expenditure function
b. Expenditure minimization problem
c. Indifference curve
d. Utility maximization problem

25.

In mathematics, a _____ of a real-valued function *f* of *n* variables is a set of the form

$$\{ [x_1,...,x_n] \mid f[x_1,...,x_n] = c \}$$

where c is a constant. That is, it is the set where the function takes on a given constant value.

When the number of variables is two, this is a **level curve** (contour line), if it is three this is a **level surface**, and for higher values of n the _____ is a **level hypersurface**.

a. Level set
b. Differentiation operator
c. Shift theorem
d. Multivariable calculus

26. In linear algebra, a _____ is a set of vectors that, in a linear combination, can represent every vector in a given vector space or free module, and such that no element of the set can be represented as a linear combination of the others. In other words, a _____ is a linearly independent spanning set. This picture illustrates the standard _____ in R^2.

a. Basis
b. Chiral
c. Conchoid
d. Dot plot

27. In mathematics, the notion of _____ refers to a basis of an algebraic structure which is canonical in a sense that depends on the precise context:

- In a coordinate space, and more generally in a free module, it refers to the standard basis defined by the Kronecker delta.
- In a polynomial ring, it refers to its standard basis given by the monomials, i.
- For finite extension fields, it means the polynomial basis.
- In representation theory, Lusztig's _____ and closely related Kashiwara's crystal basis in quantum groups and their representations.

- Canonical
- Canonical form
- Normal form
- Polynomial basis
- Normal basis
- Change of bases

a. Row space
b. Complex conjugate vector space
c. Canonical basis
d. Schmidt decomposition

28. In mathematics, the _____ or Pythagoras' theorem is a relation in Euclidean geometry among the three sides of a right triangle. The theorem is named after the Greek mathematician Pythagoras, who by tradition is credited with its discovery and proof, although it is often argued that knowledge of the theory predates him.. The theorem is as follows:

In any right triangle, the area of the square whose side is the hypotenuse is equal to the sum of the areas of the squares whose sides are the two legs.

a. 1-center problem
b. Pythagorean Theorem
c. 2-3 heap
d. 120-cell

Chapter 13. Functions of Several Variables

29. In mathematics, a _____ is a curve obtained by intersecting a cone with a plane. A _____ is therefore a restriction of a quadric surface to the plane. The _____s were named and studied as long ago as 200 BC, when Apollonius of Perga undertook a systematic study of their properties.
   - a. Conic section
   - b. Directrix
   - c. Dandelin sphere
   - d. Parabola

30. A _____ is a concept in geometry. It is a higher-dimensional generalization of the concepts of a line in Euclidean plane geometry and a plane in 3-dimensional Euclidean geometry. The most familiar kinds of _____ are affine and linear _____s; less familiar is the projective _____.
   - a. Homological mirror symmetry
   - b. Special affine group
   - c. Great grand stellated 120-cell
   - d. Hyperplane

31. If ε is a vector of n random variables, and Λ is an n-dimensional symmetric square matrix, then the scalar quantity ε'Λε is known as a _____ in ε.

It can be shown that

$$E[\epsilon'\Lambda\epsilon] = \operatorname{tr}[\Lambda\Sigma] + \mu'\Lambda\mu$$

where μ and Σ are the expected value and variance-covariance matrix of ε, respectively, and tr denotes the trace of a matrix. This result only depends on the existence of μ and Σ; in particular, normality of ε is not required.

   - a. Complex conjugate vector space
   - b. Field of values
   - c. Quadratic form
   - d. Gram-Schmidt process

32. In statistics, _____ has two related meanings:

   - the arithmetic _____.
   - the expected value of a random variable, which is also called the population _____.

It is sometimes stated that the '_____' _____s average. This is incorrect if '_____' is taken in the specific sense of 'arithmetic _____' as there are different types of averages: the _____, median, and mode. For instance, average house prices almost always use the median value for the average.

For a real-valued random variable X, the _____ is the expectation of X.

   - a. Statistical population
   - b. Proportional hazards model
   - c. Probability
   - d. Mean

33. In calculus, the _____ states, roughly, that given a section of a smooth curve, there is at least one point on that section at which the derivative of the curve is equal to the 'average' derivative of the section. It is used to prove theorems that make global conclusions about a function on an interval starting from local hypotheses about derivatives at points of the interval.

This theorem can be understood concretely by applying it to motion: if a car travels one hundred miles in one hour, so that its average speed during that time was 100 miles per hour, then at some time its instantaneous speed must have been exactly 100 miles per hour.

    a. Fundamental Theorem of Calculus
    c. Calculus controversy
    b. Mean Value Theorem
    d. Functional integration

34. In several fields of mathematics the term _____ is used with different but closely related meanings. They all relate to the notion of mapping the elements of a set to other elements of the same set, i.e., exchanging elements of a set.

The general concept of _____ can be defined more formally in different contexts:

In combinatorics, a _____ is usually understood to be a sequence containing each element from a finite set once, and only once.

    a. Cyclic permutation
    c. Linearly independent
    b. Tensor product
    d. Permutation

35. In mathematics, in matrix theory, a _____ is a square-matrix that has exactly one entry 1 in each row and each column and 0's elsewhere. Each such matrix represents a specific permutation of m elements and, when used to multiply another matrix, can produce that permutation in the rows or columns of the other matrix.

Given a permutation π of m elements,

$$\pi : \{1, \ldots, m\} \to \{1, \ldots, m\}$$

given in two-line form by

$$\begin{pmatrix} 1 & 2 & \cdots & m \\ \pi(1) & \pi(2) & \cdots & \pi(m) \end{pmatrix},$$

its _____ is the m × m matrix P_π whose entries are all 0 except that in row i, the entry equals 1.

    a. Cartan matrix
    c. Partitioned matrix
    b. Hessenberg matrix
    d. Permutation Matrix

Chapter 13. Functions of Several Variables

36. In mathematics, the word _____ means two different things in the context of polynomials:

- The first meaning is a product of powers of variables, or formally any value obtained from 1 by finitely many multiplications by a variable. If only a single variable x is considered this means that any _____ is either 1 or a power x^n of x, with n a positive integer. If several variables are considered, say, x, y, z, then each can be given an exponent, so that any _____ is of the form $x^a y^b z^c$ with a,b,c nonnegative integers.
- The second meaning of _____ includes _____s in the first sense, but also allows multiplication by any constant, so that $-7x^5$ and $4yz^{13}$ are also considered to be _____s.

With either definition, the set of _____s is a subset of all polynomials that is closed under multiplication.

a. Power sum symmetric polynomial
b. Diagonal form
c. Homogeneous polynomial
d. Monomial

37. In mathematics, a _____ is an expression constructed from variables and constants, using the operations of addition, subtraction, multiplication, and constant non-negative whole number exponents. For example, $x^2 - 4x + 7$ is a _____, but $x^2 - 4/x + 7x^{3/2}$ is not, because its second term involves division by the variable x and also because its third term contains an exponent that is not a whole number.

_____s are one of the most important concepts in algebra and throughout mathematics and science.

a. Coimage
b. Semifield
c. Group extension
d. Polynomial

38. In probability theory, a probability distribution is called _____ if its cumulative distribution function is _____. That is equivalent to saying that for random variables X with the distribution in question, Pr[X = a] = 0 for all real numbers a. If the distribution of X is _____ then X is called a _____ random variable.

a. Continuous phase modulation
b. Conull set
c. Concatenated codes
d. Continuous

39. This article will state and prove the _____ for differentiation, and then use it to prove these two formulas.

The _____ for differentiation states that for every natural number n, the derivative of $f(x) = x^n$ is $f'(x) = nx^{n-1}$, that is,

$$(x^n)' = nx^{n-1}.$$

The _____ for integration

$$\int x^n \, dx = \frac{x^{n+1}}{n+1} + C$$

for natural n is then an easy consequence. One just needs to take the derivative of this equality and use the _____ and linearity of differentiation on the right-hand side.

a. Standard part function
b. Functional integration
c. Power Rule
d. Periodic function

40. In mathematics, the image of a _____ under a given function is the set of all possible function outputs when taking each element of the _____, successively, as the function's argument.

If f : X → Y is a function from set X to set Y and x is a member of X, then f

a. Horizontal line test
b. Preimage
c. Cartesian product
d. Set of all sets

41. In descriptive statistics, the _____ is the length of the smallest interval which contains all the data. It is calculated by subtracting the smallest observations from the greatest and provides an indication of statistical dispersion.

It is measured in the same units as the data.

a. Kernel
b. Bandwidth
c. Class
d. Range

42. In mathematics, an _____ is a function which associates distinct arguments with distinct values.

An _____ is called an injection, and is also said to be an information-preserving or one-to-one function.

A function f that is not injective is sometimes called many-to-one.

a. A chemical equation
b. A Mathematical Theory of Communication
c. Unary function
d. Injective function

43. In mathematics, the _____ of a number n is the number that, when added to n, yields zero. The _____ of n is denoted −n. For example, 7 is −7, because 7 + (−7) = 0, and the _____ of −0.3 is 0.3, because −0.3 + 0.3 = 0.
a. Arity
b. Additive inverse
c. Algebraic structure
d. Associativity

44. In economics, an _____ is a function that maps the quantity of output supplied to the market price for that output.

In mathematical terms, if the demand function is , then the _____ is f^{-1}

a. Arrow-Debreu model
b. Internal rate of return
c. Enterprise value
d. Inverse demand function

Chapter 13. Functions of Several Variables

45. In mathematics, a function f is said to be surjective or _____, if its values span its whole codomain; that is, for every y in the codomain, there is at least one x in the domain such that f(x) = y .

Said another way, a function f: X → Y is surjective if and only if its range f(X) is equal to its codomain Y. A surjective function is called a surjection.

   a. A Mathematical Theory of Communication
   b. A chemical equation
   c. A posteriori
   d. Onto

46. In mathematics, a function f is said to be _____ or onto, if its values span its whole codomain; that is, for every y in the codomain, there is at least one x in the domain such that f

Said another way, a function f: X → Y is _____ if and only if its range f

   a. High-dimensional model representation
   b. Linear map
   c. Rotation of axes
   d. Surjective

47. A _____ number is a positive integer which has a positive divisor other than one or itself. By definition, every integer greater than one is either a prime number or a _____ number.zero and one are considered to be neither prime nor _____. For example, the integer 14 is a _____ number because it can be factored as 2 × 7.
   a. Basis
   b. Composite
   c. Key server
   d. Discontinuity

Chapter 14. Calculus of Several Variables

1. _____ is an important concept in economics with broad applications in game theory, engineering and the social sciences. The term is named after Vilfredo Pareto, an Italian economist who used the concept in his studies of economic efficiency and income distribution.

Given a set of alternative allocations of, say, goods or income for a set of individuals, a change from one allocation to another that can make at least one individual better off without making any other individual worse off is called a Pareto improvement.

    a. Multiunit auction   b. Quasi-perfect equilibrium
    c. Pareto efficiency   d. Pursuit-evasion

2. _____ is a fundamental construction of differential calculus and admits many possible generalizations within the fields of mathematical analysis, combinatorics, algebra, and geometry.

In real, complex, and functional analysis, _____s are generalized to functions of several real or complex variables and functions between topological vector spaces. An important case is the variational _____ in the calculus of variations.

    a. Lin-Tsien equation   b. Functional derivative
    c. Derivative   d. Metric derivative

3. In mathematics, a _____ of a function of several variables is its derivative with respect to one of those variables with the others held constant. _____s are useful in vector calculus and differential geometry.

The _____ of a function f with respect to the variable x is written as f_x, $\partial_x f$, or $\partial f / \partial x$.

    a. Partial derivative   b. Critical number
    c. Laplacian   d. Laplace invariant

4. In economics, the _____ functional form of production functions is widely used to represent the relationship of an output to inputs. It was proposed by Knut Wicksell, and tested against statistical evidence by Paul Douglas and Charles Cobb in 1928.
    a. Burden of proof   b. Cobb-Douglas
    c. State price vector   d. State price

5. The Condorcet candidate or _____ of an election is the candidate who, when compared with every other candidate, is preferred by more voters. Informally, the _____ is the person who would win a two-candidate election against each of the other candidates. A _____ will not always exist in a given set of votes, which is known as Condorcet's voting paradox.
    a. Condorcet winner   b. Psephology
    c. 120-cell   d. 1-center problem

6. The _____ governs the differentiation of products of differentiable functions.
    a. 1-center problem   b. Reciprocal Rule
    c. Product Rule   d. 120-cell

7. _____ (CES) is a property of some production functions and utility functions.

Chapter 14. Calculus of Several Variables

More precisely, it refers to a particular type of aggregator function which combines two or more types of consumption, or two or more types of productive inputs into an aggregate quantity. This aggregator function exhibits _____.

a. Constant elasticity of substitution
b. Production function
c. 1-center problem
d. Short-run

8. The mathematical concept of a _____ expresses the intuitive idea of deterministic dependence between two quantities, one of which is viewed as primary and the other as secondary. A _____ then is a way to associate a unique output for each input of a specified type, for example, a real number or an element of a given set.

a. Going up
b. Grill
c. Function
d. Coherent

9. _____ (MPK) is the additional output resulting from the use of an additional unit of capital (ceteris paribus assuming all other factors are fixed.) It equals to 1 divided by the Incremental Capital-Output Ratio.

- Production theory basics

a. 1-center problem
b. 120-cell
c. 2-3 heap
d. Marginal product of capital

10. In economics, a _____ is a function that specifies the output of a firm, an industry, or an entire economy for all combinations of inputs. A meta-_____ compares the practice of the existing entities converting inputs X into output y to determine the most efficient practice _____ of the existing entities, whether the most efficient feasible practice production or the most efficient actual practice production. In either case, the maximum output of a technologically-determined production process is a mathematical function of input factors of production.

a. Production function
b. 1-center problem
c. Short-run
d. Long-run

11. In mathematics, an _____ is a generalization for the concept of a function in which the dependent variable has not been given 'explicitly' in terms of the independent variable. To give a function f explicitly is to provide a prescription for determining the value of the function y in terms of the input value x:

$$y = f$$

a. Ordinary differential equation
b. Implicit Function
c. Inflection point
d. Implicit differentiation

12. In the branch of mathematics called multivariable calculus, the _____ is a tool which allows relations to be converted to functions. It does this by representing the relation as the graph of a function. There may not be a single function whose graph is the entire relation, but there may be such a function on a restriction of the domain of the relation.

a. Inverse function theorem
b. A chemical equation
c. A Mathematical Theory of Communication
d. Implicit Function Theorem

Chapter 14. Calculus of Several Variables

13. In mathematics, a _____ is a statement that can be proved on the basis of explicitly stated or previously agreed assumptions.
    a. Logical value
    b. Boolean function
    c. Disjunction introduction
    d. Theorem

14. In economics, the cross elasticity of demand and _____ measures the responsiveness of the quantity demanded of a good to a change in the price of another good.

    It is measured as the percentage change in quantity demanded for the first good that occurs in response to a percentage change in price of the second good. For example, if, in response to a 10% increase in the price of fuel, the quantity of new cars that are fuel inefficient demanded decreased by 20%, the cross elasticity of demand would be -20%/10% = -2.

    a. Supply and demand
    b. 1-center problem
    c. Marginal rate of substitution
    d. Cross price elasticity of demand

15. In mathematics, the concept of a _____ tries to capture the intuitive idea of a geometrical one-dimensional and continuous object. A simple example is the circle. In everyday use of the term '_____', a straight line is not curved, but in mathematical parlance _____s include straight lines and line segments.
    a. Kappa curve
    b. Negative pedal curve
    c. Quadrifolium
    d. Curve

16. Price _____ is defined as the measure of responsivenesses in the quantity demanded for a commodity as a result of change in price of the same commodity. In other words, it is percentage change in quantity demanded as per the percentage change in price of the same commodity. In economics and business studies, the price _____ is a measure of the sensitivity of quantity demanded to changes in price. It is measured as elasticity, that is it measures the relationship as the ratio of percentage changes between quantity demanded of a good and changes in its price.
    a. A Mathematical Theory of Communication
    b. A posteriori
    c. Elasticity of demand
    d. A chemical equation

17. In mathematics, the interior of a set S consists of all points of S that are intuitively 'not on the edge of S'. A point that is in the interior of S is an _____ of S.

    The exterior of a set is the interior of its complement; it consists of the points that are not in the set or its boundary.

    a. A posteriori
    b. A Mathematical Theory of Communication
    c. A chemical equation
    d. Interior point

18. _____ is defined as the measure of responsiveness in the quantity demanded for a commodity as a result of change in price of the same commodity. In other words, it is percentage change in quantity demanded as per the percentage change in price of the same commodity. In economics and business studies, the _____ (PED) is a measure of the sensitivity of quantity demanded to changes in price.
    a. 1-center problem
    b. 120-cell
    c. 2-3 heap
    d. Price elasticity of demand

Chapter 14. Calculus of Several Variables

19. In discrete mathematics and predominantly in set theory, a _____ is a concept used in comparisons of sets to refer to the unique values of one set in relation to another. The terms 'absolute' and 'relative' _____ refer to more specific applications of the concept, with universal _____s referring to elements unique to the universal set and the latter referring to the unique elements of one set in relation to another. In this image, the universal set is represented by the border of the image, and the set A as a disc.
   a. Derivative algebra
   b. Kernel
   c. Huge
   d. Complement

20. In economics, the _____ measures the responsiveness of the quantity demanded of a good to the change in the income of the people demanding the good. It is calculated as the ratio of the percent change in quantity demanded to the percent change in income. For example, if, in response to a 10% increase in income, the quantity of a good demanded increased by 20%, the _____ would be 20%/10% = 2.
   a. Expenditure function
   b. Utility maximization problem
   c. Expenditure minimization problem
   d. Income elasticity of demand

21. In mathematics, a _____ is, informally, an infinitely vast and infinitely thin sheet. _____s may be thought of as objects in some higher dimensional space, or they may be considered without any outside space, as in the setting of Euclidean geometry
   a. Blocking
   b. Group
   c. Bandwidth
   d. Plane

22. In trigonometry, the _____ is a function defined as $\tan x = \sin x / \cos x$. The function is so-named because it can be defined as the length of a certain segment of a _____ (in the geometric sense) to the unit circle. In plane geometry, a line is _____ to a curve, at some point, if both line and curve pass through the point with the same direction.
   a. Tangent
   b. Conformal geometry
   c. Projective connection
   d. Hopf conjectures

23. In mathematics, the _____ is a representation of a function as an infinite sum of terms calculated from the values of its derivatives at a single point. It may be regarded as the limit of the Taylor polynomials. _____ are named after English mathematician Brook Taylor.
   a. C^r topology
   b. Local linearity
   c. 1-center problem
   d. Taylor series

24. Suppose that $\varphi : M \to N$ is a smooth map between smooth manifolds; then the _____ of φ at a point x is, in some sense, the best linear approximation of φ near x. It can be viewed as generalization of the total derivative of ordinary calculus. Explicitly, it is a linear map from the tangent space of M at x to the tangent space of N at φ
   a. Grill
   b. Concurrent
   c. Boundary
   d. Differential

25. _____s is concerned with the tasks of developing and applying quantitative or statistical methods to the study and elucidation of economic principles. _____s combines economic theory with statistics to analyze and test economic relationships. Theoretical _____s considers questions about the statistical properties of estimators and tests, while applied _____s is concerned with the application of _____ methods to assess economic theories.
   a. Economic
   b. Econometric
   c. A Mathematical Theory of Communication
   d. A chemical equation

26. In mathematics and in the sciences, a _____ (plural: _____e, formulæ or _____s) is a concise way of expressing information symbolically (as in a mathematical or chemical _____), or a general relationship between quantities. One of many famous _____e is Albert Einstein's E = mc² (see special relativity

In mathematics, a _____ is a key to solve an equation with variables. For example, the problem of determining the volume of a sphere is one that requires a significant amount of integral calculus to solve.

a. 1-center problem
b. 2-3 heap
c. 120-cell
d. Formula

27. In mathematics, a _____ is often represented as the sum of a sequence of terms. That is, a _____ is represented as a list of numbers with addition operations between them, for example this arithmetic sequence:

    1 + 2 + 3 + 4 + 5 + ... + 99 + 100

In most cases of interest the terms of the sequence are produced according to a certain rule, such as by a formula, by an algorithm, by a sequence of measurements, or even by a random number generator.

a. Blind
b. Concavity
c. Contact
d. Series

28. In mathematics, a _____ is a certain kind of ordinary differential equation which is widely used in physics and engineering.

Given a simply connected and open subset D of R² and two functions I and J which are continuous on D then an implicit first-order ordinary differential equation of the form

$$I(x,y)\,dx + J(x,y)\,dy = 0,$$

is called exact differential equation if there exists a continuously differentiable function F, called the potential function, so that

$$\frac{\partial F}{\partial x}(x,y) = I$$

and

$$\frac{\partial F}{\partial y}(x,y) = J.$$

The nomenclature of 'exact differential equation' refers to the exact derivative (or total derivative) of a function. For a function F $(x_0, x_1, ..., x_{n-1}, x_n)$, the exact or total derivative with respect to x_0 is given by

$$\frac{dF}{dx_0} = \frac{\partial F}{\partial x_0} + \sum_{i=1}^{n} \frac{\partial F}{\partial x_i} \frac{dx_i}{dx_0}.$$

The function

$$F(x, y) := \frac{1}{2}(x^2 + y^2)$$

is a potential function for the differential equation

$$xx' + yy' = 0.$$

In physical applications the functions I and J are usually not only continuous but even continuously differentiable.

a. Total differential equation
b. Sturm-Liouville equation
c. Riccati equation
d. Wronskian

29. In mathematics, _____ are functions which can be used to prove the stability of a certain fixed point in a dynamical system or autonomous differential equation. Named after the Russian mathematician Aleksandr Mikhailovich Lyapunov, _____ are important to stability theory and control theory.

Functions which might prove the stability of some equilibrium are called Lyapunov-candidate-functions.

a. 120-cell
b. 1-center problem
c. Lyapunov functions
d. Butterfly effect

30. In vector calculus, the _____ is shorthand for either the _____ matrix or its determinant, the _____ determinant.

In algebraic geometry the _____ of a curve means the _____ variety: a group variety associated to the curve, in which the curve can be embedded.

These concepts are all named after the mathematician Carl Gustav Jacob Jacobi.

a. Monkey saddle
b. Shift theorem
c. Surface integral
d. Jacobian

Chapter 14. Calculus of Several Variables

31. In physics and in _____ calculus, a _____ is a concept characterized by a magnitude and a direction. A _____ can be thought of as an arrow in Euclidean space, drawn from an initial point A pointing to a terminal point B.
    a. Dominance
    b. Vector
    c. Constraint
    d. Deviation

32. _____ of an object is its speed in a particular direction.
    a. Maxima
    b. Velocity
    c. Rolle's Theorem
    d. Discontinuity

33. In singularity theory a _____ is a singular point of a curve. Spinode is an alternative name, but this is less commonly used today.

For a curve defined as the zero set of a function of two variables f, the _____ s on the curve will have the following properties:

1. $f(x, y) = 0$
2. $\frac{\partial f}{\partial x} = \frac{\partial f}{\partial y} = 0$
3. The Hessian matrix of second derivatives has zero determinant.

A classic example of a curve that exhibits a _____ is the curve defined by

$$x^3 - y^2 = 0.$$

This curve can be expressed parametrically by the equations

$$x = t^2, y = t^3.$$

This curve has a _____ at the origin.

   a. Dense
   b. Cusp
   c. Character
   d. Brute Force

34. In mathematics, the _____ or Pythagoras' theorem is a relation in Euclidean geometry among the three sides of a right triangle. The theorem is named after the Greek mathematician Pythagoras, who by tradition is credited with its discovery and proof, although it is often argued that knowledge of the theory predates him.. The theorem is as follows:

In any right triangle, the area of the square whose side is the hypotenuse is equal to the sum of the areas of the squares whose sides are the two legs.

   a. 2-3 heap
   b. 1-center problem
   c. 120-cell
   d. Pythagorean Theorem

Chapter 14. Calculus of Several Variables

35. In mathematical analysis, a _____ is a classification of functions according to the properties of their derivatives. Higher order _____ es correspond to the existence of more derivatives. Functions that have derivatives of all orders are called smooth.

   a. Logarithmic derivative
   b. Differentiability class
   c. Directional derivative
   d. Metric derivative

36. _____ of the difference quotient as h approaches zero, if this limit exists. If the limit exists, then f is _____ at a. Here f' (a) is one of several common notations for the derivative

   a. 1-center problem
   b. 2-3 heap
   c. 120-cell
   d. Differentiable

37. In mathematics, the _____ of a multivariate differentiable function along a given vector V at a given point P intuitively represents the instantaneous rate of change of the function, moving through P, in the direction of V. It therefore generalizes the notion of a partial derivative, in which the direction is always taken parallel to one of the coordinate axes.

   The _____ is a special case of the Gâteaux derivative.

   a. Directional derivative
   b. Second derivative test
   c. Gradient
   d. Metric derivative

38. The Gompertz-Makeham law states that death rate is a sum of age-independent component and age-dependent component, which increases exponentially with age. In a protected environment where external causes of death are rare the age-independent mortality component is often negligible, and in this case the formula simplifies to a _____ of mortality with exponential increase in death rates with age.

   The Gompertz-Makeham law of mortality describes the age dynamics of human mortality rather accurately in the age window of about 30-80 years.

   a. 1-center problem
   b. 120-cell
   c. Gompertz-Makeham law of mortality
   d. Gompertz law

39. In vector calculus, the _____ of a scalar field is a vector field which points in the direction of the greatest rate of increase of the scalar field, and whose magnitude is the greatest rate of change.

   A generalization of the _____ for functions on a Euclidean space which have values in another Euclidean space is the Jacobian. A further generalization for a function from one Banach space to another is the Fréchet derivative.

   a. Directional derivative
   b. Metric derivative
   c. Stationary point
   d. Gradient

40. In calculus, the _____ is a formula for the derivative of the composite of two functions.

Chapter 14. Calculus of Several Variables

In intuitive terms, if a variable, y, depends on a second variable, u, which in turn depends on a third variable, x, then the rate of change of y with respect to x can be computed as the rate of change of y with respect to u multiplied by the rate of change of u with respect to x. Schematically,

$$\frac{dy}{dx} = \frac{dy}{du} \cdot \frac{du}{dx}.$$

For an explanation of notation used in this section, see Function composition.

The _____ states that, under appropriate conditions,

$$(f \circ g)'(x) = f'(g(x))g'(x),$$

which in short form is written as

$$(f \circ g)' = f' \circ g \cdot g'.$$

Alternatively, in the Leibniz notation, the _____ is

$$\frac{dy}{dx} = \frac{dy}{du} \cdot \frac{du}{dx}.$$

In integration, the counterpart to the _____ is the substitution rule.

a. Chain Rule
c. Product rule
b. 120-cell
d. 1-center problem

41. In Boolean algebra, any Boolean function can be expressed in a _____ using the dual concepts of minterms and maxterms. All logical functions are expressible in _____, both as a 'sum of minterms' and as a 'product of maxterms'. This allows for greater analysis into the simplification of these functions, which is of great importance in the minimization of digital circuits.
a. Multiplicative digital root
c. Reduct
b. Topological module
d. Canonical form

42. In mathematics, the _____ is the square matrix of second-order partial derivatives of a function; that is, it describes the local curvature of a function of many variables. The _____ was developed in the 19th century by the German mathematician Ludwig Otto Hesse and later named after him. Hesse himself had used the term 'functional determinants'.
a. Jacobian
c. Partial derivative
b. Hessian matrix
d. Multivariable calculus

Chapter 14. Calculus of Several Variables

43. In statistics, _____ has two related meanings:

- the arithmetic _____.
- the expected value of a random variable, which is also called the population _____.

It is sometimes stated that the '_____' _____s average. This is incorrect if '_____' is taken in the specific sense of 'arithmetic _____' as there are different types of averages: the _____, median, and mode. For instance, average house prices almost always use the median value for the average.

For a real-valued random variable X, the _____ is the expectation of X.

a. Statistical population
c. Probability
b. Mean
d. Proportional hazards model

44. In calculus, the _____ states, roughly, that given a section of a smooth curve, there is at least one point on that section at which the derivative of the curve is equal to the 'average' derivative of the section. It is used to prove theorems that make global conclusions about a function on an interval starting from local hypotheses about derivatives at points of the interval.

This theorem can be understood concretely by applying it to motion: if a car travels one hundred miles in one hour, so that its average speed during that time was 100 miles per hour, then at some time its instantaneous speed must have been exactly 100 miles per hour.

a. Calculus controversy
c. Functional integration
b. Mean Value Theorem
d. Fundamental Theorem of Calculus

45. In mathematics, a _____ is a rectangular table of elements, which may be numbers or, more generally, any abstract quantities that can be added and multiplied. Matrices are used to describe linear equations, keep track of the coefficients of linear transformations and to record data that depend on multiple parameters. Matrices are described by the field of _____ theory.

a. Coherent
c. Matrix
b. Double counting
d. Compression

46. The _____ theory of wages, also referred to as the marginal revenue product of labor, is the change in total revenue earned by a firm that results from employing one more unit of labor. It is a neoclassical model that determines, under some conditions, the optimal number of workers to employ at an exogenously determined market wage rate. See Daniel S.

a. Marginal revenue productivity
c. Coordinate rotations and reflections
b. Continuum hypothesis
d. Continuous wave

47. _____ in economics refers to measures of output from production processes, per unit of input. Labor _____, for example, is typically measured as a ratio of output per labor-hour, an input. _____ may be conceived of as a measure of the technical or engineering efficiency of production.

a. 1-center problem
c. 2-3 heap
b. 120-cell
d. Productivity

48. In linear algebra, a _____ is a square matrix, A, that is equal to its transpose

$$A = A^T.$$

The entries of a _____ are symmetric with respect to the main diagonal. So if the entries are written as A =, then

$$a_{ij} = a_{ji}$$

for all indices i and j. The following 3×3 matrix is symmetric:

$$\begin{bmatrix} 1 & 2 & 3 \\ 2 & 4 & -5 \\ 3 & -5 & 6 \end{bmatrix}.$$

A matrix is called skew-symmetric or antisymmetric if its transpose is the same as its negative.

a. Broken-line graph
c. Contour integration
b. Conway triangle notation
d. Symmetric matrix

Chapter 15. Implicit Functions and Their Derivatives

1. _____ describes the property of operations in mathematics and computer science which means that multiple applications of the operation does not change the result. The concept of _____ arises in a number of places in abstract algebra.

There are several meanings of _____, depending on what the concept is applied to:

- A unary operation is called idempotent if, whenever it is applied twice to any value, it gives the same result as if it were applied once. For example, the absolute value function is idempotent as a function from the set of real numbers to the set of real numbers: ab = ab.
- A binary operation is called idempotent if, whenever it is applied to two equal values, it gives that value as the result. For example, the operation giving the maximum value of two values is idempotent: ma = x.
- Given a binary operation, an idempotent element for the operation is a value for which the operation, when given that value for both of its operands, gives the value as the result. For example, the number 1 is an idempotent of multiplication: 1 × 1 = 1.

A unary operation f that is a map from some set S into itself is called idempotent if, for all x in S,

   f

In particular, the identity function id_S, defined by
id_S, is idempotent, as is the constant function K_c, where c is an element of S, defined by $K_c(x) = c$.

a. Antiisomorphism
b. Ordered exponential
c. Absorption law
d. Idempotence

2. In mathematics, a _____ is a rectangular table of elements, which may be numbers or, more generally, any abstract quantities that can be added and multiplied. Matrices are used to describe linear equations, keep track of the coefficients of linear transformations and to record data that depend on multiple parameters. Matrices are described by the field of _____ theory.

a. Double counting
b. Compression
c. Coherent
d. Matrix

3. The mathematical concept of a _____ expresses the intuitive idea of deterministic dependence between two quantities, one of which is viewed as primary and the other as secondary. A _____ then is a way to associate a unique output for each input of a specified type, for example, a real number or an element of a given set.

a. Going up
b. Coherent
c. Function
d. Grill

4. In mathematics, an _____ is a generalization for the concept of a function in which the dependent variable has not been given 'explicitly' in terms of the independent variable. To give a function f explicitly is to provide a prescription for determining the value of the function y in terms of the input value x:

   y = f

a. Implicit function
b. Inflection point
c. Ordinary differential equation
d. Implicit differentiation

5. In mathematics, a _____ is a statement that can be proved on the basis of explicitly stated or previously agreed assumptions.
   a. Logical value
   b. Disjunction introduction
   c. Boolean function
   d. Theorem

6. The Condorcet candidate or _____ of an election is the candidate who, when compared with every other candidate, is preferred by more voters. Informally, the _____ is the person who would win a two-candidate election against each of the other candidates. A _____ will not always exist in a given set of votes, which is known as Condorcet's voting paradox.
   a. 1-center problem
   b. Condorcet winner
   c. 120-cell
   d. Psephology

7. In the branch of mathematics called multivariable calculus, the _____ is a tool which allows relations to be converted to functions. It does this by representing the relation as the graph of a function. There may not be a single function whose graph is the entire relation, but there may be such a function on a restriction of the domain of the relation.
   a. Inverse function theorem
   b. A Mathematical Theory of Communication
   c. A chemical equation
   d. Implicit Function Theorem

8. In mathematics, the _____ or Pythagoras' theorem is a relation in Euclidean geometry among the three sides of a right triangle. The theorem is named after the Greek mathematician Pythagoras, who by tradition is credited with its discovery and proof, although it is often argued that knowledge of the theory predates him.. The theorem is as follows:

In any right triangle, the area of the square whose side is the hypotenuse is equal to the sum of the areas of the squares whose sides are the two legs.

   a. Pythagorean Theorem
   b. 2-3 heap
   c. 1-center problem
   d. 120-cell

9. In mathematics, the concept of a _____ tries to capture the intuitive idea of a geometrical one-dimensional and continuous object. A simple example is the circle. In everyday use of the term '_____', a straight line is not curved, but in mathematical parlance _____s include straight lines and line segments.
   a. Negative pedal curve
   b. Kappa curve
   c. Quadrifolium
   d. Curve

10. A _____ is a mathematical space in which every point has a neighborhood which resembles Euclidean space, but in which the global structure may be more complicated. In discussing _____s, the idea of dimension is important. For example, lines are one-dimensional, and planes two-dimensional.
    a. Band sum
    b. Borel algebra
    c. Trivial topology
    d. Manifold

11. The _____, first developed by Sir John Hicks and Alvin Hansen, has been used from 1937 onwards to summarize a major part of Keynesian macroeconomics. IS/LM stands for Investment Saving / Liquidity preference Money supply.

Chapter 15. Implicit Functions and Their Derivatives

The _____ was born at the Econometric Conference held in Oxford during September, 1936.

a. A posteriori
c. A Mathematical Theory of Communication
b. A chemical equation
d. IS/LM model

12. In microeconomic theory, an _____ is a graph showing different bundles of goods, each measured as to quantity, between which a consumer is indifferent. That is, at each point on the curve, the consumer has no preference for one bundle over another. In other words, they are all equally preferred. One can equivalently refer to each point on the _____ as rendering the same level of utility for the consumer.

a. Expenditure function
c. Expenditure minimization problem
b. Utility maximization problem
d. Indifference curve

13. In economics, the _____ is the rate at which a consumer is ready to give up one good in exchange for another good while maintaining the same level of satisfaction.

Under the standard assumption of neoclassical economics that goods and services are continuously divisible, the marginal rates of substitution will be the same regardless of the direction of exchange, and will correspond to the slope of an indifference curve passing through the consumption bundle in question, at that point. MRS of Y for X is the amount of Y for that a consumer is willing to exchange for X locally.

a. Marginal rate of substitution
c. Supply and demand
b. 1-center problem
d. Cross price elasticity of demand

14. In economics, the _____ or the Technical Rate of Substitution is the amount by which the quantity of one input has to be reduced when one extra unit of another input is used, so that output remains constant.

$$MRTS(x_1, x_2) = \frac{\Delta x_2}{\Delta x_1} = -\frac{MP_1}{MP_2}$$

where MP_1 and MP_2 are the marginal products of input 1 and input 2, respectively.

Along an isoquant, the MRTS shows the rate at which one input may be substituted for another, while maintaining the same level of output.

a. Consumer surplus
c. Returns to scale
b. Producer surplus
d. Marginal rate of technical substitution

15. In mathematics, specifically in topology, a _____ is a two-dimensional manifold. The most familiar examples are those that arise as the boundaries of solid objects in ordinary three-dimensional Euclidean space, EÂ³. On the other hand, there are also more exotic _____s, that are so 'contorted' that they cannot be embedded in three-dimensional space at all.

a. Homoeoid
c. Standard torus
b. Cross-cap
d. Surface

16. In economics, the _____ functional form of production functions is widely used to represent the relationship of an output to inputs. It was proposed by Knut Wicksell, and tested against statistical evidence by Paul Douglas and Charles Cobb in 1928.
   a. Burden of proof
   b. State price
   c. State price vector
   d. Cobb-Douglas

17. The _____ governs the differentiation of products of differentiable functions.
   a. Product Rule
   b. 120-cell
   c. Reciprocal Rule
   d. 1-center problem

18. In economics, _____ is the comparison of two different equilibrium states, before and after a change in some underlying exogenous parameter. As a study of statics it compares two different unchanging points, after they have changed. It does not study the motion towards equilibrium, nor the process of the change itself.
   a. Producer surplus
   b. Marginal rate of technical substitution
   c. Consumer surplus
   d. Comparative statics

19. In mathematics the concept of a _____ generalizes notions such as 'length', 'area', and 'volume'. Informally, given some base set, a '_____' is any consistent assignment of 'sizes' to the subsets of the base set. Depending on the application, the 'size' of a subset may be interpreted as its physical size, the amount of something that lies within the subset, or the probability that some random process will yield a result within the subset.
   a. Lattice
   b. Cusp
   c. Congruent
   d. Measure

20. In statistics and mathematical epidemiology, _____ is the risk of an event relative to exposure. _____ is a ratio of the probability of the event occurring in the exposed group versus a non-exposed group.

$$RR = \frac{p_{\text{exposed}}}{p_{\text{non-exposed}}}$$

For example, if the probability of developing lung cancer among smokers was 20% and among non-smokers 1%, then the _____ of cancer associated with smoking would be 20.

   a. Mendelian randomization
   b. Statistical epidemiology
   c. 1-center problem
   d. Relative risk

21. _____ is a concept in economics, finance, and psychology related to the behaviour of consumers and investors under uncertainty. _____ is the reluctance of a person to accept a bargain with an uncertain payoff rather than another bargain with a more certain, but possibly lower, expected payoff.

The inverse of a person's _____ is sometimes called their risk tolerance.

   a. Life table
   b. Ruin theory
   c. Risk aversion
   d. Stochastic modelling

22. In mathematics, an _____ is a function which associates distinct arguments with distinct values.

Chapter 15. Implicit Functions and Their Derivatives

An _____ is called an injection, and is also said to be an information-preserving or one-to-one function.

A function f that is not injective is sometimes called many-to-one.

a. Injective function
b. A chemical equation
c. Unary function
d. A Mathematical Theory of Communication

23. In mathematics, a phenomenon is sometimes said to occur _____ if, roughly speaking, it occurs on sufficiently small or arbitrarily small neighborhoods of points.

A topological space is sometimes said to exhibit a property _____ if the property is exhibited 'near' each point in one of the following different senses:

1. Each point has a neighborhood exhibiting the property;
2. Each point has a neighborhood base of sets exhibiting the property.

Sense (2) is in general stronger than sense (1), and caution must be taken to distinguish between the two senses. For example, some variation in the definition of _____ compact arises from different senses of the term _____.

- _____ compact topological spaces
- _____ connected and _____ path-connected topological spaces
- _____ Hausdorff, _____ regular, _____ normal etc...
- _____ metrizable

Given some notion of equivalence (e.g., homeomorphism, diffeomorphism, isometry) between topological spaces, two spaces are _____ equivalent if every point of the first space has a neighborhood which is equivalent to a neighborhood of the second space.

For instance, the circle and the line are very different objects.

a. Locally Hausdorff space
b. Locally
c. Pseudo-Anosov map
d. Countable tightness

24. In mathematics, a function f is said to be surjective or _____, if its values span its whole codomain; that is, for every y in the codomain, there is at least one x in the domain such that f(x) = y.

Said another way, a function f: X → Y is surjective if and only if its range f(X) is equal to its codomain Y. A surjective function is called a surjection.

a. A chemical equation
b. A posteriori
c. A Mathematical Theory of Communication
d. Onto

25. In mathematics, a function f is said to be _____ or onto, if its values span its whole codomain; that is, for every y in the codomain, there is at least one x in the domain such that f

Said another way, a function f: X → Y is _____ if and only if its range f

    a. High-dimensional model representation   b. Surjective
    c. Linear map   d. Rotation of axes

26. In microeconomics, a consumer's _____ function is the demand of a consumer over a bundle of goods that minimizes their expenditure while delivering a fixed level of utility. The function is named after John Hicks.

Mathematically,

$$h(p, \bar{u}) = \arg\min_x \sum_i p_i x_i$$
$$\text{such that} \quad u(x) > \bar{u}$$

where h is the _____ function, or commodity bundle demanded, at price level p and utility level $\bar{u}$.

    a. Precautionary demand   b. Marshallian demand function
    c. 1-center problem   d. Hicksian demand

27. In mathematics, the _____ of a number n is the number that, when added to n, yields zero. The _____ of n is denoted −n. For example, 7 is −7, because 7 + (−7) = 0, and the _____ of −0.3 is 0.3, because −0.3 + 0.3 = 0.
    a. Associativity   b. Additive inverse
    c. Arity   d. Algebraic structure

28. An _____ is a function which does the reverse of a given function.
    a. Empty set   b. A Mathematical Theory of Communication
    c. Empty function   d. Inverse Function

29. In mathematics, the _____ gives sufficient conditions for a vector-valued function to be invertible on an open region containing a point in its domain. Further, the theorem shows the total derivative of the inverse function exists and gives a formula for it. The theorem can be generalized to maps defined on manifolds, and on infinite dimensional Banach spaces.
    a. A chemical equation   b. Isoperimetric inequality
    c. A Mathematical Theory of Communication   d. Inverse Function Theorem

30. In mathematics, a _____ is an isomorphism of smooth manifolds. It is an invertible function that maps one differentiable manifold to another, such that both the function and its inverse are smooth. The image of a rectangular grid on a square under a _____ from the square onto itself.

Chapter 15. Implicit Functions and Their Derivatives

Given two manifolds M and N, a bijective map f from M to N is called a _____ if both

$$f : M \to N$$

and its inverse

$$f^{-1} : N \to M$$

are differentiable.

a. 1-center problem
b. 120-cell
c. 2-3 heap
d. Diffeomorphism

31. In mathematics and in the sciences, a _____ (plural: _____ e, formulæ or _____ s) is a concise way of expressing information symbolically (as in a mathematical or chemical _____), or a general relationship between quantities. One of many famous _____ e is Albert Einstein's E = mc² (see special relativity

In mathematics, a _____ is a key to solve an equation with variables. For example, the problem of determining the volume of a sphere is one that requires a significant amount of integral calculus to solve.

a. 2-3 heap
b. 120-cell
c. 1-center problem
d. Formula

32. In the mathematical field of topology, a _____ or topological isomorphism = similar and μορφÎ® = shape = form) is a bicontinuous function between two topological spaces. _____ s are the isomorphisms in the category of topological spaces -- that is, they are the mappings which preserve all the topological properties of a given space. Two spaces with a _____ between them are called homeomorphic, and from a topological viewpoint they are the same.

a. 2-3 heap
b. Homeomorphism
c. 120-cell
d. 1-center problem

33. _____ is the probability of some event A, given the occurrence of some other event B. _____ is written P[A│B], and is read 'the probability of A, given B'.

Joint probability is the probability of two events in conjunction. That is, it is the probability of both events together. The joint probability of A and B is written $P(A \cap B)$ or $P(A,B)$.

a. Quantile
b. Sample space
c. Renewal theory
d. Conditional probability

34. _____ is the likelihood or chance that something is the case or will happen. Theoretical _____ is used extensively in areas such as statistics, mathematics, science and philosophy to draw conclusions about the likelihood of potential events and the underlying mechanics of complex systems.

The word _____ does not have a consistent direct definition.

a. Statistical significance
b. Standardized moment
c. Discrete random variable
d. Probability

35. In statistics, the _____ one-way analysis of variance by ranks is a non-parametric method for testing equality of population medians among groups. Intuitively, it is identical to a one-way analysis of variance with the data replaced by their ranks. It is an extension of the Mann-Whitney U test to 3 or more groups.
   a. Kruskal-Wallis
   b. Sign test
   c. P-rep
   d. Lilliefors test

Chapter 16. Quadratic Forms and Definite Matrices

1. In mathematics, the _____ or Pythagoras' theorem is a relation in Euclidean geometry among the three sides of a right triangle. The theorem is named after the Greek mathematician Pythagoras, who by tradition is credited with its discovery and proof, although it is often argued that knowledge of the theory predates him.. The theorem is as follows:

In any right triangle, the area of the square whose side is the hypotenuse is equal to the sum of the areas of the squares whose sides are the two legs.

a. 1-center problem
b. 2-3 heap
c. 120-cell
d. Pythagorean Theorem

2. Georg Friedrich Bernhard _____ was a German mathematician who made important contributions to analysis and differential geometry, some of them paving the way for the later development of general relativity.

_____ was born in Breselenz, a village near Dannenberg in the Kingdom of Hanover in what is today Germany. His father, Friedrich Bernhard _____, was a poor Lutheran pastor in Breselenz who fought in the Napoleonic Wars.

a. Riemann
b. Brook Taylor
c. Gustave Bertrand
d. Paul C. van Oorschot

3. In mathematics, a _____ is a method for approximating the total area underneath a curve on a graph, otherwise known as an integral. It may also be used to define the integration operation. The sums are named after the German mathematician Bernhard Riemann.

a. Solid of revolution
b. Multiple integral
c. Riemann sum
d. Singular measure

4. In mathematics, a _____ is a statement that can be proved on the basis of explicitly stated or previously agreed assumptions.

a. Disjunction introduction
b. Boolean function
c. Logical value
d. Theorem

5. If ε is a vector of n random variables, and Λ is an n-dimensional symmetric square matrix, then the scalar quantity ε'Λε is known as a _____ in ε.

It can be shown that

$$E[\epsilon'\Lambda\epsilon] = \text{tr}[\Lambda\Sigma] + \mu'\Lambda\mu$$

where μ and Σ are the expected value and variance-covariance matrix of ε, respectively, and tr denotes the trace of a matrix. This result only depends on the existence of μ and Σ; in particular, normality of ε is not required.

a. Complex conjugate vector space
b. Field of values
c. Quadratic form
d. Gram-Schmidt process

Chapter 16. Quadratic Forms and Definite Matrices

6. The mathematical concept of a _____ expresses the intuitive idea of deterministic dependence between two quantities, one of which is viewed as primary and the other as secondary. A _____ then is a way to associate a unique output for each input of a specified type, for example, a real number or an element of a given set.
   - a. Coherent
   - b. Grill
   - c. Going up
   - d. Function

7. In mathematics, an _____ is a generalization for the concept of a function in which the dependent variable has not been given 'explicitly' in terms of the independent variable. To give a function f explicitly is to provide a prescription for determining the value of the function y in terms of the input value x:

   y = f

   - a. Implicit Function
   - b. Inflection point
   - c. Implicit differentiation
   - d. Ordinary differential equation

8. In the branch of mathematics called multivariable calculus, the _____ is a tool which allows relations to be converted to functions. It does this by representing the relation as the graph of a function. There may not be a single function whose graph is the entire relation, but there may be such a function on a restriction of the domain of the relation.
   - a. Inverse function theorem
   - b. A chemical equation
   - c. A Mathematical Theory of Communication
   - d. Implicit Function Theorem

9. In mathematics, a _____ is a rectangular table of elements, which may be numbers or, more generally, any abstract quantities that can be added and multiplied. Matrices are used to describe linear equations, keep track of the coefficients of linear transformations and to record data that depend on multiple parameters. Matrices are described by the field of _____ theory.
   - a. Double counting
   - b. Matrix
   - c. Compression
   - d. Coherent

10. In several fields of mathematics the term _____ is used with different but closely related meanings. They all relate to the notion of mapping the elements of a set to other elements of the same set, i.e., exchanging elements of a set.

    The general concept of _____ can be defined more formally in different contexts:

    In combinatorics, a _____ is usually understood to be a sequence containing each element from a finite set once, and only once.

    - a. Linearly independent
    - b. Permutation
    - c. Cyclic permutation
    - d. Tensor product

11. In mathematics, in matrix theory, a _____ is a square-matrix that has exactly one entry 1 in each row and each column and 0's elsewhere. Each such matrix represents a specific permutation of m elements and, when used to multiply another matrix, can produce that permutation in the rows or columns of the other matrix.

Chapter 16. Quadratic Forms and Definite Matrices

Given a permutation π of m elements,

$$\pi : \{1, \ldots, m\} \rightarrow \{1, \ldots, m\}$$

given in two-line form by

$$\begin{pmatrix} 1 & 2 & \cdots & m \\ \pi(1) & \pi(2) & \cdots & \pi(m) \end{pmatrix},$$

its _____ is the m × m matrix P_π whose entries are all 0 except that in row i, the entry equals 1.

a. Partitioned matrix
b. Hessenberg matrix
c. Cartan matrix
d. Permutation Matrix

12. In grammatical theory, definiteness is a feature of noun phrases, distinguishing between entities which are specific and identifiable in a given context (_____ noun phrases) and entities which are not (indefinite noun phrases Examples are:

- Free form: English the boy.
- Phrasal clitic: as in Basque: Cf. emakume ('woman'), emakume-a (woman-ART: 'the woman'), emakume ederr-a (woman beautiful-ART: 'the beautiful woman')
- Noun affix: as in Romanian: om ('man'), om-ul (man-ART: 'the man'); om-ul bun (man-ART good: 'the good man')
- Prefix on both noun and adjective: Arabic الكتاب الكبير (al-kitāb al-kabīr) with two instances of al- (DEF-book-DEF-big, literally, 'the book the big')

Germanic, Romance, Celtic, Semitic, and auxiliary languages generally have a _____ article, sometimes used as a postposition. Many other languages do not.

a. 1-center problem
b. Definite
c. Sentence diagram
d. Syntax

13. In mathematics, a definite bilinear form is a bilinear form B over some vector space V (with real or complex scalar field) such that the associated quadratic form

$$Q(x) = B(x,x)$$

is definite, that is, has a real value with the same sign (positive or negative) for all non-zero x. According to that sign, B is called positive definite or _____. If Q takes both positive and negative values, the bilinear form B is called indefinite.

a. Paravector
b. Multilinear map
c. Negative definite
d. Multiple cross product

Chapter 16. Quadratic Forms and Definite Matrices

14. In linear algebra, a _____ is a matrix which in many ways is analogous to a positive real number. The notion is closely related to a positive-definite symmetric bilinear form.

An n × n real symmetric matrix M is positive definite if $z^TMz > 0$ for all non-zero vectors z with real entries, where z^T denotes the transpose of z.

a. Positive-definite matrix
b. Diagonalizable
c. Vandermonde matrix
d. Partitioned matrix

15. In microeconomics, a consumer's _____ specifies what the consumer would buy in each price and wealth situation, assuming it perfectly solves the utility maximization problem. Marshallian demand is sometimes called Walrasian demand or uncompensated demand function instead, because the original Marshallian analysis ignored wealth effects.

According to the utility maximization problem, there are L commodities with prices p.

a. Hicksian demand function
b. 1-center problem
c. Precautionary demand
d. Marshallian demand function

16. In economics, the _____ functional form of production functions is widely used to represent the relationship of an output to inputs. It was proposed by Knut Wicksell, and tested against statistical evidence by Paul Douglas and Charles Cobb in 1928.

a. Burden of proof
b. State price
c. State price vector
d. Cobb-Douglas

17. In mathematics, a _____ is the negative of a convex function. A _____ is also synonymously called concave downwards, concave down or convex cap.

Formally, a real-valued function f defined on an interval is called concave, if for any two points x and y in its domain C and any t in [0,1], we have

$$f(tx + (1-t)y) \geq tf(x) + (1-t)f(y).$$

Also, f−f

a. Darboux function
b. Dirichlet kernel
c. Weight function
d. Concave function

18. This article will state and prove the _____ for differentiation, and then use it to prove these two formulas.

The _____ for differentiation states that for every natural number n, the derivative of $f(x) = x^n$ is $f'(x) = nx^{n-1}$, that is,

$$(x^n)' = nx^{n-1}.$$

The _____ for integration

$$\int x^n \, dx = \frac{x^{n+1}}{n+1} + C$$

for natural n is then an easy consequence. One just needs to take the derivative of this equality and use the _____ and linearity of differentiation on the right-hand side.

a. Periodic function
c. Standard part function
b. Functional integration
d. Power Rule

19.   In linear algebra, a _____ of a matrix A is the determinant of some smaller square matrix, cut down from A by removing one or more of its rows or columns.

_____s obtained by removing just one row and one column from square matrices are required for calculating matrix cofactors, which in turn are useful for computing both the determinant and inverse of square matrices.

Let A be an m × n matrix and k an integer with 0 < k ≤ m, and k ≤ n.

a. Chiral
c. Homogeneity
b. Block size
d. Minor

20.   In mathematics, a _____ is a matrix formed by selecting certain rows and columns from a bigger matrix. That is, as an array, it is cut down to those entries constrained by row and column.

For example

$$\mathbf{A} = \begin{bmatrix} a_{11} & a_{12} & a_{13} & a_{14} \\ a_{21} & a_{22} & a_{23} & a_{24} \\ a_{31} & a_{32} & a_{33} & a_{34} \end{bmatrix}.$$

Then

$$\mathbf{A}[1,2;1,3,4] = \begin{bmatrix} a_{11} & a_{13} & a_{14} \\ a_{21} & a_{23} & a_{24} \end{bmatrix}$$

is a _____ of A formed by rows 1,2 and columns 1,3,4.

   a. Matrix unit   b. Jordan matrix
   c. Submatrix   d. Matrix decomposition

21. The _____ is a single-winner election method in which voters rank candidates in order of preference. The _____ determines the winner of an election by giving each candidate a certain number of points corresponding to the position in which he or she is ranked by each voter. Once all votes have been counted the candidate with the most points is the winner.

   a. Borda count   b. 1-center problem
   c. 2-3 heap   d. 120-cell

Chapter 17. Unconstrained Optimization

1. In economics and consumer theory, a _____ is that which people consume more of as price rises, violating the law of demand. In normal situations, as the price of such a good rises, the substitution effect causes people to purchase less of it and more of substitute goods. In the _____ situation, cheaper close substitutes are not available.
   a. 120-cell
   b. 1-center problem
   c. 2-3 heap
   d. Giffen good

2. In mathematical writing, the adjective _____ is used to modify technical terms which have multiple meanings. It indicates that the exclusive meaning of the term is to be understood. (More formally, one could say that this is the meaning which implies the other meanings.)
   a. Percentage points
   b. Well-behaved
   c. Jargon
   d. Strict

3. The mathematical concept of a _____ expresses the intuitive idea of deterministic dependence between two quantities, one of which is viewed as primary and the other as secondary. A _____ then is a way to associate a unique output for each input of a specified type, for example, a real number or an element of a given set.
   a. Grill
   b. Function
   c. Coherent
   d. Going up

4. In mathematics, an _____ is a generalization for the concept of a function in which the dependent variable has not been given 'explicitly' in terms of the independent variable. To give a function f explicitly is to provide a prescription for determining the value of the function y in terms of the input value x:

   y = f

   a. Inflection point
   b. Ordinary differential equation
   c. Implicit differentiation
   d. Implicit Function

5. In the branch of mathematics called multivariable calculus, the _____ is a tool which allows relations to be converted to functions. It does this by representing the relation as the graph of a function. There may not be a single function whose graph is the entire relation, but there may be such a function on a restriction of the domain of the relation.
   a. A Mathematical Theory of Communication
   b. Inverse function theorem
   c. A chemical equation
   d. Implicit Function Theorem

6. In microeconomics, a consumer's _____ specifies what the consumer would buy in each price and wealth situation, assuming it perfectly solves the utility maximization problem. Marshallian demand is sometimes called Walrasian demand or uncompensated demand function instead, because the original Marshallian analysis ignored wealth effects.

   According to the utility maximization problem, there are L commodities with prices p.

   a. Marshallian demand function
   b. Hicksian demand function
   c. 1-center problem
   d. Precautionary demand

7. In mathematics, a _____ is a statement that can be proved on the basis of explicitly stated or previously agreed assumptions.
   a. Theorem
   b. Boolean function
   c. Disjunction introduction
   d. Logical value

Chapter 17. Unconstrained Optimization

8. In mathematics, a _____ is a point on the domain of a function where:

   - one dimension: the derivative is equal to zero or a point where the function ceases to be differentiable.
   - in general: there are two distinct concepts: either the derivative vanishes, or it is not of full rank; these agree in one dimension.

Note that in one dimension, a critical value or critical number x of function f is the domain element at which the derivative is zero or undefined, whereas the associated ordered pair is the _____. In higher dimensions a critical value is in the range whereas a _____ is in the domain.

There are two situations in which a point becomes a _____ of a function of one variable. The first of which is that the value of the derivative is equal to zero.

a. Going up	b. Derivative algebra
c. Decimal system	d. Critical point

9. In mathematics, the interior of a set S consists of all points of S that are intuitively 'not on the edge of S'. A point that is in the interior of S is an _____ of S.

The exterior of a set is the interior of its complement; it consists of the points that are not in the set or its boundary.

a. A Mathematical Theory of Communication	b. A chemical equation
c. A posteriori	d. Interior point

10. In mathematics, the _____ is the square matrix of second-order partial derivatives of a function; that is, it describes the local curvature of a function of many variables. The _____ was developed in the 19th century by the German mathematician Ludwig Otto Hesse and later named after him. Hesse himself had used the term 'functional determinants'.

a. Jacobian	b. Hessian matrix
c. Multivariable calculus	d. Partial derivative

11. In mathematics, a _____ is a rectangular table of elements, which may be numbers or, more generally, any abstract quantities that can be added and multiplied. Matrices are used to describe linear equations, keep track of the coefficients of linear transformations and to record data that depend on multiple parameters. Matrices are described by the field of _____ theory.

a. Double counting	b. Compression
c. Matrix	d. Coherent

12. In several fields of mathematics the term _____ is used with different but closely related meanings. They all relate to the notion of mapping the elements of a set to other elements of the same set, i.e., exchanging elements of a set.

The general concept of _____ can be defined more formally in different contexts:

In combinatorics, a _____ is usually understood to be a sequence containing each element from a finite set once, and only once.

a. Permutation
b. Linearly independent
c. Tensor product
d. Cyclic permutation

13. In mathematics, in matrix theory, a _____ is a square-matrix that has exactly one entry 1 in each row and each column and 0's elsewhere. Each such matrix represents a specific permutation of m elements and, when used to multiply another matrix, can produce that permutation in the rows or columns of the other matrix.

Given a permutation π of m elements,

$$\pi : \{1, \ldots, m\} \to \{1, \ldots, m\}$$

given in two-line form by

$$\begin{pmatrix} 1 & 2 & \cdots & m \\ \pi(1) & \pi(2) & \cdots & \pi(m) \end{pmatrix},$$

its _____ is the m × m matrix P_π whose entries are all 0 except that in row i, the entry equals 1.

a. Permutation Matrix
b. Cartan matrix
c. Partitioned matrix
d. Hessenberg matrix

14. In grammatical theory, definiteness is a feature of noun phrases, distinguishing between entities which are specific and identifiable in a given context (_____ noun phrases) and entities which are not (indefinite noun phrases Examples are:

- Free form: English the boy.
- Phrasal clitic: as in Basque: Cf. emakume ('woman'), emakume-a (woman-ART: 'the woman'), emakume ederr-a (woman beautiful-ART: 'the beautiful woman')
- Noun affix: as in Romanian: om ('man'), om-ul (man-ART: 'the man'); om-ul bun (man-ART good: 'the good man')
- Prefix on both noun and adjective: Arabic اﻟﻜﺘﺎب اﻟﻜﺒﻴﺮ (al-kitÄ b al-kabÄ«r) with two instances of al- (DEF-book-DEF-big, literally, 'the book the big')

Germanic, Romance, Celtic, Semitic, and auxiliary languages generally have a _____ article, sometimes used as a postposition. Many other languages do not.

a. Definite
b. 1-center problem
c. Sentence diagram
d. Syntax

15. In mathematics, a definite bilinear form is a bilinear form B over some vector space V (with real or complex scalar field) such that the associated quadratic form

Q(x) = B(x,x)

Chapter 17. Unconstrained Optimization 135

is definite, that is, has a real value with the same sign (positive or negative) for all non-zero x. According to that sign, B is called positive definite or _____. If Q takes both positive and negative values, the bilinear form B is called indefinite.

a. Multilinear map
b. Paravector
c. Multiple cross product
d. Negative definite

16. In mathematics, a _____ is a point in the domain of a function of two variables which is a stationary point but not a local extremum. At such a point, in general, the surface resembles a saddle that curves up in one direction, and curves down in a different direction. In terms of contour lines, a _____ can be recognized, in general, by a contour that appears to intersect itself.

a. Gauss-Codazzi equations
b. Gauss map
c. Saddle point
d. 1-center problem

17. In economics, the _____ functional form of production functions is widely used to represent the relationship of an output to inputs. It was proposed by Knut Wicksell, and tested against statistical evidence by Paul Douglas and Charles Cobb in 1928.

a. State price
b. Cobb-Douglas
c. Burden of proof
d. State price vector

18. The Condorcet candidate or _____ of an election is the candidate who, when compared with every other candidate, is preferred by more voters. Informally, the _____ is the person who would win a two-candidate election against each of the other candidates. A _____ will not always exist in a given set of votes, which is known as Condorcet's voting paradox.

a. 120-cell
b. 1-center problem
c. Psephology
d. Condorcet winner

19. In mathematics, a _____ is the negative of a convex function. A _____ is also synonymously called concave downwards, concave down or convex cap.

Formally, a real-valued function f defined on an interval is called concave, if for any two points x and y in its domain C and any t in [0,1], we have

$$f(tx + (1-t)y) \geq tf(x) + (1-t)f(y).$$

Also, f-f

a. Concave function
b. Darboux function
c. Dirichlet kernel
d. Weight function

20. In mathematics, a real-valued function f defined on an interval is called _____, concave upwards, concave up or _____ cup, if for any two points x and y in its domain C and any t in [0,1], we have

Chapter 17. Unconstrained Optimization

$$f(tx + (1-t)y) \leq tf(x) + (1-t)f(y).$$

_____ function on an interval.

In other words, a function is _____ if and only if its epigraph is a _____ set.

Pictorially, a function is called '_____' if the function lies below the straight line segment connecting two points, for any two points in the interval.

A function is called strictly _____ if

$$f(tx + (1-t)y) < tf(x) + (1-t)f(y)$$

for any t in and $x \neq y$.

A function f is said to be concave if − f is _____.

a. Continuous wavelet
c. Continuum
b. Convex
d. Contrapositive

21. In mathematics and in the sciences, a _____ (plural: _____e, formulæ or _____s) is a concise way of expressing information symbolically (as in a mathematical or chemical _____), or a general relationship between quantities. One of many famous _____e is Albert Einstein's E = mc² (see special relativity

In mathematics, a _____ is a key to solve an equation with variables. For example, the problem of determining the volume of a sphere is one that requires a significant amount of integral calculus to solve.

a. 1-center problem
c. 2-3 heap
b. 120-cell
d. Formula

22. In mathematics, the _____ of a number n is the number that, when added to n, yields zero. The _____ of n is denoted −n. For example, 7 is −7, because 7 + (−7) = 0, and the _____ of −0.3 is 0.3, because −0.3 + 0.3 = 0.

a. Algebraic structure
c. Associativity
b. Arity
d. Additive inverse

23. In economics, an _____ is a function that maps the quantity of output supplied to the market price for that output.

In mathematical terms, if the demand function is , then the _____ is f⁻¹

a. Internal rate of return
c. Arrow-Debreu model
b. Inverse demand function
d. Enterprise value

24.

Chapter 17. Unconstrained Optimization

Under perfect competition, _____ is equal to marginal physical product (extra unit produced as a result of a new employment) multiplied by price.

$$MRP = MP \times \text{Price}$$

This is because the firm in perfect competition is a price taker. It does not have to lower the price in order to sell additional units of the good.

   a. Marginal revenue product
   b. Fisher hypothesis
   c. 120-cell
   d. 1-center problem

25. In economics, a _____ exists when a specific individual or enterprise has sufficient control over a particular product or service to determine significantly the terms on which other individuals shall have access to it. Monopolies are thus characterized by a lack of economic competition for the good or service that they provide and a lack of viable substitute goods. The verb 'monopolize' refers to the process by which a firm gains persistently greater market share than what is expected under perfect competition.
   a. 120-cell
   b. Monopoly
   c. 2-3 heap
   d. 1-center problem

26. In mathematics, the _____ or Pythagoras' theorem is a relation in Euclidean geometry among the three sides of a right triangle. The theorem is named after the Greek mathematician Pythagoras, who by tradition is credited with its discovery and proof, although it is often argued that knowledge of the theory predates him.. The theorem is as follows:

In any right triangle, the area of the square whose side is the hypotenuse is equal to the sum of the areas of the squares whose sides are the two legs.

   a. 1-center problem
   b. 120-cell
   c. Pythagorean Theorem
   d. 2-3 heap

27. The method of _____ or ordinary _____ is used to solve overdetermined systems. _____ is often applied in statistical contexts, particularly regression analysis.

_____ can be interpreted as a method of fitting data.

   a. Non-linear least squares
   b. Rata Die
   c. Least squares
   d. System equivalence

28. The _____ fallacy is an informal fallacy. It ascribes cause where none exists. The flaw is failing to account for natural fluctuations.
   a. Depth
   b. Degrees of freedom
   c. Differential
   d. Regression

29. In statistics, _____ is a collective name for techniques for the modeling and analysis of numerical data consisting of values of a dependent variable and of one or more independent variables. The dependent variable in the regression equation is modeled as a function of the independent variables, corresponding parameters, and an error term. The error term is treated as a random variable.

    a. 2-3 heap
    b. 120-cell
    c. 1-center problem
    d. Regression analysis

30. A _____ is an ornament, character or spacer used in typesetting, sometimes more formally known as a 'printer's ornament' or 'printer's character'. The term supposedly originated as onomatopoeia in old style metal-type print shops, where extra space around text or illustrations would be filled by dinging an ornament into the space then bating tight to be ready for inking.

The term continued to be used in the computer industry to describe fonts that had symbols and shapes in the positions designated for alphabetical or numeric characters.

    a. 2-3 heap
    b. 1-center problem
    c. 120-cell
    d. Dingbat

Chapter 18. Constrained Optimization I: First Order Conditions

1. The Condorcet candidate or _____ of an election is the candidate who, when compared with every other candidate, is preferred by more voters. Informally, the _____ is the person who would win a two-candidate election against each of the other candidates. A _____ will not always exist in a given set of votes, which is known as Condorcet's voting paradox.
   a. 120-cell
   b. Psephology
   c. 1-center problem
   d. Condorcet winner

2. The _____ is a basic theorem used to solve maximization problems in microeconomics. It may be used to prove Hotelling's lemma, Shephard's lemma, and Roy's identity. The statement of the theorem is:

Consider an arbitrary maximization problem where the objective function (f) depends on some parameter (a):

$$M(a) = \max_x f(x, a)$$

where the function M(a) gives the maximized value of the objective function (f) as a function of the parameter (a.)

   a. Envelope Theorem
   b. A posteriori
   c. A chemical equation
   d. A Mathematical Theory of Communication

3. The mathematical concept of a _____ expresses the intuitive idea of deterministic dependence between two quantities, one of which is viewed as primary and the other as secondary. A _____ then is a way to associate a unique output for each input of a specified type, for example, a real number or an element of a given set.
   a. Function
   b. Coherent
   c. Grill
   d. Going up

4. In mathematics, an _____ is a generalization for the concept of a function in which the dependent variable has not been given 'explicitly' in terms of the independent variable. To give a function f explicitly is to provide a prescription for determining the value of the function y in terms of the input value x:

   $$y = f$$

   a. Inflection point
   b. Ordinary differential equation
   c. Implicit differentiation
   d. Implicit Function

5. In the branch of mathematics called multivariable calculus, the _____ is a tool which allows relations to be converted to functions. It does this by representing the relation as the graph of a function. There may not be a single function whose graph is the entire relation, but there may be such a function on a restriction of the domain of the relation.
   a. Implicit Function Theorem
   b. Inverse function theorem
   c. A chemical equation
   d. A Mathematical Theory of Communication

6. In mathematics, a _____ is a statement that can be proved on the basis of explicitly stated or previously agreed assumptions.
   a. Disjunction introduction
   b. Logical value
   c. Boolean function
   d. Theorem

Chapter 18. Constrained Optimization I: First Order Conditions

7. In mathematics, a _____ is a condition that a solution to an optimization problem must satisfy. There are two types of _____s: equality _____s and inequality _____s. The set of solutions that satisfy all _____s is called the feasible set.

   a. Constraint
   b. Decidable
   c. Foci
   d. Concurrent

8. In mathematics, an _____ is a statement about the relative size or order of two objects, or about whether they are the same or not

   - The notation a < b means that a is less than b.
   - The notation a > b means that a is greater than b.
   - The notation a ≠ b means that a is not equal to b, but does not say that one is bigger than the other or even that they can be compared in size.

   In all these cases, a is not equal to b, hence, '_____'.

   These relations are known as strict _____

   - The notation a ≤ b means that a is less than or equal to b;
   - The notation a ≥ b means that a is greater than or equal to b;

   An additional use of the notation is to show that one quantity is much greater than another, normally by several orders of magnitude.

   - The notation a << b means that a is much less than b.
   - The notation a >> b means that a is much greater than b.

   If the sense of the _____ is the same for all values of the variables for which its members are defined, then the _____ is called an 'absolute' or 'unconditional' _____. If the sense of an _____ holds only for certain values of the variables involved, but is reversed or destroyed for other values of the variables, it is called a conditional _____.

   An _____ may appear unsolvable because it only states whether a number is larger or smaller than another number; but it is possible to apply the same operations for equalities to inequalities. For example, to find x for the _____ 10x > 23 one would divide 23 by 10.

   a. A Mathematical Theory of Communication
   b. A posteriori
   c. Inequality
   d. A chemical equation

9. An _____ is a tree data structure in which each internal node has up to eight children. _____s are most often used to partition a three dimensional space by recursively subdividing it into eight octants. _____s are the three-dimensional analog of quadtrees.

   a. Interval tree
   b. Adaptive k-d tree
   c. External node
   d. Octree

10. The _____ governs the differentiation of products of differentiable functions.
   a. Product Rule
   b. Reciprocal Rule
   c. 1-center problem
   d. 120-cell

11. In mathematics, the concept of a _____ tries to capture the intuitive idea of a geometrical one-dimensional and continuous object. A simple example is the circle. In everyday use of the term '_____', a straight line is not curved, but in mathematical parlance _____s include straight lines and line segments.
   a. Kappa curve
   b. Curve
   c. Quadrifolium
   d. Negative pedal curve

12. In mathematical optimization, the method of _____s is a method for finding the maximum/minimum of a function subject to constraints.

For example if we want to solve:

$$\text{maximize } f(x, y)$$
$$\text{subject to } g(x, y) = c$$

We introduce a new variable called a _____ to rewrite the problem as:

$$\text{maximize } f(x, y) + \lambda(g(x, y) - c)$$

Solving this new unconstrained problem for x, y, and λ will give us the solution for our original constrained problem.

Introduction

Consider a two-dimensional case.

   a. 1-center problem
   b. Radfar ratio
   c. 120-cell
   d. Lagrange multiplier

13. The _____, L, of a dynamical system is a function that summarizes the dynamics of the system. It is named after Joseph Louis Lagrange. The concept of a _____ was originally introduced in a reformulation of classical mechanics known as _____ mechanics.
   a. Fermi-Dirac statistics
   b. Van der Waals equation
   c. Renormalization
   d. Lagrangian

14. In Fourier analysis, a _____ is a kind of linear operator, or transformation of functions. These operators multiply the Fourier coefficients of a function by a specified function, hence the name. Among the multipliers one can count some simple operators, such as translations and differentiation, but also some more complicated ones such as the convolutions, Hilbert transform, and others.
   a. Modulated complex lapped transform
   b. Reality condition
   c. Poisson summation formula
   d. Fourier multiplier

Chapter 18. Constrained Optimization I: First Order Conditions 143

15. In vector calculus, the _____ is shorthand for either the _____ matrix or its determinant, the _____ determinant.

In algebraic geometry the _____ of a curve means the _____ variety: a group variety associated to the curve, in which the curve can be embedded.

These concepts are all named after the mathematician Carl Gustav Jacob Jacobi.

   a. Surface integral   b. Shift theorem
   c. Jacobian   d. Monkey saddle

16. In mathematics, a _____ is a point on the domain of a function where:

- one dimension: the derivative is equal to zero or a point where the function ceases to be differentiable.
- in general: there are two distinct concepts: either the derivative vanishes, or it is not of full rank; these agree in one dimension.

Note that in one dimension, a critical value or critical number x of function f is the domain element at which the derivative is zero or undefined, whereas the associated ordered pair is the _____. In higher dimensions a critical value is in the range whereas a _____ is in the domain.

There are two situations in which a point becomes a _____ of a function of one variable. The first of which is that the value of the derivative is equal to zero.

   a. Derivative algebra   b. Going up
   c. Decimal system   d. Critical point

17. _____ is a fundamental construction of differential calculus and admits many possible generalizations within the fields of mathematical analysis, combinatorics, algebra, and geometry.

In real, complex, and functional analysis, _____s are generalized to functions of several real or complex variables and functions between topological vector spaces. An important case is the variational _____ in the calculus of variations.

   a. Functional derivative   b. Lin-Tsien equation
   c. Metric derivative   d. Derivative

18. In linear algebra, _____ is an efficient algorithm for solving systems of linear equations, finding the rank of a matrix, and calculating the inverse of an invertible square matrix. _____ is named after German mathematician and scientist Carl Friedrich Gauss.

Elementary row operations are used to reduce a matrix to row echelon form.

a. Conjugate gradient method
b. Cholesky decomposition
c. Crout matrix decomposition
d. Gaussian elimination

19. In mathematics and statistics, the _____ of a list of numbers is the sum of all of the list divided by the number of items in the list. If the list is a statistical population, then the mean of that population is called a population mean. If the list is a statistical sample, we call the resulting statistic a sample mean.

a. Unsolved problems in statistics
b. Analysis of variance
c. Interval estimation
d. Arithmetic mean

20. In mathematics, an _____, or central tendency of a data set refers to a measure of the 'middle' or 'expected' value of the data set. There are many different descriptive statistics that can be chosen as a measurement of the central tendency of the data items.

An _____ is a single value that is meant to typify a list of values.

a. A Mathematical Theory of Communication
b. A posteriori
c. Average
d. A chemical equation

21. The _____, in mathematics, is a type of mean or average, which indicates the central tendency or typical value of a set of numbers. It is similar to the arithmetic mean, which is what most people think of with the word 'average,' except that instead of adding the set of numbers and then dividing the sum by the count of numbers in the set, n, the numbers are multiplied and then the nth root of the resulting product is taken.

For instance, the _____ of two numbers, say 2 and 8, is just the square root (i.e., the second root) of their product, 16, which is 4.

a. Correlation
b. Stratified sampling
c. Skewness
d. Geometric mean

22. _____ is a branch of mathematics which focuses on the study of matrices. Initially a sub-branch of linear algebra, it has grown to cover subjects related to graph theory, algebra, combinatorics, and statistics as well.

The term matrix was first coined in 1848 by J.J. Sylvester as a name of an array of numbers.

a. Segre classification
b. Pairing
c. Semi-simple operators
d. Matrix theory

23. In statistics, _____ has two related meanings:

- the arithmetic _____.
- the expected value of a random variable, which is also called the population _____.

It is sometimes stated that the '_____' _____s average. This is incorrect if '_____' is taken in the specific sense of 'arithmetic _____' as there are different types of averages: the _____, median, and mode. For instance, average house prices almost always use the median value for the average.

For a real-valued random variable X, the _____ is the expectation of X.

a. Probability
c. Statistical population
b. Proportional hazards model
d. Mean

24. In mathematics the concept of a _____ generalizes notions such as 'length', 'area', and 'volume'. Informally, given some base set, a '_____' is any consistent assignment of 'sizes' to the subsets of the base set. Depending on the application, the 'size' of a subset may be interpreted as its physical size, the amount of something that lies within the subset, or the probability that some random process will yield a result within the subset.

a. Lattice
c. Measure
b. Congruent
d. Cusp

25. In statistics and mathematical epidemiology, _____ is the risk of an event relative to exposure. _____ is a ratio of the probability of the event occurring in the exposed group versus a non-exposed group.

$$RR = \frac{p_{\text{exposed}}}{p_{\text{non-exposed}}}$$

For example, if the probability of developing lung cancer among smokers was 20% and among non-smokers 1%, then the _____ of cancer associated with smoking would be 20.

a. Mendelian randomization
c. Statistical epidemiology
b. 1-center problem
d. Relative risk

26. _____ is a concept in economics, finance, and psychology related to the behaviour of consumers and investors under uncertainty. _____ is the reluctance of a person to accept a bargain with an uncertain payoff rather than another bargain with a more certain, but possibly lower, expected payoff.

The inverse of a person's _____ is sometimes called their risk tolerance.

a. Ruin theory
c. Life table
b. Risk aversion
d. Stochastic modelling

27. In mathematics, the _____ is a representation of a function as an infinite sum of terms calculated from the values of its derivatives at a single point. It may be regarded as the limit of the Taylor polynomials. _____ are named after English mathematician Brook Taylor.

a. Local linearity
c. 1-center problem
b. C^r topology
d. Taylor series

28. In mathematics, a _____ is often represented as the sum of a sequence of terms. That is, a _____ is represented as a list of numbers with addition operations between them, for example this arithmetic sequence:

1 + 2 + 3 + 4 + 5 + ... + 99 + 100

In most cases of interest the terms of the sequence are produced according to a certain rule, such as by a formula, by an algorithm, by a sequence of measurements, or even by a random number generator.

a. Concavity
b. Blind
c. Series
d. Contact

29. In economics, the _____ functional form of production functions is widely used to represent the relationship of an output to inputs. It was proposed by Knut Wicksell, and tested against statistical evidence by Paul Douglas and Charles Cobb in 1928.

a. Burden of proof
b. State price vector
c. Cobb-Douglas
d. State price

30. _____ is an economics theory, that refers to individuals or societies gaining the maximum amount out of the resources they have available to them. The theory proposed by most economists is that _____ refers to the _____ of profit.

As some economists have begun to find out, this theory does not hold true for all people and cultures.

a. Boundary
b. Homogeneity
c. Composite
d. Maximization

31. In calculus, the _____ states, roughly, that given a section of a smooth curve, there is at least one point on that section at which the derivative of the curve is equal to the 'average' derivative of the section. It is used to prove theorems that make global conclusions about a function on an interval starting from local hypotheses about derivatives at points of the interval.

This theorem can be understood concretely by applying it to motion: if a car travels one hundred miles in one hour, so that its average speed during that time was 100 miles per hour, then at some time its instantaneous speed must have been exactly 100 miles per hour.

a. Calculus controversy
b. Fundamental Theorem of Calculus
c. Functional integration
d. Mean Value Theorem

32. In the mathematical area of order theory, every partially ordered set P gives rise to a _____ partially ordered set which is often denoted by P^{op} or P^d. This _____ order P^{op} is defined to be the set with the inverse order. It is easy to see that this construction, which can be depicted by flipping the Hasse diagram for P upside down, will indeed yield a partially ordered set.

a. Context-sensitive language
b. Contraction mapping
c. Christofides heuristics
d. Dual

33. In linear programming, the primary problem and the _____ are complementary. A solution to either one determines a solution to both.

Linear programming problems are optimization problems in which the objective function and the constraints are all linear.

a. Linear matrix inequality
b. Linear programming relaxation
c. Topological derivative
d. Dual problem

Chapter 19. Constrained Optimization II

1. The mathematical concept of a _____ expresses the intuitive idea of deterministic dependence between two quantities, one of which is viewed as primary and the other as secondary. A _____ then is a way to associate a unique output for each input of a specified type, for example, a real number or an element of a given set.
   a. Grill
   b. Coherent
   c. Function
   d. Going up

2. In mathematics, an _____ is a generalization for the concept of a function in which the dependent variable has not been given 'explicitly' in terms of the independent variable. To give a function f explicitly is to provide a prescription for determining the value of the function y in terms of the input value x:

   y = f

   a. Implicit Function
   b. Inflection point
   c. Implicit differentiation
   d. Ordinary differential equation

3. In the branch of mathematics called multivariable calculus, the _____ is a tool which allows relations to be converted to functions. It does this by representing the relation as the graph of a function. There may not be a single function whose graph is the entire relation, but there may be such a function on a restriction of the domain of the relation.
   a. A chemical equation
   b. Inverse function theorem
   c. A Mathematical Theory of Communication
   d. Implicit Function Theorem

4. In mathematics, a _____ is a statement that can be proved on the basis of explicitly stated or previously agreed assumptions.
   a. Boolean function
   b. Disjunction introduction
   c. Logical value
   d. Theorem

5. Loosely, the _____ is the change in the objective value of the optimal solution of an optimization problem obtained by relaxing the constraint by one unit. In a business application, a _____ is the maximum price that management is willing to pay for an extra unit of a given limited resource. For example, what is the price of keeping a production line operational for an additional hour if the production line is already operated at its maximum 40 hour limit? That price is the _____.
   a. Facility location
   b. Boolean model
   c. Newsvendor
   d. Shadow price

6. The _____ is a basic theorem used to solve maximization problems in microeconomics. It may be used to prove Hotelling's lemma, Shephard's lemma, and Roy's identity. The statement of the theorem is:

Consider an arbitrary maximization problem where the objective function (f) depends on some parameter (a):

$$M(a) = \max_{x} f(x, a)$$

where the function M(a) gives the maximized value of the objective function (f) as a function of the parameter (a.)

   a. A chemical equation
   b. A Mathematical Theory of Communication
   c. A posteriori
   d. Envelope Theorem

Chapter 19. Constrained Optimization II

7. In mathematics, an _____ in the sense of ring theory is a subring $\mathcal{O}$ of a ring R that satisfies the conditions

   1. R is a ring which is a finite-dimensional algebra over the rational number field $\mathbb{Q}$
   2. $\mathcal{O}$ spans R over $\mathbb{Q}$, so that $\mathbb{Q}\mathcal{O} = R$, and
   3. $\mathcal{O}$ is a lattice in R.

The third condition can be stated more accurately, in terms of the extension of scalars of R to the real numbers, embedding R in a real vector space. In less formal terms, additively $\mathcal{O}$ should be a free abelian group generated by a basis for R over $\mathbb{Q}$.

The leading example is the case where R is a number field K and $\mathcal{O}$ is its ring of integers. In algebraic number theory there are examples for any K other than the rational field of proper subrings of the ring of integers that are also _____s.

   a. Annihilator
   b. Order
   c. Efficiency
   d. Algebraic

8. The Condorcet candidate or _____ of an election is the candidate who, when compared with every other candidate, is preferred by more voters. Informally, the _____ is the person who would win a two-candidate election against each of the other candidates. A _____ will not always exist in a given set of votes, which is known as Condorcet's voting paradox.
   a. 120-cell
   b. Condorcet winner
   c. Psephology
   d. 1-center problem

9. The _____ is a single-winner election method in which voters rank candidates in order of preference. The _____ determines the winner of an election by giving each candidate a certain number of points corresponding to the position in which he or she is ranked by each voter. Once all votes have been counted the candidate with the most points is the winner.
   a. 1-center problem
   b. 120-cell
   c. 2-3 heap
   d. Borda count

10. In mathematics, the _____ or Pythagoras' theorem is a relation in Euclidean geometry among the three sides of a right triangle. The theorem is named after the Greek mathematician Pythagoras, who by tradition is credited with its discovery and proof, although it is often argued that knowledge of the theory predates him.. The theorem is as follows:

In any right triangle, the area of the square whose side is the hypotenuse is equal to the sum of the areas of the squares whose sides are the two legs.

   a. 2-3 heap
   b. 1-center problem
   c. 120-cell
   d. Pythagorean Theorem

11. In mathematics, a _____ is a rectangular table of elements, which may be numbers or, more generally, any abstract quantities that can be added and multiplied. Matrices are used to describe linear equations, keep track of the coefficients of linear transformations and to record data that depend on multiple parameters. Matrices are described by the field of _____ theory.

a. Coherent
c. Double counting
b. Compression
d. Matrix

12. In linear algebra, a _____ of a matrix A is the determinant of some smaller square matrix, cut down from A by removing one or more of its rows or columns.

_____s obtained by removing just one row and one column from square matrices are required for calculating matrix cofactors, which in turn are useful for computing both the determinant and inverse of square matrices.

Let A be an m × n matrix and k an integer with 0 < k ≤ m, and k ≤ n.

a. Homogeneity
c. Block size
b. Chiral
d. Minor

13. In mathematics, the _____ is the square matrix of second-order partial derivatives of a function; that is, it describes the local curvature of a function of many variables. The _____ was developed in the 19th century by the German mathematician Ludwig Otto Hesse and later named after him. Hesse himself had used the term 'functional determinants'.

a. Multivariable calculus
c. Jacobian
b. Partial derivative
d. Hessian matrix

14. In mathematics, a _____ is a condition that a solution to an optimization problem must satisfy. There are two types of _____s: equality _____s and inequality _____s. The set of solutions that satisfy all _____s is called the feasible set.

a. Concurrent
c. Foci
b. Decidable
d. Constraint

15. In mathematics, _____ are functions which can be used to prove the stability of a certain fixed point in a dynamical system or autonomous differential equation. Named after the Russian mathematician Aleksandr Mikhailovich Lyapunov, _____ are important to stability theory and control theory.

Functions which might prove the stability of some equilibrium are called Lyapunov-candidate-functions.

a. Butterfly effect
c. 120-cell
b. 1-center problem
d. Lyapunov functions

16. In mathematics, _____ is a technique for optimization of a linear objective function, subject to linear equality and linear inequality constraints. Informally, _____ determines the way to achieve the best outcome in a given mathematical model given some list of requirements represented as linear equations.

More formally, given a polytope, and a real-valued affine function

$$f(x_1, x_2, \ldots, x_n) = c_1 x_1 + c_2 x_2 + \cdots + c_n x_n + d$$

defined on this polytope, a _____ method will find a point in the polytope where this function has the smallest value.

a. Descent direction
b. Lin-Kernighan
c. Linear programming relaxation
d. Linear programming

17. In mathematics, the _____ of an abelian group measures how large a group is in terms of how large a vector space over the rational numbers one would need to 'contain' it; or alternatively how large a free abelian group it can contain as a subgroup.

The _____ of a finite abelian group has a different definition.

An abelian group is often thought of as composed of its torsion subgroup T, and its torsion-free part A/T.

a. Rank
b. Chord
c. Discontinuity
d. Coherence

Chapter 20. Homogeneous and Homothetic Functions

1. In microeconomics, a consumer's _____ function is the demand of a consumer over a bundle of goods that minimizes their expenditure while delivering a fixed level of utility. The function is named after John Hicks.

Mathematically,

$$h(p, \bar{u}) = \arg\min_x \sum_i p_i x_i$$
$$\text{such that } u(x) > \bar{u}$$

where h is the _____ function, or commodity bundle demanded, at price level p and utility level $\bar{u}$.

- a. 1-center problem
- b. Precautionary demand
- c. Marshallian demand function
- d. Hicksian demand

2. In mathematics, the _____ or Pythagoras' theorem is a relation in Euclidean geometry among the three sides of a right triangle. The theorem is named after the Greek mathematician Pythagoras, who by tradition is credited with its discovery and proof, although it is often argued that knowledge of the theory predates him.. The theorem is as follows:

In any right triangle, the area of the square whose side is the hypotenuse is equal to the sum of the areas of the squares whose sides are the two legs.

- a. 1-center problem
- b. 120-cell
- c. Pythagorean Theorem
- d. 2-3 heap

3. In mathematics, a _____ is a statement that can be proved on the basis of explicitly stated or previously agreed assumptions.
- a. Logical value
- b. Disjunction introduction
- c. Boolean function
- d. Theorem

4. In mathematics, a quasiconvex function is a real-valued function defined on an interval or on a convex subset of a real vector space such that the inverse image of any set of the form $(-\infty, a)$ is a convex set.

Equivalently, a function $f : S \to \mathbb{R}$ defined on a convex subset S of a real vector space is quasiconvex if whenever $x, y \in S$ and $\lambda \in [0, 1]$ then

$$f(\lambda x + (1 - \lambda)y) \leq \max(f(x), f(y)).$$

If instead

$$f(\lambda x + (1 - \lambda)y) < \max(f(x), f(y))$$

for any $x \neq y$ and $\lambda \in (0,1)$, then f is strictly quasiconvex.

A _____ function is a function whose negative is quasiconvex, and a strictly _____ function is a function whose negative is strictly quasiconvex.

- a. 1-center problem
- b. Quasiconcave
- c. 2-3 heap
- d. 120-cell

5. The Condorcet candidate or _____ of an election is the candidate who, when compared with every other candidate, is preferred by more voters. Informally, the _____ is the person who would win a two-candidate election against each of the other candidates. A _____ will not always exist in a given set of votes, which is known as Condorcet's voting paradox.
  - a. Psephology
  - b. 1-center problem
  - c. 120-cell
  - d. Condorcet winner

6. In mathematics, a _____ is a rectangular table of elements, which may be numbers or, more generally, any abstract quantities that can be added and multiplied. Matrices are used to describe linear equations, keep track of the coefficients of linear transformations and to record data that depend on multiple parameters. Matrices are described by the field of _____ theory.
  - a. Coherent
  - b. Compression
  - c. Double counting
  - d. Matrix

7. In several fields of mathematics the term _____ is used with different but closely related meanings. They all relate to the notion of mapping the elements of a set to other elements of the same set, i.e., exchanging elements of a set.

The general concept of _____ can be defined more formally in different contexts:

In combinatorics, a _____ is usually understood to be a sequence containing each element from a finite set once, and only once.

- a. Linearly independent
- b. Tensor product
- c. Cyclic permutation
- d. Permutation

8. In mathematics, in matrix theory, a _____ is a square-matrix that has exactly one entry 1 in each row and each column and 0's elsewhere. Each such matrix represents a specific permutation of m elements and, when used to multiply another matrix, can produce that permutation in the rows or columns of the other matrix.

Given a permutation π of m elements,

$$\pi : \{1,\ldots,m\} \to \{1,\ldots,m\}$$

given in two-line form by

$$\begin{pmatrix} 1 & 2 & \cdots & m \\ \pi(1) & \pi(2) & \cdots & \pi(m) \end{pmatrix},$$

its _____ is the m × m matrix P_π whose entries are all 0 except that in row i, the entry equals 1.

a. Partitioned matrix
c. Cartan matrix
b. Hessenberg matrix
d. Permutation Matrix

9. A _____ is a three-dimensional geometric shape that tapers smoothly from a flat, round base to a point called the apex or vertex. More precisely, it is the solid figure bounded by a plane base and the surface formed by the locus of all straight line segments joining the apex to the perimeter of the base. The term '_____' sometimes refers just to the surface of this solid figure, or just to the lateral surface.

a. Gravity waves
c. Characteristic
b. Cone
d. Blocking

10. The mathematical concept of a _____ expresses the intuitive idea of deterministic dependence between two quantities, one of which is viewed as primary and the other as secondary. A _____ then is a way to associate a unique output for each input of a specified type, for example, a real number or an element of a given set.

a. Going up
c. Coherent
b. Function
d. Grill

11. In mathematics, a _____ is a function with multiplicative scaling behaviour: if the argument is multiplied by a factor, then the result is multiplied by some power of this factor.

Suppose that $f : V \to W$ is a function between two vector spaces over a field F.

We say that f is homogeneous of degree k if

$$f(\alpha \mathbf{v}) = \alpha^k f(\mathbf{v})$$

for all nonzero $\alpha \in F$ and $\mathbf{v} \in V$.

a. Homogeneous function
c. Matrix pencil
b. Segre classification
d. Sarrus' rule

12. In geometry, a closed _____ is one of the 2^n subsets of an n-dimensional Euclidean space defined by constraining each Cartesian coordinate axis to be nonnegative or nonpositive. That is, a closed _____ is the analogue of a closed quadrant in the plane and a closed octant in three-dimensional space. A closed _____ is defined by a system of inequalities

$\varepsilon_i x_i \geq 0$ for $1 \leq i \leq n$

on the coordinates x_i, where each ε_i is +1 or −1.

a. Equal incircles theorem
b. Euclidean space
c. Ortsbogen theorem
d. Orthant

13. In mathematics, an _____ is a generalization for the concept of a function in which the dependent variable has not been given 'explicitly' in terms of the independent variable. To give a function f explicitly is to provide a prescription for determining the value of the function y in terms of the input value x:

y = f

a. Implicit differentiation
b. Inflection point
c. Ordinary differential equation
d. Implicit Function

14. In the branch of mathematics called multivariable calculus, the _____ is a tool which allows relations to be converted to functions. It does this by representing the relation as the graph of a function. There may not be a single function whose graph is the entire relation, but there may be such a function on a restriction of the domain of the relation.

a. A chemical equation
b. A Mathematical Theory of Communication
c. Inverse function theorem
d. Implicit Function Theorem

15. In calculus, a function f defined on a subset of the real numbers with real values is called monotonic (also monotonically increasing or non-_____), if for all x and y such that x ≤ y one has f(x) ≤ f(y), so f preserves the order. In layman's terms, the sign of the slope is always positive (the curve tending upwards) or zero (i.e., non-_____, or asymptotic, or depicted as a horizontal, flat line) Likewise, a function is called monotonically _____ (non-increasing) if, whenever x ≤ y, then f(x) ≥ f(y), so it reverses the order.

a. Decreasing
b. Dual pair
c. Circular convolution
d. Tensor product of Hilbert spaces

16. In economics, _____ and economies of scale are related terms that describe what happens as the scale of production increases. They are different terms and are not to be used interchangeably.

_____ refers to a technical property of production that examines changes in output subsequent to a proportional change in all inputs (where all inputs increase by a constant factor.)

a. Producer surplus
b. Consumer surplus
c. Marginal rate of technical substitution
d. Returns to scale

17. In economics, the _____ functional form of production functions is widely used to represent the relationship of an output to inputs. It was proposed by Knut Wicksell, and tested against statistical evidence by Paul Douglas and Charles Cobb in 1928.

Chapter 20. Homogeneous and Homothetic Functions

    a. Burden of proof   b. State price
    c. State price vector   d. Cobb-Douglas

18. The _____ governs the differentiation of products of differentiable functions.
    a. 1-center problem   b. Product Rule
    c. Reciprocal Rule   d. 120-cell

19. In economics, business, retail, and accounting, a _____ is the value of money that has been used up to produce something, and hence is not available for use anymore. In business, the _____ may be one of acquisition, in which case the amount of money expended to acquire it is counted as _____. In this case, money is the input that is gone in order to acquire the thing.
    a. Cost   b. 1-center problem
    c. 2-3 heap   d. 120-cell

20. The method of _____ or ordinary _____ is used to solve overdetermined systems. _____ is often applied in statistical contexts, particularly regression analysis.

_____ can be interpreted as a method of fitting data.

    a. Rata Die   b. Non-linear least squares
    c. Least squares   d. System equivalence

21. In mathematics, a _____ is an expression constructed from variables and constants, using the operations of addition, subtraction, multiplication, and constant non-negative whole number exponents. For example, $x^2 - 4x + 7$ is a _____, but $x^2 - 4/x + 7x^{3/2}$ is not, because its second term involves division by the variable x and also because its third term contains an exponent that is not a whole number.

_____s are one of the most important concepts in algebra and throughout mathematics and science.

    a. Semifield   b. Group extension
    c. Polynomial   d. Coimage

22. In economics, the _____ or the Technical Rate of Substitution is the amount by which the quantity of one input has to be reduced when one extra unit of another input is used, so that output remains constant.

$$MRTS(x_1, x_2) = \frac{\Delta x_2}{\Delta x_1} = -\frac{MP_1}{MP_2}$$

where MP_1 and MP_2 are the marginal products of input 1 and input 2, respectively.

Along an isoquant, the MRTS shows the rate at which one input may be substituted for another, while maintaining the same level of output.

Chapter 20. Homogeneous and Homothetic Functions

a. Marginal rate of technical substitution
c. Returns to scale
b. Producer surplus
d. Consumer surplus

23. Price _____ is defined as the measure of responsivenesses in the quantity demanded for a commodity as a result of change in price of the same commodity. In other words, it is percentage change in quantity demanded as per the percentage change in price of the same commodity. In economics and business studies, the price _____ is a measure of the sensitivity of quantity demanded to changes in price. It is measured as elasticity, that is it measures the relationship as the ratio of percentage changes between quantity demanded of a good and changes in its price.
   a. A posteriori
   c. A Mathematical Theory of Communication
   b. A chemical equation
   d. Elasticity of demand

24. In economics, the _____ measures the responsiveness of the quantity demanded of a good to the change in the income of the people demanding the good. It is calculated as the ratio of the percent change in quantity demanded to the percent change in income. For example, if, in response to a 10% increase in income, the quantity of a good demanded increased by 20%, the _____ would be 20%/10% = 2.
   a. Utility maximization problem
   c. Expenditure minimization problem
   b. Expenditure function
   d. Income elasticity of demand

25. In graph theory, a _____ in a graph is a sequence of vertices such that from each of its vertices there is an edge to the next vertex in the sequence. The first vertex is called the start vertex and the last vertex is called the end vertex. Both of them are called end or terminal vertices of the _____.
   a. Class
   c. Deltoid
   b. Blinding
   d. Path

26. _____ (CES) is a property of some production functions and utility functions.

More precisely, it refers to a particular type of aggregator function which combines two or more types of consumption, or two or more types of productive inputs into an aggregate quantity. This aggregator function exhibits _____.

   a. 1-center problem
   c. Production function
   b. Constant elasticity of substitution
   d. Short-run

27. In mathematics, _____ are generalized numbers used to measure the cardinality of sets. For finite sets, the cardinality is given by a natural number, which is simply the number of elements in the set. There are also transfinite _____ that describe the sizes of infinite sets.
   a. Strong partition cardinal
   c. Cardinal numbers
   b. Suslin cardinal
   d. Cardinality of the continuum

28. In mathematics, the concept of a _____ tries to capture the intuitive idea of a geometrical one-dimensional and continuous object. A simple example is the circle. In everyday use of the term '_____', a straight line is not curved, but in mathematical parlance _____s include straight lines and line segments.
   a. Negative pedal curve
   c. Kappa curve
   b. Quadrifolium
   d. Curve

Chapter 20. Homogeneous and Homothetic Functions

29. In microeconomic theory, an _____ is a graph showing different bundles of goods, each measured as to quantity, between which a consumer is indifferent. That is, at each point on the curve, the consumer has no preference for one bundle over another. In other words, they are all equally preferred. One can equivalently refer to each point on the _____ as rendering the same level of utility for the consumer.

a. Utility maximization problem
b. Expenditure function
c. Expenditure minimization problem
d. Indifference curve

30. The _____ is a basic theorem used to solve maximization problems in microeconomics. It may be used to prove Hotelling's lemma, Shephard's lemma, and Roy's identity. The statement of the theorem is:

Consider an arbitrary maximization problem where the objective function (f) depends on some parameter (a):

$$M(a) = \max_x f(x, a)$$

where the function M(a) gives the maximized value of the objective function (f) as a function of the parameter (a.)

a. A posteriori
b. A Mathematical Theory of Communication
c. A chemical equation
d. Envelope Theorem

31. In statistics, _____ has two related meanings:

- the arithmetic _____.
- the expected value of a random variable, which is also called the population _____.

It is sometimes stated that the '_____' _____s average. This is incorrect if '_____' is taken in the specific sense of 'arithmetic _____' as there are different types of averages: the _____, median, and mode. For instance, average house prices almost always use the median value for the average.

For a real-valued random variable X, the _____ is the expectation of X.

a. Mean
b. Statistical population
c. Probability
d. Proportional hazards model

32. In calculus, the _____ states, roughly, that given a section of a smooth curve, there is at least one point on that section at which the derivative of the curve is equal to the 'average' derivative of the section. It is used to prove theorems that make global conclusions about a function on an interval starting from local hypotheses about derivatives at points of the interval.

This theorem can be understood concretely by applying it to motion: if a car travels one hundred miles in one hour, so that its average speed during that time was 100 miles per hour, then at some time its instantaneous speed must have been exactly 100 miles per hour.

a. Functional integration
b. Calculus controversy
c. Fundamental Theorem of Calculus
d. Mean Value Theorem

33. In the study of metric spaces in mathematics, there are various notions of two metrics on the same underlying space being 'the same', or _____.

In the following, M will denote a non-empty set and d_1 and d_2 will denote two metrics on M.

The two metrics d_1 and d_2 are said to be topologically _____ if they generate the same topology on M.

a. A posteriori
b. A chemical equation
c. Equivalent
d. A Mathematical Theory of Communication

34. In mathematics, a _____ function is a function which preserves the given order. This concept first arose in calculus, and was later generalized to the more abstract setting of order theory.

In calculus, a function f defined on a subset of the real numbers with real values is called _____, if for all x and y such that x ≤ y one has f≤ f

a. Negacyclic convolution
b. Monotonic
c. C_0-semigroup
d. Compact convergence

35. In mathematics, the word _____ means two different things in the context of polynomials:

- The first meaning is a product of powers of variables, or formally any value obtained from 1 by finitely many multiplications by a variable. If only a single variable x is considered this means that any _____ is either 1 or a power x^n of x, with n a positive integer. If several variables are considered, say, x, y, z, then each can be given an exponent, so that any _____ is of the form $x^a y^b z^c$ with a,b,c nonnegative integers.
- The second meaning of _____ includes _____s in the first sense, but also allows multiplication by any constant, so that − $7x^5$ and $4yz^{13}$ are also considered to be _____s.

With either definition, the set of _____s is a subset of all polynomials that is closed under multiplication.

a. Monomial
b. Diagonal form
c. Homogeneous polynomial
d. Power sum symmetric polynomial

36. In economics, a _____ is a function that specifies the output of a firm, an industry, or an entire economy for all combinations of inputs. A meta-_____ compares the practice of the existing entities converting inputs X into output y to determine the most efficient practice _____ of the existing entities, whether the most efficient feasible practice production or the most efficient actual practice production. In either case, the maximum output of a technologically-determined production process is a mathematical function of input factors of production.

a. Long-run
b. Production function
c. 1-center problem
d. Short-run

37. In mathematics, _____ are functions which can be used to prove the stability of a certain fixed point in a dynamical system or autonomous differential equation. Named after the Russian mathematician Aleksandr Mikhailovich Lyapunov, _____ are important to stability theory and control theory.

Functions which might prove the stability of some equilibrium are called Lyapunov-candidate-functions.

a. 120-cell
c. Butterfly effect
b. 1-center problem
d. Lyapunov functions

Chapter 21. Concave and Quasiconcave Functions

1. In economics, the _____ functional form of production functions is widely used to represent the relationship of an output to inputs. It was proposed by Knut Wicksell, and tested against statistical evidence by Paul Douglas and Charles Cobb in 1928.
    a. State price vector
    b. State price
    c. Burden of proof
    d. Cobb-Douglas

2. The Condorcet candidate or _____ of an election is the candidate who, when compared with every other candidate, is preferred by more voters. Informally, the _____ is the person who would win a two-candidate election against each of the other candidates. A _____ will not always exist in a given set of votes, which is known as Condorcet's voting paradox.
    a. 120-cell
    b. Psephology
    c. 1-center problem
    d. Condorcet winner

3. In mathematics, a _____ is the negative of a convex function. A _____ is also synonymously called concave downwards, concave down or convex cap.

    Formally, a real-valued function f defined on an interval is called concave, if for any two points x and y in its domain C and any t in [0,1], we have

    $$f(tx + (1-t)y) \geq tf(x) + (1-t)f(y).$$

    Also, f–f

    a. Weight function
    b. Concave function
    c. Darboux function
    d. Dirichlet kernel

4. In mathematics, a real-valued function f defined on an interval is called _____, concave upwards, concave up or _____ cup, if for any two points x and y in its domain C and any t in [0,1], we have

    $$f(tx + (1-t)y) \leq tf(x) + (1-t)f(y).$$

    _____ function on an interval.

    In other words, a function is _____ if and only if its epigraph is a _____ set.

    Pictorially, a function is called '_____' if the function lies below the straight line segment connecting two points, for any two points in the interval.

    A function is called strictly _____ if

    $$f(tx + (1-t)y) < tf(x) + (1-t)f(y)$$

    for any t in and $x \neq y$.

    A function f is said to be concave if − f is _____.

a. Contrapositive
b. Continuum
c. Continuous wavelet
d. Convex

5. The mathematical concept of a _____ expresses the intuitive idea of deterministic dependence between two quantities, one of which is viewed as primary and the other as secondary. A _____ then is a way to associate a unique output for each input of a specified type, for example, a real number or an element of a given set.
   a. Going up
   b. Coherent
   c. Grill
   d. Function

6. In mathematics, an _____ is a ring-shaped geometric figure a term used to name a ring-shaped object. The adjectival form is annular.

The open _____ is topologically equivalent to both the open cylinder $S^1 \times (0,1)$ and the punctured plane.

   a. Outcome
   b. Erlang
   c. Annulus
   d. OMAC

7. In Euclidean space, an object is convex if for every pair of points within the object, every point on the straight line segment that joins them is also within the object. For example, a solid cube is convex, but anything that is hollow or has a dent in it, for example, a crescent shape, is not convex. A function is convex if and only if the region above its graph is a _____.

Let C be a set in a real or complex vector space.

   a. Broken-line graph
   b. Biscuspid
   c. Context mixing
   d. Convex set

8. In mathematics, the _____ is the square matrix of second-order partial derivatives of a function; that is, it describes the local curvature of a function of many variables. The _____ was developed in the 19th century by the German mathematician Ludwig Otto Hesse and later named after him. Hesse himself had used the term 'functional determinants'.
   a. Partial derivative
   b. Multivariable calculus
   c. Hessian matrix
   d. Jacobian

9. In mathematics, a _____ is a rectangular table of elements, which may be numbers or, more generally, any abstract quantities that can be added and multiplied. Matrices are used to describe linear equations, keep track of the coefficients of linear transformations and to record data that depend on multiple parameters. Matrices are described by the field of _____ theory.
   a. Compression
   b. Matrix
   c. Double counting
   d. Coherent

10. In mathematics, _____ are generalized numbers used to measure the cardinality of sets. For finite sets, the cardinality is given by a natural number, which is simply the number of elements in the set. There are also transfinite _____ that describe the sizes of infinite sets.

Chapter 21. Concave and Quasiconcave Functions

a. Cardinality of the continuum
b. Strong partition cardinal
c. Suslin cardinal
d. Cardinal numbers

11. In economics and consumer theory, a _____ is that which people consume more of as price rises, violating the law of demand. In normal situations, as the price of such a good rises, the substitution effect causes people to purchase less of it and more of substitute goods. In the _____ situation, cheaper close substitutes are not available.

a. 1-center problem
b. 2-3 heap
c. 120-cell
d. Giffen good

12. In mathematics, a _____ is a point on the domain of a function where:

- one dimension: the derivative is equal to zero or a point where the function ceases to be differentiable.
- in general: there are two distinct concepts: either the derivative vanishes, or it is not of full rank; these agree in one dimension.

Note that in one dimension, a critical value or critical number x of function f is the domain element at which the derivative is zero or undefined, whereas the associated ordered pair is the _____. In higher dimensions a critical value is in the range whereas a _____ is in the domain.

There are two situations in which a point becomes a _____ of a function of one variable. The first of which is that the value of the derivative is equal to zero.

a. Decimal system
b. Derivative algebra
c. Going up
d. Critical point

13. In propositional logic, a set of Boolean operators is called _____ if it permits the realisation of any possible truth table.

Using a complete Boolean algebra which does not include XOR (such as the well-known AND OR NOT set), this function can be realised as follows:

(a or b) and not (a and b.)

However, other complete Boolean algebras are possible, such as NAND or NOR (either gate can form a complete Boolean algebra by itself - the proof is detailed on their pages.)

a. Counterfactual conditional
b. First-order predicate calculus
c. Sufficient
d. Logical biconditional

14. In mathematics and in the sciences, a _____ (plural: _____e, formulæ or _____s) is a concise way of expressing information symbolically (as in a mathematical or chemical _____), or a general relationship between quantities. One of many famous _____e is Albert Einstein's $E = mc^2$ (see special relativity

In mathematics, a _____ is a key to solve an equation with variables. For example, the problem of determining the volume of a sphere is one that requires a significant amount of integral calculus to solve.

Chapter 21. Concave and Quasiconcave Functions

a. 2-3 heap
c. Formula

b. 1-center problem
d. 120-cell

15. In economics, the _____ is the rate at which a consumer is ready to give up one good in exchange for another good while maintaining the same level of satisfaction.

Under the standard assumption of neoclassical economics that goods and services are continuously divisible, the marginal rates of substitution will be the same regardless of the direction of exchange, and will correspond to the slope of an indifference curve passing through the consumption bundle in question, at that point. MRS of Y for X is the amount of Y for that a consumer is willing to exchange for X locally.

a. Cross price elasticity of demand
c. Marginal rate of substitution

b. 1-center problem
d. Supply and demand

16. In microeconomics, the _____ describes the minimum amount of money an individual needs to achieve some level of utility, given a utility function and prices.

Formally, if there is a utility function u that describes preferences over L commodities, the _____

$$e(p, u^*) : \mathbf{R}^L_+ \times \mathbf{R} \to \mathbf{R}$$

says what amount of money is needed to achieve a utility u^* if prices are set by p. This function is defined by

$$e(p, u^*) = \min_{x \in \geq(u^*)} p \cdot x$$

where

$$\geq (u^*) = \{x \in \mathbf{R}^L_+ : u(x) \geq u^*\}$$

is the set of all packages that give utility at least as good as u^*.

a. Utility maximization problem
c. Expenditure function

b. Indifference curve
d. Expenditure minimization problem

17. In mathematics, a _____ is a statement that can be proved on the basis of explicitly stated or previously agreed assumptions.

a. Disjunction introduction
c. Boolean function

b. Logical value
d. Theorem

18. In mathematics, the _____ or Pythagoras' theorem is a relation in Euclidean geometry among the three sides of a right triangle. The theorem is named after the Greek mathematician Pythagoras, who by tradition is credited with its discovery and proof, although it is often argued that knowledge of the theory predates him.. The theorem is as follows:

In any right triangle, the area of the square whose side is the hypotenuse is equal to the sum of the areas of the squares whose sides are the two legs.

a. 120-cell
b. 2-3 heap
c. 1-center problem
d. Pythagorean Theorem

19. In mathematics, a quasiconvex function is a real-valued function defined on an interval or on a convex subset of a real vector space such that the inverse image of any set of the form $(-\infty, a)$ is a convex set.

Equivalently, a function $f : S \to \mathbb{R}$ defined on a convex subset S of a real vector space is quasiconvex if whenever $x, y \in S$ and $\lambda \in [0, 1]$ then

$$f(\lambda x + (1 - \lambda)y) \leq \max(f(x), f(y)).$$

If instead

$$f(\lambda x + (1 - \lambda)y) < \max(f(x), f(y))$$

for any $x \neq y$ and $\lambda \in (0, 1)$, then f is strictly quasiconvex.

A _____ function is a function whose negative is quasiconvex, and a strictly _____ function is a function whose negative is strictly quasiconvex.

a. 2-3 heap
b. 120-cell
c. 1-center problem
d. Quasiconcave

20. In mathematics, a _____ is a real-valued function defined on an interval or on a convex subset of a real vector space such that the inverse image of any set of the form ☒> is a convex set.

Equivalently, a function ☒> defined on a convex subset S of a real vector space is quasiconvex if whenever ☒> and ☒> then

☒>

Chapter 21. Concave and Quasiconcave Functions

If instead

$$\boxed{} >$$

for any $\boxed{} >$ and $\boxed{} >$, then f is strictly quasiconvex.

A quasiconcave function is a function whose negative is quasiconvex, and a strictly quasiconcave function is a function whose negative is strictly quasiconvex.

a. Darboux function
c. Moment problem
b. Quasiconvex function
d. Weight function

21. The _____ governs the differentiation of products of differentiable functions.
    a. Reciprocal Rule
    c. 120-cell
    b. 1-center problem
    d. Product Rule

22. In mathematics, _____ functions form an important class of functions used in complex analysis. On a Kahler manifold, _____ functions form a subset of the subharmonic functions. However, unlike subharmonic functions _____ functions can be defined in full generality on complex spaces.
    a. 1-center problem
    c. Plurisubharmonic
    b. 120-cell
    d. 2-3 heap

23. The _____ is a single-winner election method in which voters rank candidates in order of preference. The _____ determines the winner of an election by giving each candidate a certain number of points corresponding to the position in which he or she is ranked by each voter. Once all votes have been counted the candidate with the most points is the winner.
    a. 1-center problem
    c. 120-cell
    b. 2-3 heap
    d. Borda count

24. In mathematics, a _____ is a point in the domain of a function of two variables which is a stationary point but not a local extremum. At such a point, in general, the surface resembles a saddle that curves up in one direction, and curves down in a different direction. In terms of contour lines, a _____ can be recognized, in general, by a contour that appears to intersect itself.
    a. 1-center problem
    c. Saddle point
    b. Gauss-Codazzi equations
    d. Gauss map

25. In physics and in _____ calculus, a _____ is a concept characterized by a magnitude and a direction. A _____ can be thought of as an arrow in Euclidean space, drawn from an initial point A pointing to a terminal point B.
    a. Dominance
    c. Constraint
    b. Deviation
    d. Vector

26. Loosely, the _____ is the change in the objective value of the optimal solution of an optimization problem obtained by relaxing the constraint by one unit. In a business application, a _____ is the maximum price that management is willing to pay for an extra unit of a given limited resource. For example, what is the price of keeping a production line operational for an additional hour if the production line is already operated at its maximum 40 hour limit? That price is the _____.
   a. Facility location
   c. Newsvendor
   b. Boolean model
   d. Shadow price

Chapter 22. Economic Applications

1. In economics, the _____ functional form of production functions is widely used to represent the relationship of an output to inputs. It was proposed by Knut Wicksell, and tested against statistical evidence by Paul Douglas and Charles Cobb in 1928.
   a. State price
   b. State price vector
   c. Cobb-Douglas
   d. Burden of proof

2. In statistics, _____ has two related meanings:

   - the arithmetic _____.
   - the expected value of a random variable, which is also called the population _____.

   It is sometimes stated that the '_____' _____s average. This is incorrect if '_____' is taken in the specific sense of 'arithmetic _____' as there are different types of averages: the _____, median, and mode. For instance, average house prices almost always use the median value for the average.

   For a real-valued random variable X, the _____ is the expectation of X.

   a. Statistical population
   b. Proportional hazards model
   c. Probability
   d. Mean

3. In calculus, the _____ states, roughly, that given a section of a smooth curve, there is at least one point on that section at which the derivative of the curve is equal to the 'average' derivative of the section. It is used to prove theorems that make global conclusions about a function on an interval starting from local hypotheses about derivatives at points of the interval.

   This theorem can be understood concretely by applying it to motion: if a car travels one hundred miles in one hour, so that its average speed during that time was 100 miles per hour, then at some time its instantaneous speed must have been exactly 100 miles per hour.

   a. Calculus controversy
   b. Functional integration
   c. Mean Value Theorem
   d. Fundamental Theorem of Calculus

4. In mathematics, a _____ is a statement that can be proved on the basis of explicitly stated or previously agreed assumptions.
   a. Disjunction introduction
   b. Logical value
   c. Boolean function
   d. Theorem

5. The term market basket or _____ refers to a fixed list of items used specifically to track the progress of inflation in an economy or specific market.

   The most common type of market basket is the basket of consumer goods, used to define the Consumer Price Index (CPI.) Other types of baskets are used to define

   - Producer Price Index (PPI), previously known as Wholesale Price Index (WPI)
   - various commodity price indices

The term market basket analysis in the retail business refers to research that provides the retailer with information to understand the purchase behaviour of a buyer. This information will enable the retailer to understand the buyer's needs and rewrite the store's layout accordingly, develop cross-promotional programs, or even capture new buyers (much like the cross-selling concept.)

a. Commodity bundle
b. Robin Hood index
c. 1-center problem
d. Pareto index

6. In mathematics, the concept of a _____ tries to capture the intuitive idea of a geometrical one-dimensional and continuous object. A simple example is the circle. In everyday use of the term '_____', a straight line is not curved, but in mathematical parlance _____s include straight lines and line segments.
a. Negative pedal curve
b. Kappa curve
c. Quadrifolium
d. Curve

7. The mathematical concept of a _____ expresses the intuitive idea of deterministic dependence between two quantities, one of which is viewed as primary and the other as secondary. A _____ then is a way to associate a unique output for each input of a specified type, for example, a real number or an element of a given set.
a. Grill
b. Going up
c. Coherent
d. Function

8. In microeconomics, a consumer's _____ specifies what the consumer would buy in each price and wealth situation, assuming it perfectly solves the utility maximization problem. Marshallian demand is sometimes called Walrasian demand or uncompensated demand function instead, because the original Marshallian analysis ignored wealth effects.

According to the utility maximization problem, there are L commodities with prices p.

a. 1-center problem
b. Precautionary demand
c. Marshallian demand function
d. Hicksian demand function

9. In microeconomics, a consumer's _____ function is the demand of a consumer over a bundle of goods that minimizes their expenditure while delivering a fixed level of utility. The function is named after John Hicks.

Mathematically,

$$h(p, \bar{u}) = \arg\min_x \sum_i p_i x_i$$
$$\text{such that } u(x) > \bar{u}$$

where h is the _____ function, or commodity bundle demanded, at price level p and utility level $\bar{u}$.

a. Marshallian demand function
b. 1-center problem
c. Precautionary demand
d. Hicksian demand

Chapter 22. Economic Applications

10. In mathematics, an _____ is a generalization for the concept of a function in which the dependent variable has not been given 'explicitly' in terms of the independent variable. To give a function f explicitly is to provide a prescription for determining the value of the function y in terms of the input value x:

   y = f

   a. Ordinary differential equation
   b. Implicit differentiation
   c. Inflection point
   d. Implicit Function

11. In the branch of mathematics called multivariable calculus, the _____ is a tool which allows relations to be converted to functions. It does this by representing the relation as the graph of a function. There may not be a single function whose graph is the entire relation, but there may be such a function on a restriction of the domain of the relation.
   a. A chemical equation
   b. Inverse function theorem
   c. A Mathematical Theory of Communication
   d. Implicit Function Theorem

12. In mathematics, the term _____ has several different important meanings:

   - An _____ is an equality that remains true regardless of the values of any variables that appear within it, to distinguish it from an equality which is true under more particular conditions. For this, the 'triple bar' symbol ≡ is sometimes used.
   - In algebra, an _____ or _____ element of a set S with a binary operation Â· is an element e that, when combined with any element x of S, produces that same x. That is, eÂ·x = xÂ·e = x for all x in S.
     - The _____ function from a set S to itself, often denoted id or id$_S$, s the function such that i = x for all x in S. This function serves as the _____ element in the set of all functions from S to itself with respect to function composition.
     - In linear algebra, the _____ matrix of size n is the n-by-n square matrix with ones on the main diagonal and zeros elsewhere. This matrix serves as the _____ with respect to matrix multiplication.

A common example of the first meaning is the trigonometric _____

$$\sin^2 \theta + \cos^2 \theta = 1$$

which is true for all real values of θ, as opposed to

$$\cos \theta = 1,$$

which is true only for some values of θ, not all. For example, the latter equation is true when $\theta = 0$, false when $\theta = 2$

The concepts of 'additive _____' and 'multiplicative _____' are central to the Peano axioms. The number 0 is the 'additive _____' for integers, real numbers, and complex numbers. For the real numbers, for all $a \in \mathbb{R}$,

$$0 + a = a,$$

$$a + 0 = a, \text{ and}$$

$$0 + 0 = 0.$$

Similarly, The number 1 is the 'multiplicative _____' for integers, real numbers, and complex numbers.

a. Identity
c. Action

b. ARIA
d. Intersection

13. In economics, a consumer's _____ v(p,w) gives the consumer's maximal utility when faced with a price level p and an amount of income w. It represents the consumer's preferences over market conditions.

This function is called indirect because consumers usually think about their preferences in terms of what they consume rather than prices.

a. A Mathematical Theory of Communication
c. A chemical equation

b. Indirect utility function
d. Expected utility hypothesis

14. In microeconomics, the _____ describes the minimum amount of money an individual needs to achieve some level of utility, given a utility function and prices.

Formally, if there is a utility function u that describes preferences over L commodities, the _____

$$e(p, u^*) : \mathbb{R}_+^L \times \mathbb{R} \to \mathbb{R}$$

says what amount of money is needed to achieve a utility u* if prices are set by p. This function is defined by

$$e(p, u^*) = \min_{x \in \geq(u^*)} p \cdot x$$

where

$$\geq(u^*) = \{x \in \mathbb{R}_+^L : u(x) \geq u^*\}$$

is the set of all packages that give utility at least as good as u*.

a. Expenditure minimization problem
b. Utility maximization problem
c. Indifference curve
d. Expenditure function

15. In the geometry of the projective plane, _____ refers to geometric transformations that replace points by lines and lines by points while preserving incidence properties among the transformed objects. The existence of such transformations leads to a general principle, that any theorem about incidences between points and lines in the projective plane may be transformed into another theorem about lines and points, by a substitution of the appropriate words.

_____ in the projective plane is a special case of _____ for projective spaces, transformations that interchange

dimension + codimension.

a. Decidable
b. Blocking
c. Duality
d. Disk

16. The _____ in economics, named after Eugen Slutsky, relates changes in Marshallian demand to changes in Hicksian demand. It demonstrates that demand changes due to price changes are a result of two effects:

- a substitution effect, the result of a change in the exchange rate between two goods; and
- an income effect, the effect of price results in a change of the consumer's purchasing power.

Each element of the Slutsky matrix is given by

$$\frac{\partial x_i(p,w)}{\partial p_j} = \frac{\partial h_i(p,u)}{\partial p_j} - \frac{\partial x_i(p,w)}{\partial w} x_j(p,w),$$

where h is the Hicksian demand and x is the Marshallian demand, at price level p, wealth level w, and utility level u. The first term represents the substitution effect, and the second term represents the income effect.

The same equation can be rewritten in matrix form and is called the Slutsky matrix

$$D_p x(p,w) = D_p h(p,u) - D_w x(p,w) x(p,w)^\top,$$

where D_p is the derivative operator with respect to price and D_w is the derivative operator with respect to wealth.

a. Hubbert curve
b. Quintic equation
c. Scherrer Equation
d. Slutsky Equation

17. The Condorcet candidate or _____ of an election is the candidate who, when compared with every other candidate, is preferred by more voters. Informally, the _____ is the person who would win a two-candidate election against each of the other candidates. A _____ will not always exist in a given set of votes, which is known as Condorcet's voting paradox.

Chapter 22. Economic Applications

a. Condorcet winner
c. Psephology

b. 120-cell
d. 1-center problem

18. The _____ governs the differentiation of products of differentiable functions.
  a. Reciprocal Rule
  c. 1-center problem

  b. 120-cell
  d. Product Rule

19. _____ (CES) is a property of some production functions and utility functions.

More precisely, it refers to a particular type of aggregator function which combines two or more types of consumption, or two or more types of productive inputs into an aggregate quantity. This aggregator function exhibits _____.

  a. 1-center problem
  c. Constant elasticity of substitution

  b. Production function
  d. Short-run

20. In economics, a _____ is a function that specifies the output of a firm, an industry, or an entire economy for all combinations of inputs. A meta-_____ compares the practice of the existing entities converting inputs X into output y to determine the most efficient practice _____ of the existing entities, whether the most efficient feasible practice production or the most efficient actual practice production. In either case, the maximum output of a technologically-determined production process is a mathematical function of input factors of production.
  a. Short-run
  c. 1-center problem

  b. Long-run
  d. Production function

21. In physics and in _____ calculus, a _____ is a concept characterized by a magnitude and a direction. A _____ can be thought of as an arrow in Euclidean space, drawn from an initial point A pointing to a terminal point B.
  a. Deviation
  c. Vector

  b. Dominance
  d. Constraint

22. _____ is an important concept in economics with broad applications in game theory, engineering and the social sciences. The term is named after Vilfredo Pareto, an Italian economist who used the concept in his studies of economic efficiency and income distribution.

Given a set of alternative allocations of, say, goods or income for a set of individuals, a change from one allocation to another that can make at least one individual better off without making any other individual worse off is called a Pareto improvement.

  a. Pursuit-evasion
  c. Multiunit auction

  b. Pareto efficiency
  d. Quasi-perfect equilibrium

23. In mathematics, the _____ or Pythagoras' theorem is a relation in Euclidean geometry among the three sides of a right triangle. The theorem is named after the Greek mathematician Pythagoras, who by tradition is credited with its discovery and proof, although it is often argued that knowledge of the theory predates him.. The theorem is as follows:

In any right triangle, the area of the square whose side is the hypotenuse is equal to the sum of the areas of the squares whose sides are the two legs.

Chapter 22. Economic Applications

a. 2-3 heap
b. Pythagorean Theorem
c. 1-center problem
d. 120-cell

24. In economics, business, retail, and accounting, a _____ is the value of money that has been used up to produce something, and hence is not available for use anymore. In business, the _____ may be one of acquisition, in which case the amount of money expended to acquire it is counted as _____. In this case, money is the input that is gone in order to acquire the thing.

a. 2-3 heap
b. 1-center problem
c. 120-cell
d. Cost

25. In mathematics, the _____ of a number n is the number that, when added to n, yields zero. The _____ of n is denoted −n. For example, 7 is −7, because 7 + (−7) = 0, and the _____ of −0.3 is 0.3, because −0.3 + 0.3 = 0.

a. Associativity
b. Algebraic structure
c. Additive inverse
d. Arity

26. In economics, an _____ is a function that maps the quantity of output supplied to the market price for that output.

In mathematical terms, if the demand function is , then the _____ is f^{-1}

a. Enterprise value
b. Inverse demand function
c. Arrow-Debreu model
d. Internal rate of return

27. In economics, a _____ exists when a specific individual or enterprise has sufficient control over a particular product or service to determine significantly the terms on which other individuals shall have access to it. Monopolies are thus characterized by a lack of economic competition for the good or service that they provide and a lack of viable substitute goods. The verb 'monopolize' refers to the process by which a firm gains persistently greater market share than what is expected under perfect competition.

a. 120-cell
b. 2-3 heap
c. 1-center problem
d. Monopoly

28. In mathematics, in the realm of group theory, a group is said to be _____ if it equals its own commutator subgroup if the group has no nontrivial abelian quotients.

The smallest _____ group is the alternating group A_5. More generally, any non-abelian simple group is _____ since the commutator subgroup is a normal subgroup with abelian quotient.

a. Group of Lie type
b. Perfect
c. Quaternion group
d. Free product

29. In neoclassical economics and microeconomics, _____ describes a market in which no buyer or seller has market power. In the short term, such markets are productively inefficient and allocatively efficient. However, In the long term, such markets both allocatively and productively efficient.

a. 2-3 heap
b. 120-cell
c. 1-center problem
d. Perfect competition

Chapter 22. Economic Applications

30. The _____ is a basic theorem used to solve maximization problems in microeconomics. It may be used to prove Hotelling's lemma, Shephard's lemma, and Roy's identity. The statement of the theorem is:

Consider an arbitrary maximization problem where the objective function (f) depends on some parameter (a):

$$M(a) = \max_x f(x, a)$$

where the function M(a) gives the maximized value of the objective function (f) as a function of the parameter (a.)

    a. A Mathematical Theory of Communication   b. Envelope Theorem
    c. A chemical equation   d. A posteriori

31. In economics, the cross elasticity of demand and _____ measures the responsiveness of the quantity demanded of a good to a change in the price of another good.

It is measured as the percentage change in quantity demanded for the first good that occurs in response to a percentage change in price of the second good. For example, if, in response to a 10% increase in the price of fuel, the quantity of new cars that are fuel inefficient demanded decreased by 20%, the cross elasticity of demand would be -20%/10% = -2.

    a. 1-center problem   b. Cross price elasticity of demand
    c. Marginal rate of substitution   d. Supply and demand

32. In economics, _____ defines the cost-minimizing level of an input required to produce a given level of output, for given costs of various input factors. The conditional portion of this phrase refers to the fact that this function takes a given output as an argument, and is therefore conditional on this value, wages are also important in this function. This concept is similar to but distinct from the factor demand function, which is a function of prices and wages, not output.

    a. Biscuspid   b. Convex and concave
    c. Convex   d. Conditional factor demand

33. In computer science, a _____ is a description of a configuration of discrete states used as a simple model of machines. Formally, it can be defined as a tuple [N, A, S, G] where:

- N is a set of states
- A is a set of arcs connecting the states
- S is a nonempty subset of N that contains start states
- G is a nonempty subset of N that contains the goal states.

The _____ is what _____ search searches in. Graph theory is helpful in understanding and reasoning about _____s.

Chapter 22. Economic Applications

A _____ has some common properties:

- complexity, where branching factor is important
- structure of the space, see also graph theory:
    - directionality of arcs
    - tree
    - Rooted graph

- _____ (controls) for information about continuous _____ in control engineering.
- _____ (physics) for information about continuous _____ in physics.
- Phase space for information about phase state (like continuous _____) in physics and mathematics.
- Probability space for information about _____ in probability.

a. Tag system
b. State space
c. Lambda calculus
d. Deterministic finite state machine

34. In economics, _____ is the total demand for final goods and services in the economy (Y) at a given time and price level. This is the demand for the gross domestic product of a country when inventory levels are static. It is often called effective demand or abbreviated as '_____'.

a. A posteriori
b. A chemical equation
c. A Mathematical Theory of Communication
d. Aggregate demand

35. _____s is the social science that studies the production, distribution, and consumption of goods and services.

The term _____s comes from the Ancient Greek oá¼°κονομία (oikonomia, 'management of a household, administration') from oá¼¶κος (oikos, 'house') + vÏŒμος (nomos, 'custom' or 'law'), hence 'rules of the house(hold)'.

Current _____ models developed out of the broader field of political economy in the late 19th century, owing to a desire to use an empirical approach more akin to the physical sciences.

a. A chemical equation
b. Experimental economics
c. Economic
d. A Mathematical Theory of Communication

36. In calculus, a branch of mathematics, _____ essentially states that a differentiable function, which attains equal values at two points, must have a point somewhere between them where the slope is zero.

If a real-valued function f is continuous on a closed interval [a,b], differentiable on the open interval, and f

$$f'(c) = 0.$$

This version of _____ is used to prove the mean value theorem, _____ is indeed a special case of it.

A version of the theorem was first stated by the Indian astronomer BhÄ skara II in the 12th century.

a. Contingency table
b. Convex polygon
c. Continuous wave
d. Rolle's Theorem

37. There are two _____. The first states that any competitive equilibrium or Walrasian equilibrium leads to an efficient allocation of resources. The second states the converse, that any efficient allocation can be sustainable by a competitive equilibrium. Despite the apparent symmetry of the two theorems, in fact the first theorem is much more general than the second, requiring far weaker assumptions.

a. 120-cell
b. Fundamental Theorems of Welfare Economics
c. 2-3 heap
d. 1-center problem

38. Competitive market equilibrium is the traditional concept of economic equilibrium, appropriate for the analysis of commodity markets with flexible prices and many traders, and serving as the benchmark of efficiency in economic analysis. It relies crucially on the assumption of a competitive environment where each trader decides upon a quantity that is so small compared to the total quantity traded in the market that their individual transactions have no influence on the prices.

A _____ consists of a vector of prices and an allocation such that given the prices, each trader by maximizing his objective function (profit, preferences) subject to his technological possibilities and resource constraints plans to trade into his part of the proposed allocation, and such that the prices make all net trades compatible with one another ('clear the market') by equating aggregate supply and demand for the commodities which are traded.

a. Competitive equilibrium
b. 1-center problem
c. Partial equilibrium
d. 120-cell

Chapter 23. Eigenvalues and Eigenvectors

1. In linear algebra, a _____ is a square matrix in which the entries outside the main diagonal are all zero. The diagonal entries themselves may or may not be zero. Thus, the matrix D = with n columns and n rows is diagonal if:

$$d_{i,j} = 0 \text{ if } i \neq j \quad \forall i,j \in \{1, 2, \ldots, n\}$$

For example, the following matrix is diagonal:

$$\begin{bmatrix} 1 & 0 & 0 \\ 0 & 4 & 0 \\ 0 & 0 & -3 \end{bmatrix}.$$

The term _____ may sometimes refer to a rectangular _____, which is an m-by-n matrix with only the entries of the form $d_{i,i}$ possibly non-zero; for example,

$$\begin{bmatrix} 1 & 0 & 0 \\ 0 & 4 & 0 \\ 0 & 0 & -3 \\ 0 & 0 & 0 \end{bmatrix}, \text{ or } \begin{bmatrix} 1 & 0 & 0 & 0 & 0 \\ 0 & 4 & 0 & 0 & 0 \\ 0 & 0 & -3 & 0 & 0 \end{bmatrix}.$$

   a. Design matrix
   c. Transition matrix
   b. Hankel matrix
   d. Diagonal matrix

2. In mathematics and in the sciences, a _____ (plural: _____e, formulæ or _____s) is a concise way of expressing information symbolically (as in a mathematical or chemical _____), or a general relationship between quantities. One of many famous _____e is Albert Einstein's E = mc² (see special relativity

In mathematics, a _____ is a key to solve an equation with variables. For example, the problem of determining the volume of a sphere is one that requires a significant amount of integral calculus to solve.

   a. 1-center problem
   c. 120-cell
   b. 2-3 heap
   d. Formula

3. In mathematics, a _____ is a rectangular table of elements, which may be numbers or, more generally, any abstract quantities that can be added and multiplied. Matrices are used to describe linear equations, keep track of the coefficients of linear transformations and to record data that depend on multiple parameters. Matrices are described by the field of _____ theory.
   a. Compression
   c. Matrix
   b. Coherent
   d. Double counting

4. In calculus, the _____ is a formula for the derivative of the composite of two functions.

Chapter 23. Eigenvalues and Eigenvectors

In intuitive terms, if a variable, y, depends on a second variable, u, which in turn depends on a third variable, x, then the rate of change of y with respect to x can be computed as the rate of change of y with respect to u multiplied by the rate of change of u with respect to x. Schematically,

$$\frac{dy}{dx} = \frac{dy}{du} \cdot \frac{du}{dx}.$$

For an explanation of notation used in this section, see Function composition.

The _____ states that, under appropriate conditions,

$$(f \circ g)'(x) = f'(g(x))g'(x),$$

which in short form is written as

$$(f \circ g)' = f' \circ g \cdot g'.$$

Alternatively, in the Leibniz notation, the _____ is

$$\frac{dy}{dx} = \frac{dy}{du} \cdot \frac{du}{dx}.$$

In integration, the counterpart to the _____ is the substitution rule.

a. 1-center problem
c. Product rule
b. 120-cell
d. Chain Rule

5. In mathematics, the _____ of a ring R, often denoted cha, is defined to be the smallest number of times one must add the ring's multiplicative identity element to itself to get the additive identity element; the ring is said to have _____ zero if this repeated sum never reaches the additive identity. That is, cha is the smallest positive number n such that

$$\underbrace{1 + \cdots + 1}_{n \text{ summands}} = 0$$

if such a number n exists, and 0 otherwise. The _____ may also be taken to be the exponent of the ring's additive group, that is, the smallest positive n such that

$$\underbrace{a + \cdots + a}_{n \text{ summands}} = 0$$

for every element a of the ring.

a. Characteristic b. Disk
c. Coherent d. Class

6. In linear algebra, one associates a polynomial to every square matrix, its _____. This polynomial encodes several important properties of the matrix, most notably its eigenvalues, its determinant and its trace.

Given a square matrix A, we want to find a polynomial whose roots are precisely the eigenvalues of A.

a. Polynomial long division b. Littlewood polynomial
c. Coefficient d. Characteristic polynomial

7. In algebra, a _____ is a function depending on n that associates a scalar, de, to every n×n square matrix A. The fundamental geometric meaning of a _____ is as the scale factor for measure when A is regarded as a linear transformation. _____s are important both in calculus, where they enter the substitution rule for several variables, and in multilinear algebra.

a. 1-center problem b. Functional determinant
c. Pfaffian d. Determinant

8. In mathematics, a _____ is an expression constructed from variables and constants, using the operations of addition, subtraction, multiplication, and constant non-negative whole number exponents. For example, $x^2 - 4x + 7$ is a _____, but $x^2 - 4/x + 7x^{3/2}$ is not, because its second term involves division by the variable x and also because its third term contains an exponent that is not a whole number.

_____s are one of the most important concepts in algebra and throughout mathematics and science.

a. Semifield b. Polynomial
c. Coimage d. Group extension

9. The _____ governs the differentiation of products of differentiable functions.

a. 1-center problem b. 120-cell
c. Reciprocal Rule d. Product Rule

10. In mathematics, given a linear transformation, an _____ of that linear transformation is a nonzero vector which, when that transformation is applied to it, may change in length, but not direction.

For each _____ of a linear transformation, there is a corresponding scalar value called an eigenvalue for that vector, which determines the amount the _____ is scaled under the linear transformation. For example, an eigenvalue of +2 means that the _____ is doubled in length and points in the same direction.

a. Angular momentum b. Ensemble
c. Uncertainty principle d. Eigenvector

11. In physics and in _____ calculus, a _____ is a concept characterized by a magnitude and a direction. A _____ can be thought of as an arrow in Euclidean space, drawn from an initial point A pointing to a terminal point B.

a. Constraint
b. Dominance
c. Vector
d. Deviation

12. In mathematics, _____ is one of the basic operations defining a vector space in linear algebra. Note that _____ is different from scalar product which is an inner product between two vectors.

More specifically, if K is a field and V is a vector space over K, then _____ is a function from K × V to V.

a. Frobenius normal form
b. Jordan normal form
c. Non-negative matrix factorization
d. Scalar multiplication

13. In linear algebra, the kernel or null space of a matrix A is the set of all vectors x for which Ax = 0. The null space of a matrix with n columns is a linear subspace of n-dimensional Euclidean space.

The _____ of the matrix A is exactly the same thing as the _____ of the linear mapping defined by the matrix-vector multiplication $x \mapsto Ax$, that is, the set of vectors that map to the zero vector.

a. Generalized singular value decomposition
b. Fundamental theorem of linear algebra
c. Generalized Pauli matrices
d. Nullspace

14. The mathematical concept of a _____ expresses the intuitive idea of deterministic dependence between two quantities, one of which is viewed as primary and the other as secondary. A _____ then is a way to associate a unique output for each input of a specified type, for example, a real number or an element of a given set.

a. Grill
b. Coherent
c. Going up
d. Function

15. In mathematics, an _____ is a generalization for the concept of a function in which the dependent variable has not been given 'explicitly' in terms of the independent variable. To give a function f explicitly is to provide a prescription for determining the value of the function y in terms of the input value x:

$$y = f$$

a. Inflection point
b. Implicit Function
c. Ordinary differential equation
d. Implicit differentiation

16. In the branch of mathematics called multivariable calculus, the _____ is a tool which allows relations to be converted to functions. It does this by representing the relation as the graph of a function. There may not be a single function whose graph is the entire relation, but there may be such a function on a restriction of the domain of the relation.

a. A Mathematical Theory of Communication
b. Inverse function theorem
c. Implicit Function Theorem
d. A chemical equation

17. _____ County lies just north of the Mexican border--sharing a border with Tijuana--and lies south of Orange County. It is home to miles of beaches, a mild Mediterranean climate and 16 military facilities hosting the United States Navy, the United States Coast Guard and the United States Marine Corps.

_____'s economy is largely composed of agriculture, biotechnology/biosciences, computer sciences, electronics manufacturing, defense-related manufacturing, financial and business services, ship-repair and construction, software development, telecommunications, and tourism.

a. 1-center problem	b. 2-3 heap
c. San Diego	d. 120-cell

18.   In mathematics, a _____ is a statement that can be proved on the basis of explicitly stated or previously agreed assumptions.

a. Disjunction introduction	b. Boolean function
c. Theorem	d. Logical value

19.   In mathematics, a recurrence relation is an equation that defines a sequence recursively: each term of the sequence is defined as a function of the preceding terms.

A _____ is a specific type of recurrence relation.

An example of a recurrence relation is the logistic map:

$$x_{n+1} = rx_n(1 - x_n).$$

Some simply defined recurrence relations can have very complex behaviours and are sometimes studied by physicists and mathematicians in a field of mathematics known as nonlinear analysis.

a. Difference equation	b. Digital root
c. Laws of Form	d. Continuant

20.   _____ is a fee, paid on borrowed capital. Assets lent include money, shares, consumer goods through hire purchase, major assets such as aircraft, and even entire factories in finance lease arrangements. The _____ is calculated upon the value of the assets in the same manner as upon money.

a. Interest expense	b. Interest sensitivity gap
c. A Mathematical Theory of Communication	d. Interest

21.   The Condorcet candidate or _____ of an election is the candidate who, when compared with every other candidate, is preferred by more voters. Informally, the _____ is the person who would win a two-candidate election against each of the other candidates. A _____ will not always exist in a given set of votes, which is known as Condorcet's voting paradox.

a. Condorcet winner	b. 120-cell
c. Psephology	d. 1-center problem

22.   A _____ is a simple shape of Euclidean geometry consisting of those points in a plane which are at a constant distance, called the radius, from a fixed point, called the center. A _____ with center A is sometimes denoted by the symbol A.

Chapter 23. Eigenvalues and Eigenvectors

A chord of a _____ is a line segment whose two endpoints lie on the _____.

a. Circular segment
b. Circumcircle
c. Circle
d. Malfatti circles

23. In mathematics, a _____ is a curve obtained by intersecting a cone with a plane. A _____ is therefore a restriction of a quadric surface to the plane. The _____s were named and studied as long ago as 200 BC, when Apollonius of Perga undertook a systematic study of their properties.

a. Parabola
b. Dandelin sphere
c. Conic section
d. Directrix

24. In mathematics an _____ , a 'falling short') is a conic section, the locus of points in a plane such that the sum of the distances to two fixed points is equal to a given constant. The two fixed points are then called foci.

Another way is to define it as the path traced out by a point whose distance from a focus maintains a constant ratio less than one with its distance from a straight line not passing through the focus, called the directrix.

a. Ellipse
b. A chemical equation
c. A Mathematical Theory of Communication
d. A posteriori

25. In several fields of mathematics the term _____ is used with different but closely related meanings. They all relate to the notion of mapping the elements of a set to other elements of the same set, i.e., exchanging elements of a set.

The general concept of _____ can be defined more formally in different contexts:

In combinatorics, a _____ is usually understood to be a sequence containing each element from a finite set once, and only once.

a. Permutation
b. Tensor product
c. Linearly independent
d. Cyclic permutation

26. In mathematics, in matrix theory, a _____ is a square-matrix that has exactly one entry 1 in each row and each column and 0's elsewhere. Each such matrix represents a specific permutation of m elements and, when used to multiply another matrix, can produce that permutation in the rows or columns of the other matrix.

Given a permutation π of m elements,

$$\pi : \{1,\ldots,m\} \to \{1,\ldots,m\}$$

given in two-line form by

$$\begin{pmatrix} 1 & 2 & \cdots & m \\ \pi(1) & \pi(2) & \cdots & \pi(m) \end{pmatrix},$$

its _____ is the m × m matrix P_π whose entries are all 0 except that in row i, the entry equals 1.

a. Hessenberg matrix
b. Cartan matrix
c. Partitioned matrix
d. Permutation Matrix

27. Crude _____ is the natality or childbirths per 1,000 people per year.

It can be represented by number of childbirths in that year, and p is the current population. This figure is combined with the crude death rate to produce the rate of natural population growth (natural in that it does not take into account net migration.)

a. 1-center problem
b. 120-cell
c. Birth rate
d. Gompertz-Makeham law of mortality

28. _____ is the study of marginal and long-term changes in the numbers, individual weights and age composition of individuals in one or several populations, and biological and environmental processes influencing those changes. _____ also attempts to study topics such as aging populations or population decline.

_____ has traditionally been the dominant branch of mathematical biology, which has a history of more than 210 years, although more recently the scope of mathematical biology has greatly expanded.

a. 120-cell
b. 1-center problem
c. Population growth
d. Population dynamics

29. In linear algebra, _____ is an efficient algorithm for solving systems of linear equations, finding the rank of a matrix, and calculating the inverse of an invertible square matrix. _____ is named after German mathematician and scientist Carl Friedrich Gauss.

Elementary row operations are used to reduce a matrix to row echelon form.

a. Cholesky decomposition
b. Conjugate gradient method
c. Crout matrix decomposition
d. Gaussian elimination

30. The _____ is a basic theorem used to solve maximization problems in microeconomics. It may be used to prove Hotelling's lemma, Shephard's lemma, and Roy's identity. The statement of the theorem is:

Chapter 23. Eigenvalues and Eigenvectors

Consider an arbitrary maximization problem where the objective function (f) depends on some parameter (a):

$$M(a) = \max_x f(x, a)$$

where the function M(a) gives the maximized value of the objective function (f) as a function of the parameter (a.)

a. A chemical equation
b. Envelope Theorem
c. A posteriori
d. A Mathematical Theory of Communication

31. _____ is a branch of mathematics which focuses on the study of matrices. Initially a sub-branch of linear algebra, it has grown to cover subjects related to graph theory, algebra, combinatorics, and statistics as well.

The term matrix was first coined in 1848 by J.J. Sylvester as a name of an array of numbers.

a. Segre classification
b. Matrix theory
c. Pairing
d. Semi-simple operators

32. In mathematics the concept of a _____ generalizes notions such as 'length', 'area', and 'volume'. Informally, given some base set, a '_____' is any consistent assignment of 'sizes' to the subsets of the base set. Depending on the application, the 'size' of a subset may be interpreted as its physical size, the amount of something that lies within the subset, or the probability that some random process will yield a result within the subset.

a. Lattice
b. Measure
c. Cusp
d. Congruent

33. In statistics and mathematical epidemiology, _____ is the risk of an event relative to exposure. _____ is a ratio of the probability of the event occurring in the exposed group versus a non-exposed group.

$$RR = \frac{p_{\text{exposed}}}{p_{\text{non-exposed}}}$$

For example, if the probability of developing lung cancer among smokers was 20% and among non-smokers 1%, then the _____ of cancer associated with smoking would be 20.

a. Statistical epidemiology
b. 1-center problem
c. Mendelian randomization
d. Relative risk

34. _____ is a concept in economics, finance, and psychology related to the behaviour of consumers and investors under uncertainty. _____ is the reluctance of a person to accept a bargain with an uncertain payoff rather than another bargain with a more certain, but possibly lower, expected payoff.

The inverse of a person's _____ is sometimes called their risk tolerance.

a. Stochastic modelling
b. Risk aversion
c. Ruin theory
d. Life table

35. In vascular plants, the _____ is the organ of a plant body that typically lies below the surface of the soil. This is not always the case, however, since a _____ can also be aerial (that is, growing above the ground) or aerating (that is, growing up above the ground or especially above water.) Furthermore, a stem normally occurring below ground is not exceptional either
   a. 120-cell
   b. 2-3 heap
   c. 1-center problem
   d. Root

36. In mathematics, a _____ of a number x is a number r such that r^2 = x, or, in other words, a number r whose square is x. Every non-negative real number x has a unique non-negative _____, called the principal _____, which is denoted with a radical symbol as $\sqrt{x}$, or, using exponent notation, as $x^{1/2}$. For example, the principal _____ of 9 is 3, denoted $\sqrt{9}$ = 3, because 3^2 = 3 × 3 = 9.
   a. Multiplicative inverse
   b. Double exponential
   c. Hyperbolic functions
   d. Square root

37. In probability theory and statistics, the _____ of a family of probability distributions is an important property which basically states that if one has a number of random variates that are 'in the family', any linear combination of these variates will also be 'in the family'. Specifically, the family of probability distributions here is a location-scale family, consisting of probability distributions that differ only in location and scale and 'in the family' means that the random variates have a distribution function that is a member of the family.

    The importance of a stable family of probability distributions is that they serve as 'attractors' for linear combinations of non-stable random variates.

   a. Torsion
   b. Convergent
   c. Secant
   d. Stability

38. In model theory, a complete theory is called _____ if it does not have too many types. One goal of classification theory is to divide all complete theories into those whose models can be classified and those whose models are too complicated to classify, and to classify all models in the cases where this can be done. Roughly speaking, if a theory is not _____ then its models are too complicated and numerous to classify, while if a theory is _____ there might be some hope of classifying its models, especially if the theory is superstable or totally transcendental.
   a. Transfer principle
   b. Spectrum of a theory
   c. Non-standard calculus
   d. Stable

39. In economics, the _____ functional form of production functions is widely used to represent the relationship of an output to inputs. It was proposed by Knut Wicksell, and tested against statistical evidence by Paul Douglas and Charles Cobb in 1928.
   a. Cobb-Douglas
   b. State price vector
   c. Burden of proof
   d. State price

40. In mathematics, the _____ is a representation of a function as an infinite sum of terms calculated from the values of its derivatives at a single point. It may be regarded as the limit of the Taylor polynomials. _____ are named after English mathematician Brook Taylor.

Chapter 23. Eigenvalues and Eigenvectors

a. Local linearity
b. 1-center problem
c. C^r topology
d. Taylor series

41. In mathematics, the _____s are an extension of the real numbers obtained by adjoining an imaginary unit, denoted i, which satisfies:

$$i^2 = -1.$$

Every _____ can be written in the form a + bi, where a and b are real numbers called the real part and the imaginary part of the _____, respectively.

_____s are a field, and thus have addition, subtraction, multiplication, and division operations. These operations extend the corresponding operations on real numbers, although with a number of additional elegant and useful properties, e.g., negative real numbers can be obtained by squaring _____s.

a. Real part
b. 1-center problem
c. 120-cell
d. Complex number

42. In mathematics, a _____ is often represented as the sum of a sequence of terms. That is, a _____ is represented as a list of numbers with addition operations between them, for example this arithmetic sequence:

1 + 2 + 3 + 4 + 5 + ... + 99 + 100

In most cases of interest the terms of the sequence are produced according to a certain rule, such as by a formula, by an algorithm, by a sequence of measurements, or even by a random number generator.

a. Concavity
b. Series
c. Contact
d. Blind

43. In linear algebra, the _____ of an n-by-n square matrix A is defined to be the sum of the elements on the main diagonal of A. wikimedia.org/math/8/2/b/82be32fa00bd97ebbc066aec3dfe72da.png">

where a$_{ij}$ represents the entry on the ith row and jth column of A. Equivalently, the _____ of a matrix is the sum of its eigenvalues, making it an invariant with respect to a change of basis.

a. Constructivism
b. Blinding
c. Lattice
d. Trace

44. In mathematics, the _____ or Pythagoras' theorem is a relation in Euclidean geometry among the three sides of a right triangle. The theorem is named after the Greek mathematician Pythagoras, who by tradition is credited with its discovery and proof, although it is often argued that knowledge of the theory predates him.. The theorem is as follows:

In any right triangle, the area of the square whose side is the hypotenuse is equal to the sum of the areas of the squares whose sides are the two legs.

a. 120-cell
c. 1-center problem

b. Pythagorean Theorem
d. 2-3 heap

45. In linear algebra, a _____ of a matrix A is a nonzero vector v, which has associated with it an eigenvalue λ having algebraic multiplicity k ≥1, satisfying

$$(A - \lambda I)^k \mathbf{v} = 0.$$

Ordinary eigenvectors are obtained for k=1.

_____s are needed to form a complete basis of a defective matrix, which is a matrix in which there are fewer linearly independent eigenvectors than eigenvalues. The _____s do form a complete basis, as follows from the Jordan form of a matrix.

a. Schmidt decomposition
c. Pseudovector

b. Rayleigh quotient
d. Generalized eigenvector

46. In Boolean algebra, any Boolean function can be expressed in a _____ using the dual concepts of minterms and maxterms. All logical functions are expressible in _____, both as a 'sum of minterms' and as a 'product of maxterms'. This allows for greater analysis into the simplification of these functions, which is of great importance in the minimization of digital circuits.

a. Reduct
c. Multiplicative digital root

b. Topological module
d. Canonical form

47. In mathematics, the _____ of a complex number is given by changing the sign of the imaginary part. Thus, the conjugate of the complex number

$$z = a + ib$$

(where a and b are real numbers) is

$$\bar{z} = a - ib.$$

The _____ is also very commonly denoted by z *. Here $\bar{z}$ is chosen to avoid confusion with the notation for the conjugate transpose of a matrix (which can be thought of as a generalization of complex conjugation.)

a. 120-cell
c. Real part

b. Complex conjugate
d. 1-center problem

48. In algebra, a _____ of an element in a quadratic extension field of a field K is its image under the unique non-identity automorphism of the extended field that fixes K. If the extension is generated by a square root of an element r of K, then the _____ of $a + b\sqrt{r}$ is $a - b\sqrt{r}$ for $a, b \in K$, and in particular in the case of the field C of complex numbers as an extension of the field R of real numbers, the complex _____ of a + bi is a − bi.

Chapter 23. Eigenvalues and Eigenvectors

Forming the sum or product of any element of the extension field with its _____ always gives an element of K.

   a. Real structure   b. Trinomial
   c. Relation algebra   d. Conjugate

49. _____ describes the property of operations in mathematics and computer science which means that multiple applications of the operation does not change the result. The concept of _____ arises in a number of places in abstract algebra.

There are several meanings of _____, depending on what the concept is applied to:

- A unary operation is called idempotent if, whenever it is applied twice to any value, it gives the same result as if it were applied once. For example, the absolute value function is idempotent as a function from the set of real numbers to the set of real numbers: ab = ab.
- A binary operation is called idempotent if, whenever it is applied to two equal values, it gives that value as the result. For example, the operation giving the maximum value of two values is idempotent: ma = x.
- Given a binary operation, an idempotent element for the operation is a value for which the operation, when given that value for both of its operands, gives the value as the result. For example, the number 1 is an idempotent of multiplication: 1 × 1 = 1.

A unary operation f that is a map from some set S into itself is called idempotent if, for all x in S,

      f

In particular, the identity function id_S, defined by
id_S, is idempotent, as is the constant function K_c, where c is an element of S, defined by $K_c(x) = c$.

   a. Antiisomorphism   b. Absorption law
   c. Ordered exponential   d. Idempotence

50. In mathematics, the _____ of a complex number z, is the second element of the ordered pair of real numbers representing z,. It is denoted by Im or $\mathfrak{I}\{z\}$, where $\mathfrak{I}$ is a capital I in the Fraktur typeface. The complex function which maps z to the _____ of z is not holomorphic.

   a. A chemical equation   b. A Mathematical Theory of Communication
   c. A posteriori   d. Imaginary part

51. In mathematics, the _____ of a complex number z, is the first element of the ordered pair of real numbers representing z. It is denoted by Re{z} or $\mathfrak{R}\{z\}$, where $\mathfrak{R}$ is a capital R in the Fraktur typeface. The complex function which maps z to the _____ of z is not holomorphic.

   a. Complex number   b. 1-center problem
   c. 120-cell   d. Real part

Chapter 23. Eigenvalues and Eigenvectors

52. In mathematics, the _____ system is a two-dimensional coordinate system in which each point on a plane is determined by an angle and a distance. The _____ system is especially useful in situations where the relationship between two points is most easily expressed in terms of angles and distance; in the more familiar Cartesian or rectangular coordinate system, such a relationship can only be found through trigonometric formulation.

As the coordinate system is two-dimensional, each point is determined by two _____s: the radial coordinate and the angular coordinate.

    a. Sir Isaac Newton   b. Vampire
    c. Sequence alignment   d. Polar coordinate

53. A _____, named after the Russian mathematician Andrey Markov, is a mathematical model for the random evolution of a memoryless system, that is, one for which the likelihood of a given future state, at any given moment, depends only on its present state, and not on any past states.

In a common description, a stochastic process with the Markov property, or memorylessness, is one for which conditional on the present state of the system, its future and past are independent.

Often, the term Markov chain is used to mean a discrete-time _____.

    a. Random measure   b. Hellinger distance
    c. Polar distribution   d. Markov process

54. _____ is the probability of some event A, given the occurrence of some other event B. _____ is written P[A | B], and is read 'the probability of A, given B'.

Joint probability is the probability of two events in conjunction. That is, it is the probability of both events together. The joint probability of A and B is written $P(A \cap B)$ or $P(A, B)$.

    a. Conditional probability   b. Sample space
    c. Quantile   d. Renewal theory

55. _____ is the likelihood or chance that something is the case or will happen. Theoretical _____ is used extensively in areas such as statistics, mathematics, science and philosophy to draw conclusions about the likelihood of potential events and the underlying mechanics of complex systems.

The word _____ does not have a consistent direct definition.

    a. Statistical significance   b. Discrete random variable
    c. Standardized moment   d. Probability

56. A _____ is the counterpart to a deterministic process in probability theory. Instead of dealing with only one possible 'reality' of how the process might evolve under time, in a stochastic or random process there is some indeterminacy in its future evolution described by probability distributions. This means that even if the initial condition is known, there are many possibilities the process might go to, but some paths are more probable and others less.

Chapter 23. Eigenvalues and Eigenvectors

a. Stochastic process
c. Mixing time

b. Stochastic simulation
d. Fractional Brownian motion

57. In mathematics, a _____, probability matrix, or transition matrix is used to describe the transitions of a Markov chain. It has found use in probability theory, statistics and linear algebra, as well as computer science. There are several different definitions and types of stochastic matrices;

A right _____ is a square matrix each of whose rows consists of nonnegative real numbers, with each row summing to 1.

a. Stochastic matrix
c. Positive-definite matrix

b. Vandermonde matrix
d. Similarity transformation

58. In mathematics, a stochastic matrix, probability matrix, or _____ is used to describe the transitions of a Markov chain. It has found use in probability theory, statistics and linear algebra, as well as computer science. There are several different definitions and types of stochastic matrices;

A right stochastic matrix is a square matrix each of whose rows consists of nonnegative real numbers, with each row summing to 1.

a. Sylvester matrix
c. Hessenberg matrix

b. Transition matrix
d. Pick matrix

59. In mathematics, a _____, named after Andrey Markov, is a stochastic process with the Markov property. Having the Markov property means that, given the present state, future states are independent of the past states. In other words, the description of the present state fully captures all the information that could influence the future evolution of the process. Future states will be reached through a probabilistic process instead of a deterministic one.

a. Possibility theory
c. Variance-to-mean ratio

b. Law of Truly Large Numbers
d. Markov chain

60. A nonnegative matrix is a matrix where all the elements are equal to or above zero

$$\mathbf{X} \geq 0, \qquad \forall_{ij}\, x_{ij} \geq 0.$$

A _____ is defined similarly. The set of positive matrices is a subset of all nonnegative matrices.

A non-negative matrix can represent a transition matrix for a Markov chain.

a. 120-cell
c. 1-center problem

b. 2-3 heap
d. Positive matrix

61. The _____ is a discrete, age-structured model of population growth that is very popular in population ecology. It was invented by and named after P. H. Leslie. The _____ is one of the best known ways to describe the growth of populations, in which a population is closed to migration and where only one sex, usually the female, is considered.

a. 1-center problem
c. 120-cell
b. Leslie matrix
d. Population growth

62. _____s is concerned with the tasks of developing and applying quantitative or statistical methods to the study and elucidation of economic principles. _____s combines economic theory with statistics to analyze and test economic relationships. Theoretical _____s considers questions about the statistical properties of estimators and tests, while applied _____s is concerned with the application of _____ methods to assess economic theories.
   a. A Mathematical Theory of Communication
   c. A chemical equation
   b. Economic
   d. Econometric

63. In linear algebra, a _____ is a square matrix, A, that is equal to its transpose

$$A = A^T.$$

The entries of a _____ are symmetric with respect to the main diagonal. So if the entries are written as A =, then

$$a_{ij} = a_{ji}$$

for all indices i and j. The following 3×3 matrix is symmetric:

$$\begin{bmatrix} 1 & 2 & 3 \\ 2 & 4 & -5 \\ 3 & -5 & 6 \end{bmatrix}.$$

A matrix is called skew-symmetric or antisymmetric if its transpose is the same as its negative.

   a. Contour integration
   c. Symmetric matrix
   b. Conway triangle notation
   d. Broken-line graph

64. In mathematics, two vectors are _____ if they are perpendicular. For example, a subway and the street above, although they do not physically intersect, are _____ if they cross at a right angle.
   a. Unique factorization domain
   c. Orthogonal
   b. Algebraic structure
   d. Additive identity

65. In matrix theory, a real _____ is a square matrix Q whose transpose is its inverse:

$$Q^T Q = Q Q^T = I.$$

A special _____ is an _____ with determinant +1:

$$\det Q = +1.$$

Chapter 23. Eigenvalues and Eigenvectors 193

An _____ is the real specialization of a unitary matrix, and thus always a normal matrix. Although we consider only real matrices here, the definition can be used for matrices with entries from any field. However, orthogonal matrices arise naturally from inner products, and for matrices of complex numbers that leads instead to the unitary requirement.

a. Alternating sign matrix
b. Unimodular polynomial matrix
c. Unitary matrix
d. Orthogonal matrix

66. In linear algebra, two vectors in an inner product space are _____ if they are orthogonal and both of unit length. A set of vectors form an _____ set if all vectors in the set are mutually orthogonal and all of unit length. An _____ set which forms a basis is called an _____ basis.
a. Orthonormal
b. Orthogonalization
c. Orthogonal Procrustes problem
d. Orthogonal complement

67. In linear algebra, _____ is the process of finding a set of orthogonal vectors that span a particular subspace. Formally, starting with a linearly independent set of vectors $\{v_1,...,v_k\}$ in an inner product space, _____ results in a set of orthogonal vectors $\{u_1,...,u_k\}$ that generate the same subspace as the vectors $v_1,...,v_k$. Every vector in the new set is orthogonal to every other vector in the new set; and the new set and the old set have the same linear span.
a. Antiunitary
b. Orthogonalization
c. Indeterminate system
d. Examples of vector spaces

68. In grammatical theory, definiteness is a feature of noun phrases, distinguishing between entities which are specific and identifiable in a given context (_____ noun phrases) and entities which are not (indefinite noun phrases Examples are:

- Free form: English the boy.
- Phrasal clitic: as in Basque: Cf. emakume ('woman'), emakume-a (woman-ART: 'the woman'), emakume ederr-a (woman beautiful-ART: 'the beautiful woman')
- Noun affix: as in Romanian: om ('man'), om-ul (man-ART: 'the man'); om-ul bun (man-ART good: 'the good man')
- Prefix on both noun and adjective: Arabic ا-لْفَتاش الْفْشَر (al-kitÄ b al-kabÄ«r) with two instances of al- (DEF-book-DEF-big, literally, 'the book the big')

Germanic, Romance, Celtic, Semitic, and auxiliary languages generally have a _____ article, sometimes used as a postposition. Many other languages do not.

a. 1-center problem
b. Sentence diagram
c. Syntax
d. Definite

69. In mathematics, a definite bilinear form is a bilinear form B over some vector space V (with real or complex scalar field) such that the associated quadratic form

$Q(x) = B(x,x)$

is definite, that is, has a real value with the same sign (positive or negative) for all non-zero x. According to that sign, B is called positive definite or _____. If Q takes both positive and negative values, the bilinear form B is called indefinite.

a. Multiple cross product
b. Multilinear map
c. Paravector
d. Negative definite

70. In linear algebra, a _____ is a matrix which in many ways is analogous to a positive real number. The notion is closely related to a positive-definite symmetric bilinear form.

An n × n real symmetric matrix M is positive definite if $z^T Mz > 0$ for all non-zero vectors z with real entries, where z^T denotes the transpose of z.

a. Vandermonde matrix
b. Positive-definite matrix
c. Partitioned matrix
d. Diagonalizable

71. This article will state and prove the _____ for differentiation, and then use it to prove these two formulas.

The _____ for differentiation states that for every natural number n, the derivative of $f(x) = x^n$ is $f'(x) = nx^{n-1}$, that is,

$$(x^n)' = nx^{n-1}.$$

The _____ for integration

$$\int x^n\, dx = \frac{x^{n+1}}{n+1} + C$$

for natural n is then an easy consequence. One just needs to take the derivative of this equality and use the _____ and linearity of differentiation on the right-hand side.

a. Standard part function
b. Periodic function
c. Functional integration
d. Power Rule

72. _____ is a vector space transform often used to reduce multidimensional data sets to lower dimensions for analysis. Depending on the field of application, it is also named the discrete Karhunen-Loève transform, the Hotelling transform or proper orthogonal decomposition.

PCA was invented in 1901 by Karl Pearson.

a. Multiple discriminant analysis
b. Tucker decomposition
c. Multivariate analysis
d. Principal component analysis

1. Suppose that φ : M → N is a smooth map between smooth manifolds; then the _____ of φ at a point x is, in some sense, the best linear approximation of φ near x. It can be viewed as generalization of the total derivative of ordinary calculus. Explicitly, it is a linear map from the tangent space of M at x to the tangent space of N at φ

   a. Boundary
   b. Grill
   c. Concurrent
   d. Differential

2. _____s arise in many problems in physics, engineering, etc. The following examples show how to solve _____s in a few simple cases when an exact solution exists.

   A separable linear ordinary _____ of the first order has the general form:

   $$\frac{dy}{dt} + f(t)y = 0$$

   where f is some known function.

   a. Nahm equations
   b. Differential equation
   c. Nullcline
   d. Homogeneous differential equation

3. In mathematics and in the sciences, a _____ (plural: _____e, formulæ or _____s) is a concise way of expressing information symbolically (as in a mathematical or chemical _____), or a general relationship between quantities. One of many famous _____e is Albert Einstein's E = mc^2 (see special relativity

   In mathematics, a _____ is a key to solve an equation with variables. For example, the problem of determining the volume of a sphere is one that requires a significant amount of integral calculus to solve.

   a. 1-center problem
   b. 2-3 heap
   c. 120-cell
   d. Formula

4. _____ is an important concept in economics with broad applications in game theory, engineering and the social sciences. The term is named after Vilfredo Pareto, an Italian economist who used the concept in his studies of economic efficiency and income distribution.

   Given a set of alternative allocations of, say, goods or income for a set of individuals, a change from one allocation to another that can make at least one individual better off without making any other individual worse off is called a Pareto improvement.

   a. Pursuit-evasion
   b. Quasi-perfect equilibrium
   c. Multiunit auction
   d. Pareto efficiency

5. In mathematics, an _____ is a relation that contains functions of only one independent variable, and one or more of its derivatives with respect to that variable.

A simple example is Newton's second law of motion, which leads to the differential equation

$$m\frac{d^2x(t)}{dt^2} = F(x(t)),$$

for the motion of a particle of mass m. In general, the force F depends upon the position of the particle at time t, and thus the unknown function appears on both sides of the differential equation, as is indicated in the notation F

    a. Implicit function   b. Inflection point
    c. Implicit differentiation   d. Ordinary differential equation

6. In mathematics, _____s are a type of differential equation. _____s are used to formulate, and thus aid the solution of, problems involving functions of several variables; such as the propagation of sound or heat, electrostatics, electrodynamics, fluid flow, and elasticity. Interestingly, seemingly distinct physical phenomena may have identical mathematical formulations, and thus be governed by the same underlying dynamic.
    a. 1-center problem   b. Partial differential equation
    c. 120-cell   d. 2-3 heap

7. The _____, first developed by Sir John Hicks and Alvin Hansen, has been used from 1937 onwards to summarize a major part of Keynesian macroeconomics. IS/LM stands for Investment Saving / Liquidity preference Money supply.

The _____ was born at the Econometric Conference held in Oxford during September, 1936.

    a. IS/LM model   b. A chemical equation
    c. A Mathematical Theory of Communication   d. A posteriori

8. In mathematics, the _____ is a representation of a function as an infinite sum of terms calculated from the values of its derivatives at a single point. It may be regarded as the limit of the Taylor polynomials. _____ are named after English mathematician Brook Taylor.
    a. Local linearity   b. C^r topology
    c. 1-center problem   d. Taylor series

9. _____ is the right to self-government. _____ is a concept found in moral, political, and bioethical philosophy. Within these contexts, it refers to the capacity of a rational individual to make an informed, un-coerced decision.
    a. A Mathematical Theory of Communication   b. A chemical equation
    c. Autonomy   d. A posteriori

10. In mathematics the concept of a _____ generalizes notions such as 'length', 'area', and 'volume'. Informally, given some base set, a '_____' is any consistent assignment of 'sizes' to the subsets of the base set. Depending on the application, the 'size' of a subset may be interpreted as its physical size, the amount of something that lies within the subset, or the probability that some random process will yield a result within the subset.
    a. Cusp   b. Congruent
    c. Lattice   d. Measure

198   *Chapter 24. Ordinary Differential Equations: Scalar Equations*

11. In mathematics, an _____ in the sense of ring theory is a subring $\mathcal{O}$ of a ring R that satisfies the conditions

   1. R is a ring which is a finite-dimensional algebra over the rational number field $\mathbb{Q}$
   2. $\mathcal{O}$ spans R over $\mathbb{Q}$, so that $\mathbb{Q}\mathcal{O} = R$, and
   3. $\mathcal{O}$ is a lattice in R.

The third condition can be stated more accurately, in terms of the extension of scalars of R to the real numbers, embedding R in a real vector space. In less formal terms, additively $\mathcal{O}$ should be a free abelian group generated by a basis for R over $\mathbb{Q}$.

The leading example is the case where R is a number field K and $\mathcal{O}$ is its ring of integers. In algebraic number theory there are examples for any K other than the rational field of proper subrings of the ring of integers that are also _____ s.

- a. Algebraic
- b. Efficiency
- c. Annihilator
- d. Order

12. In statistics and mathematical epidemiology, _____ is the risk of an event relative to exposure. _____ is a ratio of the probability of the event occurring in the exposed group versus a non-exposed group.

$$RR = \frac{p_{\text{exposed}}}{p_{\text{non-exposed}}}$$

For example, if the probability of developing lung cancer among smokers was 20% and among non-smokers 1%, then the _____ of cancer associated with smoking would be 20.

- a. Mendelian randomization
- b. 1-center problem
- c. Statistical epidemiology
- d. Relative risk

13. _____ is a concept in economics, finance, and psychology related to the behaviour of consumers and investors under uncertainty. _____ is the reluctance of a person to accept a bargain with an uncertain payoff rather than another bargain with a more certain, but possibly lower, expected payoff.

The inverse of a person's _____ is sometimes called their risk tolerance.

- a. Ruin theory
- b. Stochastic modelling
- c. Risk aversion
- d. Life table

14. In mathematics, a _____ is often represented as the sum of a sequence of terms. That is, a _____ is represented as a list of numbers with addition operations between them, for example this arithmetic sequence:

   1 + 2 + 3 + 4 + 5 + ... + 99 + 100

Chapter 24. Ordinary Differential Equations: Scalar Equations   199

In most cases of interest the terms of the sequence are produced according to a certain rule, such as by a formula, by an algorithm, by a sequence of measurements, or even by a random number generator.

a. Contact
b. Blind
c. Concavity
d. Series

15. The mathematical concept of a _____ expresses the intuitive idea of deterministic dependence between two quantities, one of which is viewed as primary and the other as secondary. A _____ then is a way to associate a unique output for each input of a specified type, for example, a real number or an element of a given set.
   a. Going up
   b. Coherent
   c. Function
   d. Grill

16. In mathematics, an _____ is a generalization for the concept of a function in which the dependent variable has not been given 'explicitly' in terms of the independent variable. To give a function f explicitly is to provide a prescription for determining the value of the function y in terms of the input value x:

   y = f

   a. Ordinary differential equation
   b. Inflection point
   c. Implicit differentiation
   d. Implicit Function

17. In the branch of mathematics called multivariable calculus, the _____ is a tool which allows relations to be converted to functions. It does this by representing the relation as the graph of a function. There may not be a single function whose graph is the entire relation, but there may be such a function on a restriction of the domain of the relation.
   a. Implicit Function Theorem
   b. A chemical equation
   c. Inverse function theorem
   d. A Mathematical Theory of Communication

18. Georg Friedrich Bernhard _____ was a German mathematician who made important contributions to analysis and differential geometry, some of them paving the way for the later development of general relativity.

   _____ was born in Breselenz, a village near Dannenberg in the Kingdom of Hanover in what is today Germany. His father, Friedrich Bernhard _____, was a poor Lutheran pastor in Breselenz who fought in the Napoleonic Wars.

   a. Paul C. van Oorschot
   b. Gustave Bertrand
   c. Brook Taylor
   d. Riemann

19. In mathematics, a _____ is a method for approximating the total area underneath a curve on a graph, otherwise known as an integral. It may also be used to define the integration operation. The sums are named after the German mathematician Bernhard Riemann.
   a. Solid of revolution
   b. Riemann sum
   c. Multiple integral
   d. Singular measure

20. In mathematics, a _____ is a statement that can be proved on the basis of explicitly stated or previously agreed assumptions.

a. Boolean function
c. Logical value
b. Theorem
d. Disjunction introduction

21. _____ is a fee, paid on borrowed capital. Assets lent include money, shares, consumer goods through hire purchase, major assets such as aircraft, and even entire factories in finance lease arrangements. The _____ is calculated upon the value of the assets in the same manner as upon money.
   a. Interest expense
   b. A Mathematical Theory of Communication
   c. Interest
   d. Interest sensitivity gap

22. Initial objects are also called _____, and terminal objects are also called final.
   a. Direct limit
   b. Coterminal
   c. Terminal object
   d. Colimit

23. In mathematics, in the field of differential equations, an _____ is an ordinary differential equation together with specified value, called the initial condition, of the unknown function at a given point in the domain of the solution. In physics or other sciences, modeling a system frequently amounts to solving an _____; in this context, the differential equation is an evolution equation specifying how, given initial conditions, the system will evolve with time.

An _____ is a differential equation

$$y'(t) = f(t, y(t)) \quad \text{with} \quad f : \mathbb{R} \times \mathbb{R} \to \mathbb{R}$$

together with a point in the domain of f

$$(t_0, y_0) \in \mathbb{R} \times \mathbb{R},$$

called the initial condition.

   a. A Mathematical Theory of Communication
   b. A chemical equation
   c. A posteriori
   d. Initial value problem

24. The _____ is a polynomial mapping of degree 2, often cited as an archetypal example of how complex, chaotic behaviour can arise from very simple non-linear dynamical equations. The map was popularized in a seminal 1976 paper by the biologist Robert May, in part as a discrete-time demographic model analogous to the logistic equation first created by Pierre François Verhulst. Mathematically, the _____ is written

$$(1) \quad x_{n+1} = r x_n (1 - x_n)$$

where:

x_n is a number between zero and one, and represents the population at year n, and hence x_0 represents the initial population

r is a positive number, and represents a combined rate for reproduction and starvation.

a. 1-center problem
c. Horseshoe map
b. Rabinovich-Fabrikant equations
d. Logistic map

25. The _____ is a basic theorem used to solve maximization problems in microeconomics. It may be used to prove Hotelling's lemma, Shephard's lemma, and Roy's identity. The statement of the theorem is:

Consider an arbitrary maximization problem where the objective function (f) depends on some parameter (a):

$$M(a) = \max_x f(x, a)$$

where the function M(a) gives the maximized value of the objective function (f) as a function of the parameter (a.)

a. A posteriori
c. A Mathematical Theory of Communication
b. A chemical equation
d. Envelope Theorem

26. In linear algebra, _____ is an efficient algorithm for solving systems of linear equations, finding the rank of a matrix, and calculating the inverse of an invertible square matrix. _____ is named after German mathematician and scientist Carl Friedrich Gauss.

Elementary row operations are used to reduce a matrix to row echelon form.

a. Crout matrix decomposition
c. Conjugate gradient method
b. Cholesky decomposition
d. Gaussian elimination

27. In mathematics, the _____ or Pythagoras' theorem is a relation in Euclidean geometry among the three sides of a right triangle. The theorem is named after the Greek mathematician Pythagoras, who by tradition is credited with its discovery and proof, although it is often argued that knowledge of the theory predates him.. The theorem is as follows:

In any right triangle, the area of the square whose side is the hypotenuse is equal to the sum of the areas of the squares whose sides are the two legs.

a. 2-3 heap
c. 120-cell
b. 1-center problem
d. Pythagorean Theorem

28. _____ County lies just north of the Mexican border--sharing a border with Tijuana--and lies south of Orange County. It is home to miles of beaches, a mild Mediterranean climate and 16 military facilities hosting the United States Navy, the United States Coast Guard and the United States Marine Corps.

_____'s economy is largely composed of agriculture, biotechnology/biosciences, computer sciences, electronics manufacturing, defense-related manufacturing, financial and business services, ship-repair and construction, software development, telecommunications, and tourism.

a. 1-center problem
c. 2-3 heap
b. 120-cell
d. San Diego

29. In microeconomics, a consumer's _____ function is the demand of a consumer over a bundle of goods that minimizes their expenditure while delivering a fixed level of utility. The function is named after John Hicks.

Mathematically,

$$h(p, \bar{u}) = \arg\min_x \sum_i p_i x_i$$
$$\text{such that } u(x) > \bar{u}$$

where h is the _____ function, or commodity bundle demanded, at price level p and utility level $\bar{u}$.

a. Hicksian demand
b. 1-center problem
c. Precautionary demand
d. Marshallian demand function

30. In mathematics, _____ are functions which can be used to prove the stability of a certain fixed point in a dynamical system or autonomous differential equation. Named after the Russian mathematician Aleksandr Mikhailovich Lyapunov, _____ are important to stability theory and control theory.

Functions which might prove the stability of some equilibrium are called Lyapunov-candidate-functions.

a. Butterfly effect
b. Lyapunov functions
c. 120-cell
d. 1-center problem

31. _____ is the frequency with which an engineered system or component fails, expressed for example in failures per hour. It is often denoted by the Greek letter λ and is important in reliability theory. In practice, the closely related Mean Time Between Failures is more commonly expressed and used for high quality components or systems.

a. Failure rate
b. Percentile rank
c. Semivariance
d. Kaplan-Meier estimator

32. In mathematics, an _____ is a function that is chosen to facilitate the solving of a given ordinary differential equation.

Consider an ordinary differential equation of the form

$$y' + a(x)y = b(x) \qquad (1)$$

where y = y is an unknown function of x, and a and b are given functions.

The _____ method works by turning the left hand side into the form of the derivative of a product.

a. Integrating factor
b. A chemical equation
c. A posteriori
d. A Mathematical Theory of Communication

33. In mathematics, a _____ is a differential equation of the form

Chapter 24. Ordinary Differential Equations: Scalar Equations

$$Ly = f$$

where the differential operator L is a linear operator, y is the unknown function, and the right hand side f is a given function. The linearity condition on L rules out operations such as taking the square of the derivative of y; but permits, for example, taking the second derivative of y. Therefore a fairly general form of such an equation would be

$$a_n(x)D^n y(x) + a_{n-1}(x)D^{n-1}y(x) + \cdots + a_1(x)Dy(x) + a_0(x)y(x) = f(x)$$

where D is the differential operator d/dx, and the a_i are given functions.

a. Petrovsky lacuna
b. Differential equation
c. Differential algebraic equations
d. Linear differential equation

34. In statistics, _____ is the consistency of a set of measurements or measuring instrument, often used to describe a test. This can either be whether the measurements of the same instrument give or are likely to give the same measurement, or in the case of more subjective instruments, such as personality or trait inventories, whether two independent assessors give similar scores. _____ is inversely related to random error.
    a. Disk
    b. Reliability
    c. Converse logic
    d. Capable

35. The survival function is a property of any random variable that maps a set of events, usually associated with mortality or failure of some system, onto time. It captures the probability that the system will survive beyond a specified time. The term _____ is common in engineering while the term survival function is used in a broader range of applications, including human mortality.
    a. Type I error
    b. False positive
    c. Chi-square distribution
    d. Reliability function

36. In probability theory and statistics, the _____ is a continuous probability distribution. It is often called the Rosin-Rammler distribution when used to describe the size distribution of particles. The distribution was introduced by P.
    a. Gumbel distribution
    b. Hyperbolic secant distribution
    c. Shifted Gompertz distribution
    d. Weibull distribution

37. In differential geometry, a discipline within mathematics, a _____ is a subset of the tangent bundle of a manifold satisfying certain properties. _____s are used to build up notions of integrability, and specifically of a foliation of a manifold
    a. Coherence
    b. Discontinuity
    c. Distribution
    d. Constraint

38. In probability theory and statistics, the _____s are a class of continuous probability distributions. They describe the times between events in a Poisson process.

The probability density function of an _____ has the form

$$f(x; \lambda) = \begin{cases} \lambda e^{-\lambda x} &, x \geq 0, \\ 0 &, x < 0. \end{cases}$$

where λ > 0 is a parameter of the distribution, often called the rate parameter.

a. A Mathematical Theory of Communication
b. A posteriori
c. A chemical equation
d. Exponential distribution

39. The Condorcet candidate or _____ of an election is the candidate who, when compared with every other candidate, is preferred by more voters. Informally, the _____ is the person who would win a two-candidate election against each of the other candidates. A _____ will not always exist in a given set of votes, which is known as Condorcet's voting paradox.

a. 1-center problem
b. Psephology
c. 120-cell
d. Condorcet winner

40. In mathematics, an algebraic field extension L/K is _____ if it can be generated by adjoining to K a set each of whose elements is a root of a _____ polynomial over K. In that case, each β in L has a _____ minimal polynomial over K.

The condition of separability is central in Galois theory.

a. Small set
b. Computational mathematics
c. Normal form
d. Separable

41. In the absence of a more specific context, convergence denotes the approach toward a definite value, as time goes on; or to a definite point, a common view or opinion, or toward a fixed or equilibrium state. _____ is the adjectival form, and also a noun meaning an iterative approximation.

In mathematics, convergence describes limiting behaviour, particularly of an infinite sequence or series, toward some limit.

a. Separable
b. Prime ideal theorem
c. Word problem
d. Convergent

42. A _____ or logistic curve is the most common sigmoid curve. It models the S-curve of growth of some set P, where P might be thought of as population. The initial stage of growth is approximately exponential; then, as saturation begins, the growth slows, and at maturity, growth stops.

a. Legendre forms
b. Spin-weighted spherical harmonics
c. Jack function
d. Logistic function

43. In mathematics, _____ is any of several methods for solving ordinary and partial differential equations, in which algebra allows one to re-write an equation so that each of two variables occurs on a different side of the equation.

Suppose a differential equation can be written in the form

$$\frac{d}{dx}f(x) = g(x)h(f(x)), \quad (1)$$

which we can write more simply by letting y = f:

$$\frac{dy}{dx} = g(x)h(y).$$

As long as h≠ 0, we can rearrange terms to obtain:

$$\frac{dy}{h(y)} = g(x)dx,$$

so that the two variables x and y have been separated.

Some who dislike Leibniz's notation may prefer to write this as

$$\frac{1}{h(y)}\frac{dy}{dx} = g(x),$$

but that fails to make it quite as obvious why this is called '_____'.

a. Wronskian
c. Normal mode
b. Sturm-Liouville equation
d. Separation of variables

44. In algebra, the _____ decomposition or _____ expansion is used to reduce the degree of either the numerator or the denominator of a rational function. The outcome of _____ expansion expresses that function as a sum of fractions, where:

- the denominator of each term is a power of an irreducible polynomial and
- the numerator is a polynomial of smaller degree than that irreducible polynomial.

See _____s in integration for an account of their use in finding antiderivatives. They are also used in calculating the inverse of transforms; such as the Laplace transform, or the Z-transform.

The basic idea behind _____s is to work backwards to separate a function.

a. Concept algebra
c. Continuant
b. Real structure
d. Partial fraction

45. The supportable population of an organism, given the food, habitat, water and other necessities available within an environment is known as the environment's _____ for that organism. For the human population, more complex variables such as sanitation and medical care are sometimes considered as part of the necessary infrastructure.

As population density increases, birth rate often increases and death rates typically decrease.

a. 1-center problem
c. 120-cell
b. Carrying capacity
d. 2-3 heap

46. In model theory, a complete theory is called _____ if it does not have too many types. One goal of classification theory is to divide all complete theories into those whose models can be classified and those whose models are too complicated to classify, and to classify all models in the cases where this can be done. Roughly speaking, if a theory is not _____ then its models are too complicated and numerous to classify, while if a theory is _____ there might be some hope of classifying its models, especially if the theory is superstable or totally transcendental.

a. Spectrum of a theory
c. Non-standard calculus
b. Transfer principle
d. Stable

47. In calculus, the _____ is a formula for the derivative of the composite of two functions.

In intuitive terms, if a variable, y, depends on a second variable, u, which in turn depends on a third variable, x, then the rate of change of y with respect to x can be computed as the rate of change of y with respect to u multiplied by the rate of change of u with respect to x. Schematically,

$$\frac{dy}{dx} = \frac{dy}{du} \cdot \frac{du}{dx}.$$

For an explanation of notation used in this section, see Function composition.

The _____ states that, under appropriate conditions,

$$(f \circ g)'(x) = f'(g(x))g'(x),$$

which in short form is written as

$$(f \circ g)' = f' \circ g \cdot g'.$$

Alternatively, in the Leibniz notation, the _____ is

$$\frac{dy}{dx} = \frac{dy}{du} \cdot \frac{du}{dx}.$$

In integration, the counterpart to the _____ is the substitution rule.

a. Product rule
b. Chain Rule
c. 120-cell
d. 1-center problem

48. In mathematics, the _____ of a ring R, often denoted cha, is defined to be the smallest number of times one must add the ring's multiplicative identity element to itself to get the additive identity element; the ring is said to have _____ zero if this repeated sum never reaches the additive identity. That is, cha is the smallest positive number n such that

$$\underbrace{1 + \cdots + 1}_{n \text{ summands}} = 0$$

if such a number n exists, and 0 otherwise. The _____ may also be taken to be the exponent of the ring's additive group, that is, the smallest positive n such that

$$\underbrace{a + \cdots + a}_{n \text{ summands}} = 0$$

for every element a of the ring.

a. Class
b. Coherent
c. Characteristic
d. Disk

49. A quadratic equation with real solutions, called roots, which may be real or complex, is given by the _____: $x = \frac{-b \pm \sqrt{b^2 - 4ac}}{2a}$.

a. Differential Algebra
b. Parametric continuity
c. Quotient
d. Quadratic formula

50. _____ is the force resisting the relative lateral (tangential) motion of solid surfaces, fluid layers, or material elements in contact. It is usually subdivided into several varieties:

- Dry _____ resists relative lateral motion of two solid surfaces in contact. Dry _____ is also subdivided into static _____ between non-moving surfaces, and kinetic _____ (sometimes called sliding _____ or dynamic _____) between moving surfaces.

- Lubricated _____ or fluid _____ resists relative lateral motion of two solid surfaces separated by a layer of gas or liquid.

- Fluid _____ is also used to describe the _____ between layers within a fluid that are moving relative to each other.

- Skin _____ is a component of drag, the force resisting the motion of a solid body through a fluid.

- Internal _____ is the force resisting motion between the elements making up a solid material while it undergoes deformation.

208 *Chapter 24. Ordinary Differential Equations: Scalar Equations*

_____ is not a fundamental force, as it is derived from electromagnetic force between charged particles, including electrons, protons, atoms, and molecules, and so cannot be calculated from first principles, but instead must be found empirically. When contacting surfaces move relative to each other, the _____ between the two surfaces converts kinetic energy into thermal energy, or heat.

a. Non-uniform circular motion
b. Simple harmonic motion
c. Stretch rule
d. Friction

51. In economics, an externality is an impact on any party not directly involved in an economic decision. An externality occurs when an economic activity causes _____ costs or _____ benefits to third party stakeholders who did not directly affect the economic transaction. Another term that often replaces externality is spillover.

a. A chemical equation
b. A posteriori
c. A Mathematical Theory of Communication
d. External

52. In the mathematical discipline of set theory, _____ is a technique invented by Paul Cohen, for proving consistency and independence results in set theory. It was first used, in 1962, to prove the independence of the continuum hypothesis and the axiom of choice from Zermelo-Fraenkel set theory. _____ was considerably reworked and simplified in the sixties, and has proven to be an extremely powerful technique both within set theory and in other areas of mathematical logic such as recursion theory.

a. Forcing
b. Bertrand paradox
c. Descent
d. Discontinuity

53. In statistics, _____ has two related meanings:

- the arithmetic _____.
- the expected value of a random variable, which is also called the population _____.

It is sometimes stated that the '_____' _____s average. This is incorrect if '_____' is taken in the specific sense of 'arithmetic _____' as there are different types of averages: the _____, median, and mode. For instance, average house prices almost always use the median value for the average.

For a real-valued random variable X, the _____ is the expectation of X.

a. Probability
b. Proportional hazards model
c. Statistical population
d. Mean

54. In calculus, the _____ states, roughly, that given a section of a smooth curve, there is at least one point on that section at which the derivative of the curve is equal to the 'average' derivative of the section. It is used to prove theorems that make global conclusions about a function on an interval starting from local hypotheses about derivatives at points of the interval.

This theorem can be understood concretely by applying it to motion: if a car travels one hundred miles in one hour, so that its average speed during that time was 100 miles per hour, then at some time its instantaneous speed must have been exactly 100 miles per hour.

a. Fundamental Theorem of Calculus
b. Functional integration
c. Mean Value Theorem
d. Calculus controversy

55. In mathematics, a _____ is a constant multiplicative factor of a certain object. For example, in the expression 9x², the _____ of x² is 9.

The object can be such things as a variable, a vector, a function, etc.

a. Multivariate division algorithm
b. Fibonacci polynomials
c. Coefficient
d. Stability radius

56. In mathematics, the _____ is an approach to finding a particular solution to certain inhomogeneous ordinary differential equations and recurrence relations. It is closely related to the annihilator method, but instead of using a particular kind of differential operator in order to find the best possible form of the particular solution, a 'guess' is made as to the appropriate form, which is then tested by differentiating the resulting equation. In this sense, the _____ is less formal but more intuitive than the annihilator method.

a. Differential algebraic equations
b. Linear differential equation
c. Method of undetermined coefficients
d. Phase line

57. In physics, _____ is the tendency of a system to oscillate at maximum amplitude at certain frequencies, known as the system's _____ frequencies. At these frequencies, even small periodic driving forces can produce large amplitude vibrations, because the system stores vibrational energy. When damping is small, the _____ frequency is approximately equal to the natural frequency of the system, which is the frequency of free vibrations.

a. Signal compression
b. Square wave
c. Sawtooth wave
d. Resonance

58. This article will state and prove the _____ for differentiation, and then use it to prove these two formulas.

The _____ for differentiation states that for every natural number n, the derivative of $f(x) = x^n$ is $f'(x) = nx^{n-1}$, that is,

$$(x^n)' = nx^{n-1}.$$

The _____ for integration

$$\int x^n \, dx = \frac{x^{n+1}}{n+1} + C$$

for natural n is then an easy consequence. One just needs to take the derivative of this equality and use the _____ and linearity of differentiation on the right-hand side.

a. Standard part function
b. Periodic function
c. Functional integration
d. Power Rule

59. In mathematics, the _____ is a special function which occurs in probability, statistics, materials science, and partial differential equations. It is defined as:

$$\mathrm{erf}(x) = \frac{2}{\sqrt{\pi}} \int_0^x e^{-t^2} dt.$$

The complementary _____, denoted erfc, is defined in terms of the _____:

$$\mathrm{erfc}(x) = 1 - \mathrm{erf}(x)$$
$$= \frac{2}{\sqrt{\pi}} \int_x^\infty e^{-t^2} dt.$$

The complex _____, denoted w

$$w(x) = e^{-x^2} \mathrm{erfc}(-ix).$$

Fig.2. Integrand ex in the complex z-plane. Fig.3.

a. Anger function
b. Incomplete polylogarithm
c. Analytical expression
d. Error function

60. In abstract algebra, a _____ is an algebraic structure in which the operations of addition, subtraction, multiplication and division may be performed in a way that satisfies some familiar rules from the arithmetic of ordinary numbers.

All _____ s are rings, but not conversely. _____ s differ from rings most importantly in the requirement that division be possible, but also, in modern definitions, by the requirement that the multiplication operation in a _____ be commutative.

a. Blind
b. Functional
c. Field
d. Chord

61. In commutative algebra, the notions of an element _____ over a ring, and of an _____ extension of rings, are a generalization of the notions in field theory of an element being algebraic over a field, and of an algebraic extension of fields.

The special case of greatest interest in number theory is that of complex numbers _____ over the ring of integers Z.

The term ring will be understood to mean commutative ring with a unit.

a. Antidifferentiation
b. Integral
c. Integral test for convergence
d. Arc length

Chapter 24. Ordinary Differential Equations: Scalar Equations

62. In mathematics, the concept of a _____ tries to capture the intuitive idea of a geometrical one-dimensional and continuous object. A simple example is the circle. In everyday use of the term '_____', a straight line is not curved, but in mathematical parlance _____s include straight lines and line segments.
   a. Quadrifolium
   b. Negative pedal curve
   c. Kappa curve
   d. Curve

63. In mathematics, a _____ is a rectangular table of elements, which may be numbers or, more generally, any abstract quantities that can be added and multiplied. Matrices are used to describe linear equations, keep track of the coefficients of linear transformations and to record data that depend on multiple parameters. Matrices are described by the field of _____ theory.
   a. Compression
   b. Coherent
   c. Double counting
   d. Matrix

64. In several fields of mathematics the term _____ is used with different but closely related meanings. They all relate to the notion of mapping the elements of a set to other elements of the same set, i.e., exchanging elements of a set.

The general concept of _____ can be defined more formally in different contexts:

In combinatorics, a _____ is usually understood to be a sequence containing each element from a finite set once, and only once.

   a. Permutation
   b. Linearly independent
   c. Tensor product
   d. Cyclic permutation

65. In mathematics, in matrix theory, a _____ is a square-matrix that has exactly one entry 1 in each row and each column and 0's elsewhere. Each such matrix represents a specific permutation of m elements and, when used to multiply another matrix, can produce that permutation in the rows or columns of the other matrix.

Given a permutation π of m elements,

$$\pi : \{1,\ldots,m\} \to \{1,\ldots,m\}$$

given in two-line form by

$$\begin{pmatrix} 1 & 2 & \cdots & m \\ \pi(1) & \pi(2) & \cdots & \pi(m) \end{pmatrix},$$

its _____ is the m × m matrix P_π whose entries are all 0 except that in row i, the entry equals 1.

   a. Hessenberg matrix
   b. Partitioned matrix
   c. Cartan matrix
   d. Permutation Matrix

66. A _____ is a geometric representation of the trajectories of a dynamical system in the phase plane. Each set of initial conditions is representated by a different curve, or point.

_____s are an invaluable tool in studying dynamical systems.

a. Phase portrait
b. X band
c. Supermultiplet
d. Coordinate-free treatment

67. In mathematics, a _____ refers to the boundary separating two modes of behaviour in a differential equation.

Consider the differential equation describing the motion of a simple pendulum:

$$\frac{d^2\theta}{dt^2} + \frac{g}{l}\sin\theta = 0.$$

where l denotes the length of the pendulum, g the gravitational acceleration and θ the angle between the pendulum and vertically downwards. In this system there is a conserved quantity H, which is given by

$$H = \frac{\dot{\theta}^2}{2} - \frac{g}{l}\cos\theta.$$

With this defined, one can plot a curve of constant H in the phase space of system.

a. Gamma test
b. Boussinesq approximation
c. Closed form
d. Separatrix

68. The Gompertz-Makeham law states that death rate is a sum of age-independent component and age-dependent component, which increases exponentially with age. In a protected environment where external causes of death are rare the age-independent mortality component is often negligible, and in this case the formula simplifies to a _____ of mortality with exponential increase in death rates with age.

The Gompertz-Makeham law of mortality describes the age dynamics of human mortality rather accurately in the age window of about 30-80 years.

a. 1-center problem
b. Gompertz-Makeham law of mortality
c. 120-cell
d. Gompertz law

69. In economics, the _____ functional form of production functions is widely used to represent the relationship of an output to inputs. It was proposed by Knut Wicksell, and tested against statistical evidence by Paul Douglas and Charles Cobb in 1928.

a. Burden of proof
b. Cobb-Douglas
c. State price
d. State price vector

Chapter 25. Ordinary Differential Equations: Systems of Equations

1. In economics, the _____ functional form of production functions is widely used to represent the relationship of an output to inputs. It was proposed by Knut Wicksell, and tested against statistical evidence by Paul Douglas and Charles Cobb in 1928.
   a. Cobb-Douglas
   b. State price vector
   c. Burden of proof
   d. State price

2. The mathematical concept of a _____ expresses the intuitive idea of deterministic dependence between two quantities, one of which is viewed as primary and the other as secondary. A _____ then is a way to associate a unique output for each input of a specified type, for example, a real number or an element of a given set.
   a. Coherent
   b. Function
   c. Going up
   d. Grill

3. The Condorcet candidate or _____ of an election is the candidate who, when compared with every other candidate, is preferred by more voters. Informally, the _____ is the person who would win a two-candidate election against each of the other candidates. A _____ will not always exist in a given set of votes, which is known as Condorcet's voting paradox.
   a. Condorcet winner
   b. 1-center problem
   c. 120-cell
   d. Psephology

4. This article will state and prove the _____ for differentiation, and then use it to prove these two formulas.

   The _____ for differentiation states that for every natural number n, the derivative of $f(x) = x^n$ is $f'(x) = nx^{n-1}$, that is,

   $$(x^n)' = nx^{n-1}.$$

   The _____ for integration

   $$\int x^n \, dx = \frac{x^{n+1}}{n+1} + C$$

   for natural n is then an easy consequence. One just needs to take the derivative of this equality and use the _____ and linearity of differentiation on the right-hand side.

   a. Standard part function
   b. Functional integration
   c. Periodic function
   d. Power Rule

5. _____ is a biological interaction between individuals of two different species, where both individuals derive a fitness benefit, for example increased survivorship. Similar interactions within a species are known as co-operation. It can be contrasted with interspecific competition, in which both species experience reduced fitness, and exploitation, in which one species benefits at the expense of the other.
   a. 120-cell
   b. 1-center problem
   c. 2-3 heap
   d. Mutualism

Chapter 25. Ordinary Differential Equations: Systems of Equations

6. In ecology, _____ describes a biological interaction where a predator (an organism that is hunting) feeds on its prey, the organism that is attacked. Predators may or may not kill their prey prior to feeding on them, but the act of _____ always results in the death of the prey. The other main category of consumption is detritivory, the consumption of dead organic material (detritus.)

 a. 120-cell
 b. Predation
 c. Predator
 d. 1-center problem

7. In linear algebra, _____ is an efficient algorithm for solving systems of linear equations, finding the rank of a matrix, and calculating the inverse of an invertible square matrix. _____ is named after German mathematician and scientist Carl Friedrich Gauss.

Elementary row operations are used to reduce a matrix to row echelon form.

 a. Conjugate gradient method
 b. Cholesky decomposition
 c. Crout matrix decomposition
 d. Gaussian elimination

8. In mathematics, an _____ is a generalization for the concept of a function in which the dependent variable has not been given 'explicitly' in terms of the independent variable. To give a function f explicitly is to provide a prescription for determining the value of the function y in terms of the input value x:

$$y = f$$

 a. Inflection point
 b. Ordinary differential equation
 c. Implicit differentiation
 d. Implicit Function

9. In the branch of mathematics called multivariable calculus, the _____ is a tool which allows relations to be converted to functions. It does this by representing the relation as the graph of a function. There may not be a single function whose graph is the entire relation, but there may be such a function on a restriction of the domain of the relation.

 a. A Mathematical Theory of Communication
 b. A chemical equation
 c. Inverse function theorem
 d. Implicit Function Theorem

10. In mathematics, the _____ is a representation of a function as an infinite sum of terms calculated from the values of its derivatives at a single point. It may be regarded as the limit of the Taylor polynomials. _____ are named after English mathematician Brook Taylor.

 a. 1-center problem
 b. C^r topology
 c. Taylor series
 d. Local linearity

11. In mathematics, a _____ is a statement that can be proved on the basis of explicitly stated or previously agreed assumptions.

 a. Boolean function
 b. Logical value
 c. Disjunction introduction
 d. Theorem

12. _____ is the right to self-government. _____ is a concept found in moral, political, and bioethical philosophy. Within these contexts, it refers to the capacity of a rational individual to make an informed, un-coerced decision.

Chapter 25. Ordinary Differential Equations: Systems of Equations

    a. Autonomy
    c. A Mathematical Theory of Communication
    b. A posteriori
    d. A chemical equation

13. Initial objects are also called _____, and terminal objects are also called final.
    a. Coterminal
    b. Terminal object
    c. Colimit
    d. Direct limit

14. In mathematics, in the field of differential equations, an _____ is an ordinary differential equation together with specified value, called the initial condition, of the unknown function at a given point in the domain of the solution. In physics or other sciences, modeling a system frequently amounts to solving an _____; in this context, the differential equation is an evolution equation specifying how, given initial conditions, the system will evolve with time.

An _____ is a differential equation

$$y'(t) = f(t, y(t)) \quad \text{with} \quad f : \mathbb{R} \times \mathbb{R} \to \mathbb{R}$$

together with a point in the domain of f

$$(t_0, y_0) \in \mathbb{R} \times \mathbb{R},$$

called the initial condition.

    a. A posteriori
    c. Initial value problem
    b. A Mathematical Theory of Communication
    d. A chemical equation

15. In mathematics the concept of a _____ generalizes notions such as 'length', 'area', and 'volume'. Informally, given some base set, a '_____' is any consistent assignment of 'sizes' to the subsets of the base set. Depending on the application, the 'size' of a subset may be interpreted as its physical size, the amount of something that lies within the subset, or the probability that some random process will yield a result within the subset.
    a. Cusp
    b. Lattice
    c. Measure
    d. Congruent

16. In mathematics, an _____ in the sense of ring theory is a subring $\mathcal{O}$ of a ring R that satisfies the conditions

    1. R is a ring which is a finite-dimensional algebra over the rational number field $\mathbb{Q}$
    2. $\mathcal{O}$ spans R over $\mathbb{Q}$, so that $\mathbb{Q}\mathcal{O} = R$, and
    3. $\mathcal{O}$ is a lattice in R.

The third condition can be stated more accurately, in terms of the extension of scalars of R to the real numbers, embedding R in a real vector space. In less formal terms, additively $\mathcal{O}$ should be a free abelian group generated by a basis for R over $\mathbb{Q}$.

The leading example is the case where R is a number field K and $\mathcal{O}$ is its ring of integers. In algebraic number theory there are examples for any K other than the rational field of proper subrings of the ring of integers that are also _____s.

- a. Algebraic
- b. Annihilator
- c. Efficiency
- d. Order

17. In statistics and mathematical epidemiology, _____ is the risk of an event relative to exposure. _____ is a ratio of the probability of the event occurring in the exposed group versus a non-exposed group.

$$RR = \frac{p_{\text{exposed}}}{p_{\text{non-exposed}}}$$

For example, if the probability of developing lung cancer among smokers was 20% and among non-smokers 1%, then the _____ of cancer associated with smoking would be 20.

- a. Statistical epidemiology
- b. Relative risk
- c. 1-center problem
- d. Mendelian randomization

18. _____ is a concept in economics, finance, and psychology related to the behaviour of consumers and investors under uncertainty. _____ is the reluctance of a person to accept a bargain with an uncertain payoff rather than another bargain with a more certain, but possibly lower, expected payoff.

The inverse of a person's _____ is sometimes called their risk tolerance.

- a. Risk aversion
- b. Stochastic modelling
- c. Life table
- d. Ruin theory

19. In mathematics, a _____ is often represented as the sum of a sequence of terms. That is, a _____ is represented as a list of numbers with addition operations between them, for example this arithmetic sequence:

1 + 2 + 3 + 4 + 5 + ... + 99 + 100

In most cases of interest the terms of the sequence are produced according to a certain rule, such as by a formula, by an algorithm, by a sequence of measurements, or even by a random number generator.

- a. Blind
- b. Contact
- c. Concavity
- d. Series

20. In mathematics, the term _____ has several different important meanings:

- An _____ is an equality that remains true regardless of the values of any variables that appear within it, to distinguish it from an equality which is true under more particular conditions. For this, the 'triple bar' symbol ≡ is sometimes used.
- In algebra, an _____ or _____ element of a set S with a binary operation Â· is an element e that, when combined with any element x of S, produces that same x. That is, eÂ·x = xÂ·e = x for all x in S.
    - The _____ function from a set S to itself, often denoted id or id$_S$, s the function such that i = x for all x in S. This function serves as the _____ element in the set of all functions from S to itself with respect to function composition.
    - In linear algebra, the _____ matrix of size n is the n-by-n square matrix with ones on the main diagonal and zeros elsewhere. This matrix serves as the _____ with respect to matrix multiplication.

A common example of the first meaning is the trigonometric _____

$$\sin^2 \theta + \cos^2 \theta = 1$$

which is true for all real values of θ, as opposed to

$$\cos \theta = 1,$$

which is true only for some values of θ, not all. For example, the latter equation is true when $\theta = 0$, false when $\theta = 2$

The concepts of 'additive _____' and 'multiplicative _____' are central to the Peano axioms. The number 0 is the 'additive _____' for integers, real numbers, and complex numbers. For the real numbers, for all $a \in \mathbb{R}$,

$$0 + a = a,$$

$$a + 0 = a, \text{ and}$$

$$0 + 0 = 0.$$

Similarly, The number 1 is the 'multiplicative _____' for integers, real numbers, and complex numbers.

a. Intersection
b. Identity
c. ARIA
d. Action

Chapter 25. Ordinary Differential Equations: Systems of Equations

21. In computer science, a _____ is a description of a configuration of discrete states used as a simple model of machines. Formally, it can be defined as a tuple [N, A, S, G] where:

- N is a set of states
- A is a set of arcs connecting the states
- S is a nonempty subset of N that contains start states
- G is a nonempty subset of N that contains the goal states.

The _____ is what _____ search searches in. Graph theory is helpful in understanding and reasoning about _____s.

A _____ has some common properties:

- complexity, where branching factor is important
- structure of the space, see also graph theory:
    - directionality of arcs
    - tree
    - Rooted graph

- _____ (controls) for information about continuous _____ in control engineering.
- _____ (physics) for information about continuous _____ in physics.
- Phase space for information about phase state (like continuous _____) in physics and mathematics.
- Probability space for information about _____ in probability.

a. Deterministic finite state machine
b. Tag system
c. Lambda calculus
d. State space

22. A _____ is an element of the set of variables that describe the state of a dynamical system.

In case of simple mechanical systems, position coordinates and their derivates are typical _____s. Temperature, pressure, internal energy, enthalpy, entropy are examples of _____s in a thermodynamics system.

a. Filter
b. Deltoid
c. Boussinesq approximation
d. State variable

23. In mathematics, _____ are functions which can be used to prove the stability of a certain fixed point in a dynamical system or autonomous differential equation. Named after the Russian mathematician Aleksandr Mikhailovich Lyapunov, _____ are important to stability theory and control theory.

Functions which might prove the stability of some equilibrium are called Lyapunov-candidate-functions.

Chapter 25. Ordinary Differential Equations: Systems of Equations

a. 1-center problem
c. Butterfly effect
b. 120-cell
d. Lyapunov functions

24.   A _____ is a mathematical model of a system based on the use of a linear operator. _____s typically exhibit features and properties that are much simpler than the general, nonlinear case. As a mathematical abstraction or idealization, _____s find important applications in automatic control theory, signal processing, and telecommunications.
a. Predispositioning Theory
c. Hybrid system
b. Percolation
d. Linear system

25.   In mathematics and in the sciences, a _____ (plural: _____e, formulæ or _____s) is a concise way of expressing information symbolically (as in a mathematical or chemical _____), or a general relationship between quantities. One of many famous _____e is Albert Einstein's E = mc² (see special relativity

In mathematics, a _____ is a key to solve an equation with variables. For example, the problem of determining the volume of a sphere is one that requires a significant amount of integral calculus to solve.

a. 2-3 heap
c. Formula
b. 1-center problem
d. 120-cell

26.   In mathematics, given a linear transformation, an _____ of that linear transformation is a nonzero vector which, when that transformation is applied to it, may change in length, but not direction.

For each _____ of a linear transformation, there is a corresponding scalar value called an eigenvalue for that vector, which determines the amount the _____ is scaled under the linear transformation. For example, an eigenvalue of +2 means that the _____ is doubled in length and points in the same direction.

a. Ensemble
c. Uncertainty principle
b. Eigenvector
d. Angular momentum

27.   In linear algebra, a _____ of a matrix A is a nonzero vector v, which has associated with it an eigenvalue λ having algebraic multiplicity k ≥1, satisfying

$$(A - \lambda I)^k \mathbf{v} = 0.$$

Ordinary eigenvectors are obtained for k=1.

_____s are needed to form a complete basis of a defective matrix, which is a matrix in which there are fewer linearly independent eigenvectors than eigenvalues. The _____s do form a complete basis, as follows from the Jordan form of a matrix.

a. Rayleigh quotient
c. Pseudovector
b. Schmidt decomposition
d. Generalized eigenvector

Chapter 25. Ordinary Differential Equations: Systems of Equations

28. _____ is an important concept in economics with broad applications in game theory, engineering and the social sciences. The term is named after Vilfredo Pareto, an Italian economist who used the concept in his studies of economic efficiency and income distribution.

Given a set of alternative allocations of, say, goods or income for a set of individuals, a change from one allocation to another that can make at least one individual better off without making any other individual worse off is called a Pareto improvement.

    a. Quasi-perfect equilibrium   b. Multiunit auction
    c. Pursuit-evasion   d. Pareto efficiency

29. Georg Friedrich Bernhard _____ was a German mathematician who made important contributions to analysis and differential geometry, some of them paving the way for the later development of general relativity.

_____ was born in Breselenz, a village near Dannenberg in the Kingdom of Hanover in what is today Germany. His father, Friedrich Bernhard _____, was a poor Lutheran pastor in Breselenz who fought in the Napoleonic Wars.

    a. Paul C. van Oorschot   b. Brook Taylor
    c. Gustave Bertrand   d. Riemann

30. In mathematics, a _____ is a method for approximating the total area underneath a curve on a graph, otherwise known as an integral. It may also be used to define the integration operation. The sums are named after the German mathematician Bernhard Riemann.

    a. Solid of revolution   b. Riemann sum
    c. Multiple integral   d. Singular measure

31. The _____ is a basic theorem used to solve maximization problems in microeconomics. It may be used to prove Hotelling's lemma, Shephard's lemma, and Roy's identity. The statement of the theorem is:

Consider an arbitrary maximization problem where the objective function (f) depends on some parameter (a):

$$M(a) = \max_x f(x, a)$$

where the function M(a) gives the maximized value of the objective function (f) as a function of the parameter (a.)

    a. A chemical equation   b. A Mathematical Theory of Communication
    c. A posteriori   d. Envelope Theorem

32. In mathematics, the _____ or Pythagoras' theorem is a relation in Euclidean geometry among the three sides of a right triangle. The theorem is named after the Greek mathematician Pythagoras, who by tradition is credited with its discovery and proof, although it is often argued that knowledge of the theory predates him.. The theorem is as follows:

In any right triangle, the area of the square whose side is the hypotenuse is equal to the sum of the areas of the squares whose sides are the two legs.

Chapter 25. Ordinary Differential Equations: Systems of Equations 221

a. 2-3 heap
c. Pythagorean Theorem
b. 120-cell
d. 1-center problem

33. _____ County lies just north of the Mexican border--sharing a border with Tijuana--and lies south of Orange County. It is home to miles of beaches, a mild Mediterranean climate and 16 military facilities hosting the United States Navy, the United States Coast Guard and the United States Marine Corps.

_____'s economy is largely composed of agriculture, biotechnology/biosciences, computer sciences, electronics manufacturing, defense-related manufacturing, financial and business services, ship-repair and construction, software development, telecommunications, and tourism.

a. 2-3 heap
c. 1-center problem
b. 120-cell
d. San Diego

34. In economics and consumer theory, a _____ is that which people consume more of as price rises, violating the law of demand. In normal situations, as the price of such a good rises, the substitution effect causes people to purchase less of it and more of substitute goods. In the _____ situation, cheaper close substitutes are not available.
 a. 1-center problem
 c. 120-cell
 b. Giffen good
 d. 2-3 heap

35. In mathematics, the concept of a _____ tries to capture the intuitive idea of a geometrical one-dimensional and continuous object. A simple example is the circle. In everyday use of the term '_____', a straight line is not curved, but in mathematical parlance _____s include straight lines and line segments.
 a. Curve
 c. Kappa curve
 b. Quadrifolium
 d. Negative pedal curve

36. In model theory, a complete theory is called _____ if it does not have too many types. One goal of classification theory is to divide all complete theories into those whose models can be classified and those whose models are too complicated to classify, and to classify all models in the cases where this can be done. Roughly speaking, if a theory is not _____ then its models are too complicated and numerous to classify, while if a theory is _____ there might be some hope of classifying its models, especially if the theory is superstable or totally transcendental.
 a. Transfer principle
 c. Stable
 b. Non-standard calculus
 d. Spectrum of a theory

37. In probability theory and statistics, the _____ of a family of probability distributions is an important property which basically states that if one has a number of random variates that are 'in the family', any linear combination of these variates will also be 'in the family'. Specifically, the family of probability distributions here is a location-scale family, consisting of probability distributions that differ only in location and scale and 'in the family' means that the random variates have a distribution function that is a member of the family.

The importance of a stable family of probability distributions is that they serve as 'attractors' for linear combinations of non-stable random variates.

a. Secant
c. Torsion
b. Stability
d. Convergent

Chapter 25. Ordinary Differential Equations: Systems of Equations

38. In mathematics, a _____ is a system which is not linear. Less technically, a _____ is any problem where the variabl to be solved for cannot be written as a linear sum of independent components. A nonhomogenous system, which is linear apart from the presence of a function of the independent variables, is nonlinear according to a strict definition, but such systems are usually studied alongside linear systems, because they can be transformed to a linear system as long as a particular solution is known.
   a. 1-center problem
   b. George Dantzig
   c. Metric system
   d. Nonlinear system

39. In abstract algebra, a _____ is an algebraic structure in which the operations of addition, subtraction, multiplication and division may be performed in a way that satisfies some familiar rules from the arithmetic of ordinary numbers.

   All _____s are rings, but not conversely. _____s differ from rings most importantly in the requirement that division be possible, but also, in modern definitions, by the requirement that the multiplication operation in a _____ be commutative.

   a. Functional
   b. Chord
   c. Blind
   d. Field

40. In physics and in _____ calculus, a _____ is a concept characterized by a magnitude and a direction. A _____ can be thought of as an arrow in Euclidean space, drawn from an initial point A pointing to a terminal point B.
   a. Deviation
   b. Constraint
   c. Dominance
   d. Vector

41. In mathematics a _____ is a construction in vector calculus which associates a vector to every point in a Euclidean space.

   _____s are often used in physics to model, for example, the speed and direction of a moving fluid throughout space, or the strength and direction of some force, such as the magnetic or gravitational force, as it changes from point to point.

   In the rigorous mathematical treatment, _____s are defined on manifolds as sections of a manifold's tangent bundle.

   a. Vector field
   b. 2-3 heap
   c. 1-center problem
   d. 120-cell

42. In mathematics, a _____ is a rectangular table of elements, which may be numbers or, more generally, any abstract quantities that can be added and multiplied. Matrices are used to describe linear equations, keep track of the coefficients of linear transformations and to record data that depend on multiple parameters. Matrices are described by the field of _____ theory.
   a. Double counting
   b. Matrix
   c. Compression
   d. Coherent

43. In several fields of mathematics the term _____ is used with different but closely related meanings. They all relate to the notion of mapping the elements of a set to other elements of the same set, i.e., exchanging elements of a set.

Chapter 25. Ordinary Differential Equations: Systems of Equations

The general concept of _____ can be defined more formally in different contexts:

In combinatorics, a _____ is usually understood to be a sequence containing each element from a finite set once, and only once.

a. Permutation
b. Linearly independent
c. Tensor product
d. Cyclic permutation

44. In mathematics, in matrix theory, a _____ is a square-matrix that has exactly one entry 1 in each row and each column and 0's elsewhere. Each such matrix represents a specific permutation of m elements and, when used to multiply another matrix, can produce that permutation in the rows or columns of the other matrix.

Given a permutation π of m elements,

$$\pi : \{1,\ldots,m\} \to \{1,\ldots,m\}$$

given in two-line form by

$$\begin{pmatrix} 1 & 2 & \cdots & m \\ \pi(1) & \pi(2) & \cdots & \pi(m) \end{pmatrix},$$

its _____ is the m × m matrix P_π whose entries are all 0 except that in row i, the entry equals 1.

a. Partitioned matrix
b. Permutation Matrix
c. Cartan matrix
d. Hessenberg matrix

45. A _____ is a 2D geometric symbolic representation of information according to some visualization technique. Sometimes, the technique uses a 3D visualization which is then projected onto the 2D surface. The word graph is sometimes used as a synonym for _____.

a. 120-cell
b. 2-3 heap
c. Diagram
d. 1-center problem

46. In physics, an _____ is the gravitationally curved path of one object around a point or another body, for example the gravitational _____ of a planet around a star.

Historically, the apparent motion of the planets were first understood in terms of epicycles, which are the sums of numerous circular motions. This predicted the path of the planets quite well, until Johannes Kepler was able to show that the motion of the planets were in fact elliptical motions.

a. Equatorial coordinate system
b. A Mathematical Theory of Communication
c. Orbital resonance
d. Orbit

Chapter 25. Ordinary Differential Equations: Systems of Equations

47. In mathematics and physics, a _____, introduced by Willard Gibbs in 1901, is a space in which all possible states of a system are represented, with each possible state of the system corresponding to one unique point in the _____. For mechanical systems, the _____ usually consists of all possible values of position and momentum variables. A plot of position and momentum variables as a function of time is sometimes called a phase plot or a phase diagram.

a. Renormalization
b. Moment of inertia
c. Thermodynamic limit
d. Phase space

48. A _____ is a geometric representation of the trajectories of a dynamical system in the phase plane. Each set of initial conditions is represented by a different curve, or point.

_____s are an invaluable tool in studying dynamical systems.

a. X band
b. Supermultiplet
c. Coordinate-free treatment
d. Phase portrait

49. In mathematics, a _____ is a number that can be expressed as an integral of an algebraic function over an algebraic domain. Kontsevich and Zagier define a _____ as a complex number whose real and imaginary parts are values of absolutely convergent integrals of rational functions with rational coefficients, over domains in given by polynomial inequalities with rational coefficients.

a. Period
b. Disk
c. Boussinesq approximation
d. Closeness

50. The _____, first developed by Sir John Hicks and Alvin Hansen, has been used from 1937 onwards to summarize a major part of Keynesian macroeconomics. IS/LM stands for Investment Saving / Liquidity preference Money supply.

The _____ was born at the Econometric Conference held in Oxford during September, 1936.

a. IS/LM model
b. A Mathematical Theory of Communication
c. A posteriori
d. A chemical equation

51. In mathematics, a _____ refers to the boundary separating two modes of behaviour in a differential equation.

Consider the differential equation describing the motion of a simple pendulum:

$$\frac{d^2\theta}{dt^2} + \frac{g}{l}\sin\theta = 0.$$

where l denotes the length of the pendulum, g the gravitational acceleration and θ the angle between the pendulum and vertically downwards. In this system there is a conserved quantity H, which is given by

$$H = \frac{\dot{\theta}^2}{2} - \frac{g}{l}\cos\theta.$$

With this defined, one can plot a curve of constant H in the phase space of system.

a. Separatrix
c. Gamma test
b. Closed form
d. Boussinesq approximation

52. _____ is a fundamental construction of differential calculus and admits many possible generalizations within the fields of mathematical analysis, combinatorics, algebra, and geometry.

In real, complex, and functional analysis, _____s are generalized to functions of several real or complex variables and functions between topological vector spaces. An important case is the variational _____ in the calculus of variations.

a. Lin-Tsien equation
c. Derivative
b. Functional derivative
d. Metric derivative

53. In commutative algebra, the notions of an element _____ over a ring, and of an _____ extension of rings, are a generalization of the notions in field theory of an element being algebraic over a field, and of an algebraic extension of fields.

The special case of greatest interest in number theory is that of complex numbers _____ over the ring of integers Z.

The term ring will be understood to mean commutative ring with a unit.

a. Antidifferentiation
c. Arc length
b. Integral test for convergence
d. Integral

54. In physics, the law of _____ states that the total amount of energy in an isolated system remains constant. A consequence of this law is that energy cannot be created or destroyed. The only thing that can happen with energy in an isolated system is that it can change form, that is to say for instance kinetic energy can become thermal energy.

a. Conservation of energy
c. 2-3 heap
b. 120-cell
d. 1-center problem

55. In signal processing, the _____ E_s of a continuous-time signal x

$$E_s = \langle x(t), x(t) \rangle = \int_{-\infty}^{\infty} |x(t)|^2 dt$$

_____ in this context is not, strictly speaking, the same as the conventional notion of _____ in physics and the other sciences. The two concepts are, however, closely related, and it is possible to convert from one to the other:

$$E = \frac{E_s}{Z} = \frac{1}{Z}\int_{-\infty}^{\infty} |x(t)|^2 dt$$

where Z represents the magnitude, in appropriate units of measure, of the load driven by the signal.

For example, if x

226   *Chapter 25. Ordinary Differential Equations: Systems of Equations*

a. Energy
c. Audio signal processing

b. Essential bandwidth
d. Emphasis

56.

- _____ difference
- _____ energy

a. Potential
c. 120-cell

b. 1-center problem
d. 2-3 heap

57. In mathematics, stability theory deals with the stability of solutions for differential equations and dynamical systems.

Let be a real dynamical system with R the real numbers, X a locally compact Hausdorff space and Φ the evolution function. For a Φ-invariant, non-empty and closed subset M of X we call

$$A_\omega(M) := \{x \in X : \lim_\omega \gamma_x \neq \varnothing \text{ and } \lim_\omega \gamma_x \subset M\} \cup M$$

the ω-_____ and

$$A_\alpha(M) := \{x \in X : \lim_\alpha \gamma_x \neq \varnothing \text{ and } \lim_\alpha \gamma_x \subset M\} \cup M$$

the α-_____ and

$$A(M) := A_\omega(M) \cup A_\alpha(M)$$

the _____.

a. 120-cell
c. Basin of attraction

b. 1-center problem
d. Lyapunov functions

58. _____ is the force resisting the relative lateral (tangential) motion of solid surfaces, fluid layers, or material elements in contact. It is usually subdivided into several varieties:

- Dry _____ resists relative lateral motion of two solid surfaces in contact. Dry _____ is also subdivided into static _____ between non-moving surfaces, and kinetic _____ (sometimes called sliding _____ or dynamic _____) between moving surfaces.

- Lubricated _____ or fluid _____ resists relative lateral motion of two solid surfaces separated by a layer of gas or liquid.

- Fluid _____ is also used to describe the _____ between layers within a fluid that are moving relative to each other.

- Skin _____ is a component of drag, the force resisting the motion of a solid body through a fluid.

- Internal _____ is the force resisting motion between the elements making up a solid material while it undergoes deformation.

_____ is not a fundamental force, as it is derived from electromagnetic force between charged particles, including electrons, protons, atoms, and molecules, and so cannot be calculated from first principles, but instead must be found empirically. When contacting surfaces move relative to each other, the _____ between the two surfaces converts kinetic energy into thermal energy, or heat.

a. Stretch rule
c. Simple harmonic motion
b. Friction
d. Non-uniform circular motion

Chapter 26. Determinants: The Details

1. In algebra, a _____ is a function depending on n that associates a scalar, de, to every n×n square matrix A. The fundamental geometric meaning of a _____ is as the scale factor for measure when A is regarded as a linear transformation. _____s are important both in calculus, where they enter the substitution rule for several variables, and in multilinear algebra.
   - a. 1-center problem
   - b. Pfaffian
   - c. Functional determinant
   - d. Determinant

2. In mathematics and in the sciences, a _____ (plural: _____e, formulæ or _____s) is a concise way of expressing information symbolically (as in a mathematical or chemical _____), or a general relationship between quantities. One of many famous _____e is Albert Einstein's $E = mc^2$ (see special relativity

   In mathematics, a _____ is a key to solve an equation with variables. For example, the problem of determining the volume of a sphere is one that requires a significant amount of integral calculus to solve.
   - a. 2-3 heap
   - b. 120-cell
   - c. 1-center problem
   - d. Formula

3. In economics, the _____ functional form of production functions is widely used to represent the relationship of an output to inputs. It was proposed by Knut Wicksell, and tested against statistical evidence by Paul Douglas and Charles Cobb in 1928.
   - a. State price vector
   - b. Burden of proof
   - c. State price
   - d. Cobb-Douglas

4. The mathematical concept of a _____ expresses the intuitive idea of deterministic dependence between two quantities, one of which is viewed as primary and the other as secondary. A _____ then is a way to associate a unique output for each input of a specified type, for example, a real number or an element of a given set.
   - a. Function
   - b. Grill
   - c. Coherent
   - d. Going up

5. In mathematics, an _____ is a generalization for the concept of a function in which the dependent variable has not been given 'explicitly' in terms of the independent variable. To give a function f explicitly is to provide a prescription for determining the value of the function y in terms of the input value x:

   y = f

   - a. Implicit differentiation
   - b. Inflection point
   - c. Ordinary differential equation
   - d. Implicit Function

6. In the branch of mathematics called multivariable calculus, the _____ is a tool which allows relations to be converted to functions. It does this by representing the relation as the graph of a function. There may not be a single function whose graph is the entire relation, but there may be such a function on a restriction of the domain of the relation.
   - a. Inverse function theorem
   - b. A chemical equation
   - c. A Mathematical Theory of Communication
   - d. Implicit Function Theorem

7. In statistics, _____ has two related meanings:

- the arithmetic _____.
- the expected value of a random variable, which is also called the population _____.

It is sometimes stated that the '_____' _____s average. This is incorrect if '_____' is taken in the specific sense of 'arithmetic _____' as there are different types of averages: the _____, median, and mode. For instance, average house prices almost always use the median value for the average.

For a real-valued random variable X, the _____ is the expectation of X.

a. Proportional hazards model   b. Probability
c. Statistical population   d. Mean

8. In calculus, the _____ states, roughly, that given a section of a smooth curve, there is at least one point on that section at which the derivative of the curve is equal to the 'average' derivative of the section. It is used to prove theorems that make global conclusions about a function on an interval starting from local hypotheses about derivatives at points of the interval.

This theorem can be understood concretely by applying it to motion: if a car travels one hundred miles in one hour, so that its average speed during that time was 100 miles per hour, then at some time its instantaneous speed must have been exactly 100 miles per hour.

a. Functional integration   b. Calculus controversy
c. Fundamental Theorem of Calculus   d. Mean Value Theorem

9. In mathematics, a _____ is a statement that can be proved on the basis of explicitly stated or previously agreed assumptions.

a. Boolean function   b. Disjunction introduction
c. Logical value   d. Theorem

10. A recursive definition or _____ is one that defines something in terms of itself (that is, recursively), albeit in a useful way. For it to work, the definition in any given case must be well-founded, avoiding an infinite regress.

In simple terms, the recursive definition is one that grows an awareness and clarity upon itself toward a conclusive end, with each recurrence contributing something new toward the end definition.

a. A posteriori   b. A chemical equation
c. A Mathematical Theory of Communication   d. Inductive definition

11. In linear algebra, a _____ of a matrix A is the determinant of some smaller square matrix, cut down from A by removing one or more of its rows or columns.

_____s obtained by removing just one row and one column from square matrices are required for calculating matrix cofactors, which in turn are useful for computing both the determinant and inverse of square matrices.

Let A be an m × n matrix and k an integer with 0 < k ≤ m, and k ≤ n.

a. Chiral
b. Minor
c. Homogeneity
d. Block size

12. _____ describes the property of operations in mathematics and computer science which means that multiple applications of the operation does not change the result. The concept of _____ arises in a number of places in abstract algebra.

There are several meanings of _____, depending on what the concept is applied to:

- A unary operation is called idempotent if, whenever it is applied twice to any value, it gives the same result as if it were applied once. For example, the absolute value function is idempotent as a function from the set of real numbers to the set of real numbers: ab = ab.
- A binary operation is called idempotent if, whenever it is applied to two equal values, it gives that value as the result. For example, the operation giving the maximum value of two values is idempotent: ma = x.
- Given a binary operation, an idempotent element for the operation is a value for which the operation, when given that value for both of its operands, gives the value as the result. For example, the number 1 is an idempotent of multiplication: 1 × 1 = 1.

A unary operation f that is a map from some set S into itself is called idempotent if, for all x in S,

   f

In particular, the identity function id_S, defined by
id_S, is idempotent, as is the constant function K_c, where c is an element of S, defined by $K_c(x) = c$.

a. Idempotence
b. Absorption law
c. Antiisomorphism
d. Ordered exponential

13. In mathematics, a _____ is a rectangular table of elements, which may be numbers or, more generally, any abstract quantities that can be added and multiplied. Matrices are used to describe linear equations, keep track of the coefficients of linear transformations and to record data that depend on multiple parameters. Matrices are described by the field of _____ theory.

a. Compression
b. Double counting
c. Coherent
d. Matrix

14. This article will state and prove the _____ for differentiation, and then use it to prove these two formulas.

The _____ for differentiation states that for every natural number n, the derivative of $f(x) = x^n$ is $f'(x) = nx^{n-1}$, that is,

$$(x^n)' = nx^{n-1}.$$

The _____ for integration

$$\int x^n \, dx = \frac{x^{n+1}}{n+1} + C$$

for natural n is then an easy consequence. One just needs to take the derivative of this equality and use the _____ and linearity of differentiation on the right-hand side.

a. Periodic function
c. Power Rule

b. Standard part function
d. Functional integration

15. In mathematics, the term _____ has several different important meanings:

- An _____ is an equality that remains true regardless of the values of any variables that appear within it, to distinguish it from an equality which is true under more particular conditions. For this, the 'triple bar' symbol ≡ is sometimes used.
- In algebra, an _____ or _____ element of a set S with a binary operation Â· is an element e that, when combined with any element x of S, produces that same x. That is, eÂ·x = xÂ·e = x for all x in S.
    - The _____ function from a set S to itself, often denoted id or id_s, s the function such that i = x for all x in S. This function serves as the _____ element in the set of all functions from S to itself with respect to function composition.
    - In linear algebra, the _____ matrix of size n is the n-by-n square matrix with ones on the main diagonal and zeros elsewhere. This matrix serves as the _____ with respect to matrix multiplication.

A common example of the first meaning is the trigonometric _____

$$\sin^2 \theta + \cos^2 \theta = 1$$

which is true for all real values of θ, as opposed to

$$\cos \theta = 1,$$

which is true only for some values of θ, not all. For example, the latter equation is true when $\theta = 0$, false when $\theta = 2$

The concepts of 'additive _____' and 'multiplicative _____' are central to the Peano axioms. The number 0 is the 'additive _____' for integers, real numbers, and complex numbers. For the real numbers, for all $a \in \mathbb{R}$,

$$0 + a = a,$$

$a + 0 = a$, and

$$0 + 0 = 0.$$

Similarly, The number 1 is the 'multiplicative _____' for integers, real numbers, and complex numbers.

a. Intersection
b. Action
c. ARIA
d. Identity

16. In linear algebra, the _____ or unit matrix of size n is the n-by-n square matrix with ones on the main diagonal and zeros elsewhere. It is denoted by I_n, or simply by I if the size is immaterial or can be trivially determined by the context. (In some fields, such as quantum mechanics, the _____ is denoted by a boldface one, 1; otherwise it is identical to I.)
a. Arity
b. Associativity
c. Unital
d. Identity matrix

17. _____ is a method of mathematical proof typically used to establish that a given statement is true of all natural numbers. It is done by proving that the first statement in the infinite sequence of statements is true, and then proving that if any one statement in the infinite sequence of statements is true, then so is the next one.

The method can be extended to prove statements about more general well-founded structures, such as trees; this generalization, known as structural induction, is used in mathematical logic and computer science.

a. Finitary
b. Mathematical induction
c. Ground expression
d. Herbrand structure

18. In computational complexity theory, the complexity class _____ is the union of the classes in the exponential hierarchy.

$$\text{ELEMENTARY} = \text{EXP} \cup \text{2EXP} \cup \text{3EXP} \cup \cdots$$
$$= \text{DTIME}(2^n) \cup \text{DTIME}(2^{2^n}) \cup \text{DTIME}(2^{2^{2^n}}) \cup \cdots$$

The name was coined by Laszlo Kalmar, in the context of recursive functions and undecidability; most problems in it are far from _____. Some natural recursive problems lie outside _____, and are thus NONELEMENTARY.

a. A posteriori	b. A Mathematical Theory of Communication
c. A chemical equation	d. Elementary

19. In linear algebra a matrix is in _____ if

- All nonzero rows are above any rows of all zeroes, and
- The leading coefficient of a row is always strictly to the right of the leading coefficient of the row above it.

This is the definition used in this article, but some texts add a third condition:

- The leading coefficient of each nonzero row is one.

A matrix is in reduced _____ if it satisfies the above three conditions, and if, in addition

- Every leading coefficient is the only nonzero entry in its column.

The first non-zero entry in each row is called a pivot.

This matrix is in reduced _____:

$$\begin{bmatrix} 0 & 1 & 4 & 0 & 0 \\ 0 & 0 & 0 & 1 & 0 \\ 0 & 0 & 0 & 0 & 1 \\ 0 & 0 & 0 & 0 & 0 \end{bmatrix}.$$

The following matrix is also in _____, but not in reduced row form:

$$\begin{bmatrix} 1 & 1 & 1 & 1 \\ 0 & 9 & 0 & 2 \\ 0 & 0 & 0 & 3 \end{bmatrix}.$$

However, this matrix is not in _____, as the leading coefficient of row 3 is not strictly to the right of the leading coefficient of row 2.

$$\begin{bmatrix} 1 & 2 & 3 & 4 \\ 0 & 3 & 7 & 2 \\ 0 & 2 & 0 & 0 \end{bmatrix}$$

Every non-zero matrix can be reduced to an infinite number of echelon forms via elementary matrix transformations.

a. Reduced row echelon form
b. Portable, Extensible Toolkit for Scientific Computation
c. Gaussian elimination
d. Row echelon form

20. In mathematics, the _____ is a representation of a function as an infinite sum of terms calculated from the values of its derivatives at a single point. It may be regarded as the limit of the Taylor polynomials. _____ are named after English mathematician Brook Taylor.

a. C^r topology
b. Taylor series
c. 1-center problem
d. Local linearity

21. In linear algebra, a _____ is a square matrix in which the entries outside the main diagonal are all zero. The diagonal entries themselves may or may not be zero. Thus, the matrix D = with n columns and n rows is diagonal if:

$$d_{i,j} = 0 \text{ if } i \neq j \quad \forall i,j \in \{1,2,\ldots,n\}$$

For example, the following matrix is diagonal:

$$\begin{bmatrix} 1 & 0 & 0 \\ 0 & 4 & 0 \\ 0 & 0 & -3 \end{bmatrix}.$$

The term _____ may sometimes refer to a rectangular _____, which is an m-by-n matrix with only the entries of the form $d_{i,i}$ possibly non-zero; for example,

$$\begin{bmatrix} 1 & 0 & 0 \\ 0 & 4 & 0 \\ 0 & 0 & -3 \\ 0 & 0 & 0 \end{bmatrix}, \text{ or } \begin{bmatrix} 1 & 0 & 0 & 0 & 0 \\ 0 & 4 & 0 & 0 & 0 \\ 0 & 0 & -3 & 0 & 0 \end{bmatrix}.$$

a. Diagonal matrix
b. Design matrix
c. Transition matrix
d. Hankel matrix

22. In mathematics, a _____ is often represented as the sum of a sequence of terms. That is, a _____ is represented as a list of numbers with addition operations between them, for example this arithmetic sequence:

1 + 2 + 3 + 4 + 5 + ... + 99 + 100

In most cases of interest the terms of the sequence are produced according to a certain rule, such as by a formula, by an algorithm, by a sequence of measurements, or even by a random number generator.

a. Blind
b. Concavity
c. Contact
d. Series

23. In the mathematical discipline of linear algebra, a _____ is a special kind of square matrix where the entries either below or above the main diagonal are zero. Because matrix equations with triangular matrices are easier to solve they are very important in numerical analysis. The LU decomposition gives an algorithm to decompose any invertible matrix A into a normed lower triangle matrix L and an upper triangle matrix U.
   a. Rayleigh quotient iteration
   b. Crout matrix decomposition
   c. Successive over-relaxation
   d. Triangular matrix

24. If $A_1, A_2, ..., A_n$ are _____ square matrices over a field, then

$$(A_1 A_2 \cdots A_n)^{-1} = A_n^{-1} A_{n-1}^{-1} \cdots A_1^{-1}.$$

It becomes evident why this is the case if one attempts to find an inverse for the product of the A_is from first principles, that is, that we wish to determine B such that

$$(A_1 A_2 \cdots A_n) B = I$$

where B is the inverse matrix of the product. To remove A_1 from the product, we can then write

$$A_1^{-1} (A_1 A_2 \cdots A_n) B = A_1^{-1} I$$

which would reduce the equation to

$$(A_2 A_3 \cdots A_n) B = A_1^{-1} I.$$

Likewise, then, from

$$A_2^{-1} (A_2 A_3 \cdots A_n) B = A_2^{-1} A_1^{-1} I$$

which simplifies to

$$(A_3 A_4 \cdots A_n) B = A_2^{-1} A_1^{-1} I.$$

If one repeat the process up to A_n, the equation becomes

$$B = A_n^{-1} A_{n-1}^{-1} \cdots A_2^{-1} A_1^{-1} I$$

$$B = A_n^{-1} A_{n-1}^{-1} \cdots A_2^{-1} A_1^{-1}$$

but B is the inverse matrix, i.e. $\mathbf{B} = (\mathbf{A}_1 \mathbf{A}_2 \cdots \mathbf{A}_n)^{-1}$ so the property is established.

Over the field of real numbers, the set of singular n-by-n matrices, considered as a subset of $R^{n \times n}$, is a null set, i.e., has Lebesgue measure zero.

a. Projection-valued measure
b. Matrix pencil
c. Jordan normal form
d. Nonsingular

25. In mathematics, two vectors are _____ if they are perpendicular. For example, a subway and the street above, although they do not physically intersect, are _____ if they cross at a right angle.

a. Algebraic structure
b. Unique factorization domain
c. Orthogonal
d. Additive identity

26. In matrix theory, a real _____ is a square matrix Q whose transpose is its inverse:

$$Q^T Q = Q Q^T = I.$$

A special _____ is an _____ with determinant +1:

$$\det Q = +1.$$

An _____ is the real specialization of a unitary matrix, and thus always a normal matrix. Although we consider only real matrices here, the definition can be used for matrices with entries from any field. However, orthogonal matrices arise naturally from inner products, and for matrices of complex numbers that leads instead to the unitary requirement.

a. Alternating sign matrix
b. Unitary matrix
c. Unimodular polynomial matrix
d. Orthogonal matrix

27. _____ or _____ lines lie on different planes. They are neither parallel nor intersecting.

- In geometry, straight lines in a space referred to as _____ if they are neither parallel nor intersecting.
- In statistics, _____ is sometimes used as an alternative term to skewness to refer to the degree of asymmetry of a distribution. It can mean distortion in a positive or negative direction.
- In parallel transmission, the difference in arrival time of bits transmitted at the same time.
- For data recorded on multichannel magnetic tape, the difference between reading times of bits recorded in a single transverse line.

Nte: _____ is usually interpreted to mean the difference in reading times between bits recorded on the tracks at the extremities, or edges, of the tape.

a. Genus
b. P-wave
c. Skew
d. Common operator notation

28. In linear algebra, a _____ matrix is a square matrix A whose transpose is also its negative; that is, it satisfies the equation:

A^T = − A

or in component form, if A = :

a_{ij} = − a_{ji} for all i and j.

For example, the following matrix is _____:

$$\begin{bmatrix} 0 & 2 & -1 \\ -2 & 0 & -4 \\ 1 & 4 & 0 \end{bmatrix}.$$

Compare this with a symmetric matrix whose transpose is the same as the matrix

$$A^T = A,$$

or to an orthogonal matrix, the transpose of which is equal to its inverse:

$$A^T = A^{-1}.$$

Sums and scalar products of _____ matrices are again _____. Hence, the _____ matrices form a vector space. Its dimension is $\frac{n(n-1)}{2}$.

a. Skew-symmetric
b. Dispersion
c. Dominance
d. Foci

29. In linear algebra, a _____ is a square matrix, A, that is equal to its transpose

$$A = A^T.$$

The entries of a _____ are symmetric with respect to the main diagonal. So if the entries are written as A =, then

$$a_{ij} = a_{ji}$$

for all indices i and j. The following 3×3 matrix is symmetric:

$$\begin{bmatrix} 1 & 2 & 3 \\ 2 & 4 & -5 \\ 3 & -5 & 6 \end{bmatrix}.$$

A matrix is called skew-symmetric or antisymmetric if its transpose is the same as its negative.

- a. Contour integration
- b. Broken-line graph
- c. Symmetric matrix
- d. Conway triangle notation

30. In mathematics, the conjugate transpose, Hermitian transpose, or _____ of an m-by-n matrix A with complex entries is the n-by-m matrix A* obtained from A by taking the transpose and then taking the complex conjugate of each entry. The conjugate transpose is formally defined by

$$(A^*)_{ij} = \overline{A_{ji}}$$

where the subscripts denote the i,j-th entry, for 1 ≤ i ≤ n and 1 ≤ j ≤ m, and the overbar denotes a scalar complex conjugate.

This definition can also be written as

$$A^* = (\overline{A})^{\mathrm{T}} = \overline{A^{\mathrm{T}}}$$

where A^{T} denotes the transpose and $\overline{A}$ denotes the matrix with complex conjugated entries.

- a. Independent equation
- b. Adjoint matrix
- c. Invariant subspace
- d. Orthogonal Procrustes problem

31. _____ is an important concept in economics with broad applications in game theory, engineering and the social sciences. The term is named after Vilfredo Pareto, an Italian economist who used the concept in his studies of economic efficiency and income distribution.

Given a set of alternative allocations of, say, goods or income for a set of individuals, a change from one allocation to another that can make at least one individual better off without making any other individual worse off is called a Pareto improvement.

- a. Pursuit-evasion
- b. Multiunit auction
- c. Quasi-perfect equilibrium
- d. Pareto efficiency

Chapter 26. Determinants: The Details

32. A _____ is a type of economic equilibrium, where the clearance on the market of some specific goods is obtained independently from prices and quantities demanded and supplied in other markets. In other words, the prices of all substitutes and complements, as well as income levels of consumers are constant. Here the dynamic process is that prices adjust until supply equals demand.
   a. 120-cell
   b. Partial equilibrium
   c. Walrasian auction
   d. 1-center problem

33. In discrete mathematics and predominantly in set theory, a _____ is a concept used in comparisons of sets to refer to the unique values of one set in relation to another. The terms 'absolute' and 'relative' _____ refer to more specific applications of the concept, with universal _____s referring to elements unique to the universal set and the latter referring to the unique elements of one set in relation to another. In this image, the universal set is represented by the border of the image, and the set A as a disc.
   a. Derivative algebra
   b. Kernel
   c. Complement
   d. Huge

34. In mathematics, specifically in combinatorial commutative algebra, a convex lattice polytope P is called _____ if it has the following property: given any positive integer n, every lattice point of the dilation nP, obtained from P by scaling its vertices by the factor n and taking the convex hull of the resulting points, can be written as the sum of exactly n lattice points in P. This property plays an important role in the theory of toric varieties, where it corresponds to projective normality of the toric variety determined by P.

The simplex in R^k with the vertices at the origin and along the unit coordinate vectors is _____.

   a. Normal
   b. Hypercube
   c. Polytetrahedron
   d. Demihypercubes

35. In economics, _____s are any goods for which demand increases when income increases and falls when income decreases but price remains constant. The term does not necessarily refer to the quality of the good.

Depending on the indifference curves, the amount of a good bought can either increase, decrease, or stay the same when income increases.

   a. Normal good
   b. Partnership game
   c. Sequential game
   d. Holding period return

36. In mathematics, when X a finite set of at least two elements, the permutations of X fall into two classes of equal size: the _____ and the odd permutations. If any total ordering of X is fixed, the parity of a permutation σ of X can be defined as the parity of the number of inversions for σ.

The sign or signature of a permutation σ is denoted sg and defined as +1 if σ is even and −1 if σ is odd.

   a. Inner automorphism
   b. Even permutations
   c. Outer automorphism group
   d. Induced representation

37. In several fields of mathematics the term _____ is used with different but closely related meanings. They all relate to the notion of mapping the elements of a set to other elements of the same set, i.e., exchanging elements of a set.

The general concept of _____ can be defined more formally in different contexts:

In combinatorics, a _____ is usually understood to be a sequence containing each element from a finite set once, and only once.

   a. Tensor product   b. Linearly independent
   c. Cyclic permutation   d. Permutation

Chapter 27. Subspaces Attached to a Matrix

1. In mathematics, the _____ or Pythagoras' theorem is a relation in Euclidean geometry among the three sides of a right triangle. The theorem is named after the Greek mathematician Pythagoras, who by tradition is credited with its discovery and proof, although it is often argued that knowledge of the theory predates him.. The theorem is as follows:

In any right triangle, the area of the square whose side is the hypotenuse is equal to the sum of the areas of the squares whose sides are the two legs.

 a. 2-3 heap
 c. 120-cell
 b. Pythagorean Theorem
 d. 1-center problem

2. _____ County lies just north of the Mexican border--sharing a border with Tijuana--and lies south of Orange County. It is home to miles of beaches, a mild Mediterranean climate and 16 military facilities hosting the United States Navy, the United States Coast Guard and the United States Marine Corps.

_____'s economy is largely composed of agriculture, biotechnology/biosciences, computer sciences, electronics manufacturing, defense-related manufacturing, financial and business services, ship-repair and construction, software development, telecommunications, and tourism.

 a. San Diego
 c. 1-center problem
 b. 120-cell
 d. 2-3 heap

3. In mathematics, a _____ is a statement that can be proved on the basis of explicitly stated or previously agreed assumptions.
 a. Logical value
 c. Boolean function
 b. Disjunction introduction
 d. Theorem

4. In mathematics and in the sciences, a _____ (plural: _____e, formulæ or _____s) is a concise way of expressing information symbolically (as in a mathematical or chemical _____), or a general relationship between quantities. One of many famous _____e is Albert Einstein's E = mc^2 (see special relativity

In mathematics, a _____ is a key to solve an equation with variables. For example, the problem of determining the volume of a sphere is one that requires a significant amount of integral calculus to solve.

 a. 120-cell
 c. 1-center problem
 b. 2-3 heap
 d. Formula

5. In the various branches of mathematics that fall under the heading of abstract algebra, the _____ of a homomorphism measures the degree to which the homomorphism fails to be injective. An important special case is the _____ of a matrix, also called the null space.

The definition of _____ takes various forms in various contexts.

 a. Bertrand paradox
 c. Leibniz formula
 b. Constructivism
 d. Kernel

6. In linear algebra, the kernel or null space of a matrix A is the set of all vectors x for which Ax = 0. The null space of a matrix with n columns is a linear subspace of n-dimensional Euclidean space.

The _____ of the matrix A is exactly the same thing as the _____ of the linear mapping defined by the matrix-vector multiplication $\mathbf{x} \mapsto \mathbf{Ax}$, that is, the set of vectors that map to the zero vector.

a. Fundamental theorem of linear algebra
b. Generalized singular value decomposition
c. Generalized Pauli matrices
d. Nullspace

7. In mathematics, the _____ of an abelian group measures how large a group is in terms of how large a vector space over the rational numbers one would need to 'contain' it; or alternatively how large a free abelian group it can contain as a subgroup.

The _____ of a finite abelian group has a different definition.

An abelian group is often thought of as composed of its torsion subgroup T, and its torsion-free part A/T.

a. Coherence
b. Chord
c. Rank
d. Discontinuity

8. In calculus, the _____ is a formula for the derivative of the composite of two functions.

In intuitive terms, if a variable, y, depends on a second variable, u, which in turn depends on a third variable, x, then the rate of change of y with respect to x can be computed as the rate of change of y with respect to u multiplied by the rate of change of u with respect to x. Schematically,

$$\frac{dy}{dx} = \frac{dy}{du} \cdot \frac{du}{dx}.$$

For an explanation of notation used in this section, see Function composition.

The _____ states that, under appropriate conditions,

$$(f \circ g)'(x) = f'(g(x))g'(x),$$

which in short form is written as

$$(f \circ g)' = f' \circ g \cdot g'.$$

Alternatively, in the Leibniz notation, the _____ is

$$\frac{dy}{dx} = \frac{dy}{du} \cdot \frac{du}{dx}.$$

In integration, the counterpart to the _____ is the substitution rule.

a. 1-center problem
b. 120-cell
c. Product rule
d. Chain Rule

9. In economics, the _____ functional form of production functions is widely used to represent the relationship of an output to inputs. It was proposed by Knut Wicksell, and tested against statistical evidence by Paul Douglas and Charles Cobb in 1928.
   a. Burden of proof
   b. State price vector
   c. State price
   d. Cobb-Douglas

10. In mathematics the _____ of a set which is equipped with the operation of addition is an element which, when added to any element x in the set, yields x. One of the most familiar additive identities is the number 0 from elementary mathematics, but additive identities occur in other mathematical structures where addition is defined, such as in groups and rings.

    - The _____ familiar from elementary mathematics is zero, denoted 0. For example,

    $5 + 0 = 5 = 0 + 5$.

    - In the natural numbers N and all of its supersets, the _____ is 0. Thus for any one of these numbers n,

    $n + 0 = n = 0 + n$.

    Let N be a set which is closed under the operation of addition, denoted +. An _____ for N is any element e such that for any element n in N,

    $e + n = n = n + e$.

    a. Unique factorization domain
    b. Unit ring
    c. Algebraically independent
    d. Additive identity

11. In mathematics, the _____ of a number n is the number that, when added to n, yields zero. The _____ of n is denoted −n. For example, 7 is −7, because 7 + (−7) = 0, and the _____ of −0.3 is 0.3, because −0.3 + 0.3 = 0.
    a. Associativity
    b. Arity
    c. Algebraic structure
    d. Additive inverse

12. In mathematics, _____ is a property that a binary operation can have. It means that, within an expression containing two or more of the same associative operators in a row, the order that the operations are performed does not matter as long as the sequence of the operands is not changed. That is, rearranging the parentheses in such an expression will not change its value.
    a. Unital
    b. Associativity
    c. Algebraically closed
    d. Idempotence

13. In mathematics, a set is said to be _____ if the operation on members of the set produces a member of the set. For example, the real numbers are closed under subtraction, but the natural numbers are not: 3 and 7 are both natural numbers, but the result of 3 − 7 is not.

Similarly, a set is said to be closed under a collection of operations if it is closed under each of the operations individually.

   a. Continuous linear extension
   b. Closed under some operation
   c. Contingency table
   d. Control chart

14. The _____ is a rule which states that when you add or multiply numbers, changing the order doesn't change the result.
   a. Commutative law
   b. Coimage
   c. Conditional event algebra
   d. Semigroupoid

15. In mathematics, and in particular in abstract algebra, distributivity is a property of binary operations that generalises the _____ law from elementary algebra.
   a. General linear group
   b. Distributive
   c. Permutation
   d. Closure with a twist

16. The mathematical concept of a _____ expresses the intuitive idea of deterministic dependence between two quantities, one of which is viewed as primary and the other as secondary. A _____ then is a way to associate a unique output for each input of a specified type, for example, a real number or an element of a given set.
   a. Coherent
   b. Going up
   c. Grill
   d. Function

17. In mathematics, the term _____ has several different important meanings:

   - An _____ is an equality that remains true regardless of the values of any variables that appear within it, to distinguish it from an equality which is true under more particular conditions. For this, the 'triple bar' symbol ≡ is sometimes used.
   - In algebra, an _____ or _____ element of a set S with a binary operation Â· is an element e that, when combined with any element x of S, produces that same x. That is, eÂ·x = xÂ·e = x for all x in S.
     - The _____ function from a set S to itself, often denoted id or id$_S$, s the function such that i = x for all x in S. This function serves as the _____ element in the set of all functions from S to itself with respect to function composition.
     - In linear algebra, the _____ matrix of size n is the n-by-n square matrix with ones on the main diagonal and zeros elsewhere. This matrix serves as the _____ with respect to matrix multiplication.

A common example of the first meaning is the trigonometric _____

$$\sin^2 \theta + \cos^2 \theta = 1$$

which is true for all real values of θ, as opposed to

$$\cos \theta = 1,$$

which is true only for some values of θ, not all. For example, the latter equation is true when $\theta = 0$, false when $\theta = 2$

The concepts of 'additive _____' and 'multiplicative _____' are central to the Peano axioms. The number 0 is the 'additive _____' for integers, real numbers, and complex numbers. For the real numbers, for all $a \in \mathbb{R}$,

$$0 + a = a,$$

$$a + 0 = a,$$ and

$$0 + 0 = 0.$$

Similarly, The number 1 is the 'multiplicative _____' for integers, real numbers, and complex numbers.

- a. ARIA
- b. Intersection
- c. Action
- d. Identity

18. In mathematics the concept of a _____ generalizes notions such as 'length', 'area', and 'volume'. Informally, given some base set, a '_____' is any consistent assignment of 'sizes' to the subsets of the base set. Depending on the application, the 'size' of a subset may be interpreted as its physical size, the amount of something that lies within the subset, or the probability that some random process will yield a result within the subset.
- a. Cusp
- b. Lattice
- c. Congruent
- d. Measure

19. In statistics and mathematical epidemiology, _____ is the risk of an event relative to exposure. _____ is a ratio of the probability of the event occurring in the exposed group versus a non-exposed group.

$$RR = \frac{p_{\text{exposed}}}{p_{\text{non-exposed}}}$$

For example, if the probability of developing lung cancer among smokers was 20% and among non-smokers 1%, then the _____ of cancer associated with smoking would be 20.

- a. Relative risk
- b. 1-center problem
- c. Statistical epidemiology
- d. Mendelian randomization

20. _____ is a concept in economics, finance, and psychology related to the behaviour of consumers and investors under uncertainty. _____ is the reluctance of a person to accept a bargain with an uncertain payoff rather than another bargain with a more certain, but possibly lower, expected payoff.

The inverse of a person's _____ is sometimes called their risk tolerance.

a. Life table
b. Stochastic modelling
c. Ruin theory
d. Risk aversion

21. A _____ is the counterpart to a deterministic process in probability theory. Instead of dealing with only one possible 'reality' of how the process might evolve under time, in a stochastic or random process there is some indeterminacy in its future evolution described by probability distributions. This means that even if the initial condition is known, there are many possibilities the process might go to, but some paths are more probable and others less.

a. Fractional Brownian motion
b. Stochastic simulation
c. Mixing time
d. Stochastic process

22. In physics and in _____ calculus, a _____ is a concept characterized by a magnitude and a direction. A _____ can be thought of as an arrow in Euclidean space, drawn from an initial point A pointing to a terminal point B.

a. Dominance
b. Constraint
c. Deviation
d. Vector

23. In mathematics, a _____ is a collection of objects called vectors that may be scaled and added. These two operations must adhere to a number of axioms that generalize common properties of tuples of real numbers such as vectors in the plane or three-dimensional Euclidean space. _____s are a keystone of linear algebra, and much of their theory is of a linear nature.

a. Minkowski space
b. Geodesic
c. Moment of inertia
d. Vector space

24. In mathematics, _____ are functions which can be used to prove the stability of a certain fixed point in a dynamical system or autonomous differential equation. Named after the Russian mathematician Aleksandr Mikhailovich Lyapunov, _____ are important to stability theory and control theory.

Functions which might prove the stability of some equilibrium are called Lyapunov-candidate-functions.

a. 120-cell
b. 1-center problem
c. Butterfly effect
d. Lyapunov functions

25. Georg Friedrich Bernhard _____ was a German mathematician who made important contributions to analysis and differential geometry, some of them paving the way for the later development of general relativity.

_____ was born in Breselenz, a village near Dannenberg in the Kingdom of Hanover in what is today Germany. His father, Friedrich Bernhard _____, was a poor Lutheran pastor in Breselenz who fought in the Napoleonic Wars.

a. Brook Taylor
b. Paul C. van Oorschot
c. Gustave Bertrand
d. Riemann

26. In mathematics, a _____ is a method for approximating the total area underneath a curve on a graph, otherwise known as an integral. It may also be used to define the integration operation. The sums are named after the German mathematician Bernhard Riemann.

Chapter 27. Subspaces Attached to a Matrix

a. Multiple integral
b. Solid of revolution
c. Singular measure
d. Riemann sum

27. In combinatorial mathematics, a _____ is an un-ordered collection of distinct elements, usually of a prescribed size and taken from a given set. Given such a set S, a _____ of elements of S is just a subset of S, where as always forsets the order of the elements is not taken into account. Also, as always forsets, no elements can be repeated more than once in a _____; this is often referred to as a 'collection without repetition'.
a. Sparsity
b. Fill-in
c. Heawood number
d. Combination

28. In mathematics, _____ are a concept central to linear algebra and related fields of mathematics

Suppose that K is a field and V is a vector space over K.

a. Polarization
b. Setoid
c. Linear combinations
d. Linear span

29. In linear algebra, a _____ is a set of vectors that, in a linear combination, can represent every vector in a given vector space or free module, and such that no element of the set can be represented as a linear combination of the others. In other words, a _____ is a linearly independent spanning set. This picture illustrates the standard _____ in R^2.
a. Conchoid
b. Dot plot
c. Chiral
d. Basis

30. In mathematics, a _____ is a rectangular table of elements, which may be numbers or, more generally, any abstract quantities that can be added and multiplied. Matrices are used to describe linear equations, keep track of the coefficients of linear transformations and to record data that depend on multiple parameters. Matrices are described by the field of _____ theory.
a. Double counting
b. Compression
c. Coherent
d. Matrix

31. In linear algebra, a row vector or _____ is a 1 × n matrix, that is, a matrix consisting of a single row:

$$\mathbf{x} = \begin{bmatrix} x_1 & x_2 & \ldots & x_m \end{bmatrix}.$$

The transpose of a row vector is a column vector:

$$\begin{bmatrix} x_1 \\ x_2 \\ \vdots \\ x_m \end{bmatrix} = \begin{bmatrix} x_1 & x_2 & \ldots & x_m \end{bmatrix}^T.$$

The set of all row vectors forms a vector space which is the dual space to the set of all column vectors.

Row vectors are sometimes written using the following non-standard notation:

$$\mathbf{x} = \begin{bmatrix} x_1, x_2, \ldots, x_m \end{bmatrix}.$$

- Matrix multiplication involves the action of multiplying each row vector of one matrix by each column vector of another matrix.

- The dot product of two vectors a and b is equivalent to multiplying the row vector representation of a by the column vector representation of b:

$$\mathbf{a} \cdot \mathbf{b} = \begin{bmatrix} a_1 & a_2 & a_3 \end{bmatrix} \begin{bmatrix} b_1 \\ b_2 \\ b_3 \end{bmatrix}.$$

a. Dual vector space
b. Gram-Schmidt process
c. Woodbury matrix identity
d. Row Matrix

32. In linear algebra, the _____ of a matrix is the set of all possible linear combinations of its row vectors. The _____ of an m × n matrix is a subspace of n-dimensional Euclidean space. The dimension of the _____ is called the rank of the matrix.
   a. Symplectic vector space
   b. Row space
   c. Generalized eigenvector
   d. Dot product

33. In linear algebra, the _____ of a matrix is the set of all possible linear combinations of its column vectors. The _____ of an m × n matrix is a subspace of m-dimensional Euclidean space. The dimension of the _____ is called the rank of the matrix.
   a. Schur complement
   b. Controlled invariant subspace
   c. Quadratic form
   d. Column space

34. In several fields of mathematics the term _____ is used with different but closely related meanings. They all relate to the notion of mapping the elements of a set to other elements of the same set, i.e., exchanging elements of a set.

The general concept of _____ can be defined more formally in different contexts:

In combinatorics, a _____ is usually understood to be a sequence containing each element from a finite set once, and only once.

a. Tensor product
b. Linearly independent
c. Cyclic permutation
d. Permutation

35. In mathematics, in matrix theory, a _____ is a square-matrix that has exactly one entry 1 in each row and each column and 0's elsewhere. Each such matrix represents a specific permutation of m elements and, when used to multiply another matrix, can produce that permutation in the rows or columns of the other matrix.

Given a permutation π of m elements,

$$\pi : \{1, \ldots, m\} \to \{1, \ldots, m\}$$

given in two-line form by

$$\begin{pmatrix} 1 & 2 & \cdots & m \\ \pi(1) & \pi(2) & \cdots & \pi(m) \end{pmatrix},$$

its _____ is the m × m matrix P_π whose entries are all 0 except that in row i, the entry equals 1.

a. Partitioned matrix
b. Hessenberg matrix
c. Permutation Matrix
d. Cartan matrix

36. In microeconomics, a consumer's _____ function is the demand of a consumer over a bundle of goods that minimizes their expenditure while delivering a fixed level of utility. The function is named after John Hicks.

Mathematically,

$$h(p, \bar{u}) = \arg\min_x \sum_i p_i x_i$$
$$\text{such that } u(x) > \bar{u}$$

where h is the _____ function, or commodity bundle demanded, at price level p and utility level $\bar{u}$.

a. Marshallian demand function
b. Precautionary demand
c. 1-center problem
d. Hicksian demand

37. In mathematics, the _____ is a representation of a function as an infinite sum of terms calculated from the values of its derivatives at a single point. It may be regarded as the limit of the Taylor polynomials. _____ are named after English mathematician Brook Taylor.

a. Taylor series
b. Local linearity
c. 1-center problem
d. C^r topology

38. In mathematics, a _____ is often represented as the sum of a sequence of terms. That is, a _____ is represented as a list of numbers with addition operations between them, for example this arithmetic sequence:

1 + 2 + 3 + 4 + 5 + ... + 99 + 100

250 *Chapter 27. Subspaces Attached to a Matrix*

In most cases of interest the terms of the sequence are produced according to a certain rule, such as by a formula, by an algorithm, by a sequence of measurements, or even by a random number generator.

a. Series
c. Blind
b. Contact
d. Concavity

39. In mathematics, an _____ is an abstract structure that generalises the affine-geometric properties of Euclidean space. In an _____, one can subtract points to get vectors, or add a vector to a point to get another point, but one cannot add points. In particular, there is no distinguished point that serves as an origin.
  a. A Mathematical Theory of Communication
  b. Affine space
  c. Affine transformation
  d. A chemical equation

40. In mathematics, the _____ makes several statements regarding vector spaces. These may be stated concretely in terms of the rank r of an m×n matrix A and its LDU factorization:

    PA = LDU

wherein P is a permutation matrix, L is a lower triangular matrix, D is a diagonal matrix, and U is an upper triangular matrix. At a more abstract level there is an interpretation that reads it in terms of a linear mapping and its transpose.

  a. Linear complementarity problem
  b. Purification
  c. Matrix determinant lemma
  d. Fundamental Theorem of Linear Algebra

41. _____ is the branch of mathematics concerned with the study of vectors, vector spaces, linear maps, and systems of linear equations. Vector spaces are a central theme in modern mathematics; thus, _____ is widely used in both abstract algebra and functional analysis. _____ also has a concrete representation in analytic geometry and it is generalized in operator theory.
  a. Dual basis
  b. Binomial inverse theorem
  c. Generalized eigenvector
  d. Linear Algebra

42. In mathematics, _____ is one of the basic operations defining a vector space in linear algebra. Note that _____ is different from scalar product which is an inner product between two vectors.

More specifically, if K is a field and V is a vector space over K, then _____ is a function from K × V to V.

  a. Jordan normal form
  b. Non-negative matrix factorization
  c. Scalar multiplication
  d. Frobenius normal form

43. The _____, first developed by Sir John Hicks and Alvin Hansen, has been used from 1937 onwards to summarize a major part of Keynesian macroeconomics. IS/LM stands for Investment Saving / Liquidity preference Money supply.

The _____ was born at the Econometric Conference held in Oxford during September, 1936.

a. A Mathematical Theory of Communication
c. A posteriori

b. A chemical equation
d. IS/LM model

44. In category theory, two categories C and D are _____ if there exist functors F : C → D and G : D → C which are mutually inverse to each other. This means that both the objects and the morphisms of C and D stand in a one to one correspondence to each other. Two _____ categories share all properties that are defined solely in terms of category theory; for all practical purposes, they are identical and differ only in the notation of their objects and morphisms.

a. Isomorphic
c. Automorphism group

b. Isomorphism
d. Epimorphism

45. A _____, in mathematics, is a polynomial function of the form $f(x) = ax^2 + bx + c$, where $a \neq 0$. The graph of a _____ is a parabola whose major axis is parallel to the y-axis.

The expression $ax^2 + bx + c$ in the definition of a _____ is a polynomial of degree 2 or a 2nd degree polynomial, because the highest exponent of x is 2.

a. Multivariate division algorithm
c. Discriminant

b. Laguerre polynomials
d. Quadratic function

Chapter 28. Applications of Linear Independence

1. The mathematical concept of a _____ expresses the intuitive idea of deterministic dependence between two quantities, one of which is viewed as primary and the other as secondary. A _____ then is a way to associate a unique output for each input of a specified type, for example, a real number or an element of a given set.
   a. Going up
   b. Grill
   c. Coherent
   d. Function

2. In mathematics, an _____ is a generalization for the concept of a function in which the dependent variable has not been given 'explicitly' in terms of the independent variable. To give a function f explicitly is to provide a prescription for determining the value of the function y in terms of the input value x:

   y = f

   a. Implicit differentiation
   b. Inflection point
   c. Ordinary differential equation
   d. Implicit Function

3. In the branch of mathematics called multivariable calculus, the _____ is a tool which allows relations to be converted to functions. It does this by representing the relation as the graph of a function. There may not be a single function whose graph is the entire relation, but there may be such a function on a restriction of the domain of the relation.
   a. Implicit Function Theorem
   b. A Mathematical Theory of Communication
   c. Inverse function theorem
   d. A chemical equation

4. Georg Friedrich Bernhard _____ was a German mathematician who made important contributions to analysis and differential geometry, some of them paving the way for the later development of general relativity.

   _____ was born in Breselenz, a village near Dannenberg in the Kingdom of Hanover in what is today Germany. His father, Friedrich Bernhard _____, was a poor Lutheran pastor in Breselenz who fought in the Napoleonic Wars.

   a. Gustave Bertrand
   b. Brook Taylor
   c. Paul C. van Oorschot
   d. Riemann

5. In mathematics, a _____ is a method for approximating the total area underneath a curve on a graph, otherwise known as an integral. It may also be used to define the integration operation. The sums are named after the German mathematician Bernhard Riemann.
   a. Riemann sum
   b. Solid of revolution
   c. Multiple integral
   d. Singular measure

6. In mathematics, a _____ is a statement that can be proved on the basis of explicitly stated or previously agreed assumptions.
   a. Disjunction introduction
   b. Logical value
   c. Boolean function
   d. Theorem

7. In mathematics, a _____ is a rectangular table of elements, which may be numbers or, more generally, any abstract quantities that can be added and multiplied. Matrices are used to describe linear equations, keep track of the coefficients of linear transformations and to record data that depend on multiple parameters. Matrices are described by the field of _____ theory.

a. Compression
c. Matrix
b. Coherent
d. Double counting

8. In several fields of mathematics the term _____ is used with different but closely related meanings. They all relate to the notion of mapping the elements of a set to other elements of the same set, i.e., exchanging elements of a set.

The general concept of _____ can be defined more formally in different contexts:

In combinatorics, a _____ is usually understood to be a sequence containing each element from a finite set once, and only once.

a. Cyclic permutation
c. Linearly independent
b. Permutation
d. Tensor product

9. In mathematics, in matrix theory, a _____ is a square-matrix that has exactly one entry 1 in each row and each column and 0's elsewhere. Each such matrix represents a specific permutation of m elements and, when used to multiply another matrix, can produce that permutation in the rows or columns of the other matrix.

Given a permutation π of m elements,

$$\pi : \{1, \ldots, m\} \to \{1, \ldots, m\}$$

given in two-line form by

$$\begin{pmatrix} 1 & 2 & \cdots & m \\ \pi(1) & \pi(2) & \cdots & \pi(m) \end{pmatrix},$$

its _____ is the m × m matrix P_π whose entries are all 0 except that in row i, the entry equals 1.

a. Cartan matrix
c. Permutation Matrix
b. Hessenberg matrix
d. Partitioned matrix

10. The _____ governs the differentiation of products of differentiable functions.
a. 1-center problem
c. Reciprocal Rule
b. 120-cell
d. Product Rule

11. In mathematics, the _____ or Pythagoras' theorem is a relation in Euclidean geometry among the three sides of a right triangle. The theorem is named after the Greek mathematician Pythagoras, who by tradition is credited with its discovery and proof, although it is often argued that knowledge of the theory predates him.. The theorem is as follows:

In any right triangle, the area of the square whose side is the hypotenuse is equal to the sum of the areas of the squares whose sides are the two legs.

a. 1-center problem
c. 2-3 heap
b. Pythagorean Theorem
d. 120-cell

12. In linear algebra, the kernel or null space of a matrix A is the set of all vectors x for which Ax = 0. The null space of a matrix with n columns is a linear subspace of n-dimensional Euclidean space.

The _____ of the matrix A is exactly the same thing as the _____ of the linear mapping defined by the matrix-vector multiplication $\mathbf{x} \mapsto \mathbf{Ax}$, that is, the set of vectors that map to the zero vector.

a. Generalized Pauli matrices
c. Nullspace
b. Generalized singular value decomposition
d. Fundamental theorem of linear algebra

13. In mathematics, a _____ is a number which can be expressed as a ratio of two integers. Non-integer _____s are usually written as the vulgar fraction $\frac{a}{b}$, where b is not zero. a is called the numerator, and b the denominator.

a. Tally marks
c. Rational number
b. Pre-algebra
d. Minkowski distance

14. The Condorcet candidate or _____ of an election is the candidate who, when compared with every other candidate, is preferred by more voters. Informally, the _____ is the person who would win a two-candidate election against each of the other candidates. A _____ will not always exist in a given set of votes, which is known as Condorcet's voting paradox.

a. Condorcet winner
c. Psephology
b. 1-center problem
d. 120-cell

15. The _____ is a single-winner election method in which voters rank candidates in order of preference. The _____ determines the winner of an election by giving each candidate a certain number of points corresponding to the position in which he or she is ranked by each voter. Once all votes have been counted the candidate with the most points is the winner.

a. 1-center problem
c. 120-cell
b. 2-3 heap
d. Borda count

16. In statistics, _____ has two related meanings:

- the arithmetic _____.
- the expected value of a random variable, which is also called the population _____.

It is sometimes stated that the '_____' _____s average. This is incorrect if '_____' is taken in the specific sense of 'arithmetic _____' as there are different types of averages: the _____, median, and mode. For instance, average house prices almost always use the median value for the average.

For a real-valued random variable X, the _____ is the expectation of X.

a. Statistical population
c. Probability
b. Proportional hazards model
d. Mean

17. In calculus, the _____ states, roughly, that given a section of a smooth curve, there is at least one point on that section at which the derivative of the curve is equal to the 'average' derivative of the section. It is used to prove theorems that make global conclusions about a function on an interval starting from local hypotheses about derivatives at points of the interval.

This theorem can be understood concretely by applying it to motion: if a car travels one hundred miles in one hour, so that its average speed during that time was 100 miles per hour, then at some time its instantaneous speed must have been exactly 100 miles per hour.

a. Fundamental Theorem of Calculus
c. Calculus controversy
b. Mean Value Theorem
d. Functional integration

18. This article will state and prove the _____ for differentiation, and then use it to prove these two formulas.

The _____ for differentiation states that for every natural number n, the derivative of $f(x) = x^n$ is $f'(x) = nx^{n-1}$, that is,

$$(x^n)' = nx^{n-1}.$$

The _____ for integration

$$\int x^n \, dx = \frac{x^{n+1}}{n+1} + C$$

for natural n is then an easy consequence. One just needs to take the derivative of this equality and use the _____ and linearity of differentiation on the right-hand side.

a. Standard part function
c. Functional integration
b. Periodic function
d. Power Rule

19. _____ is the word given to a number of similar team sports, all of which involve (to varying degrees) kicking a ball with the foot in an attempt to score a goal. The most popular of these sports worldwide is association _____, more commonly known as just '_____' or 'soccer'. The English language word '_____' is also applied to 'gridiron _____' (a name associated with the North American sports, especially American _____ and Canadian _____), Australian _____, Gaelic _____, rugby _____ (rugby league and rugby union), and related games.

a. 120-cell
c. 1-center problem
b. 2-3 heap
d. Football

20. A _____ is a ranked voting method in which the options receive points based on their position on each ballot, and the option with the most points wins.

Donald G. Saari has published various works that analyze _____s mathematically.

   a. 120-cell
   b. Positional voting system
   c. 1-center problem
   d. 2-3 heap

21. In physics and in _____ calculus, a _____ is a concept characterized by a magnitude and a direction. A _____ can be thought of as an arrow in Euclidean space, drawn from an initial point A pointing to a terminal point B.

   a. Constraint
   b. Deviation
   c. Dominance
   d. Vector

22. In mathematics, _____ are functions which can be used to prove the stability of a certain fixed point in a dynamical system or autonomous differential equation. Named after the Russian mathematician Aleksandr Mikhailovich Lyapunov, _____ are important to stability theory and control theory.

Functions which might prove the stability of some equilibrium are called Lyapunov-candidate-functions.

   a. Butterfly effect
   b. 120-cell
   c. Lyapunov functions
   d. 1-center problem

23. _____ is an accounting concept used in national accounts such as the United Nations System of National Accounts (UNSNA) and the NIPAs, and sometimes in corporate or government accounts.

In national accounts, _____ is equivalent to the gross value added during an accounting period when producing enterprises use inputs (labor and capital assets) to produce outputs. Gross value added is called 'gross' because it includes depreciation charges or Consumption of fixed capital.

   a. 2-3 heap
   b. 120-cell
   c. Net output
   d. 1-center problem

24. In linear algebra, _____ is an efficient algorithm for solving systems of linear equations, finding the rank of a matrix, and calculating the inverse of an invertible square matrix. _____ is named after German mathematician and scientist Carl Friedrich Gauss.

Elementary row operations are used to reduce a matrix to row echelon form.

   a. Gaussian elimination
   b. Conjugate gradient method
   c. Cholesky decomposition
   d. Crout matrix decomposition

25. The _____ is a statistical linear model. It may be written as

$$\mathbf{Y} = \mathbf{XB} + \mathbf{U},$$

where Y is a matrix with series of multivariate measurements, X is a matrix that might be a design matrix, B is a matrix containing parameters that are usually to be estimated and U is a matrix containing errors or noise. The residual is usually assumed to follow a multivariate normal distribution.

a. Pseudomedian
b. Proportional reduction in loss
c. Comparisonwise error rate
d. General linear model

26. In statistics, given a sample $(Y_i, X_{i1}, \ldots, X_{ip})$, $i = 1, \ldots, n$ the most general form of _____ is formulated as

$$Y_i = \beta_0 + \beta_1 \phi_1(X_{i1}) + \ldots + \beta_p \phi_p(X_{ip}) + \varepsilon_i \qquad i = 1, \ldots, n$$

where $\phi_1, \ldots, \phi_p$ may be nonlinear functions.

In matrix notation this model can be written as

$$Y = X\beta + \varepsilon$$

where Y is an n × 1 column vector, X is an n × matrix, β is a × 1 vector of parameters, and ε is an n × 1 vector of errors, which are uncorrelated random variables each with expected value 0 and variance σ^2. Note that depending on the context the sample can be seen as fixed, or random.

a. Life table
b. Risk aversion
c. Risk measure
d. Linear model

27. In abstract algebra, a module S over a ring R is called _____ or irreducible if it is not the zero module 0 and if its only submodules are 0 and S. Understanding the _____ modules over a ring is usually helpful because these modules form the 'building blocks' of all other modules in a certain sense.

Abelian groups are the same as Z-modules.

a. Harmonic series
b. Derivation
c. Basis
d. Simple

Chapter 29. Limits and Compact Sets

1. In mathematics, a _____, named after Augustin Cauchy, is a sequence whose elements become arbitrarily close to each other as the sequence progresses. To be more precise, by dropping enough terms from the start of the sequence, it is possible to make the maximum of the distances from any of the remaining elements to any other such element smaller than any preassigned positive value.

   In other words, suppose a pre-assigned positive real value ε is chosen.

   a. Systolic inequalities for curves on surfaces
   b. Hausdorff distance
   c. Contraction mapping
   d. Cauchy sequence

2. The _____ is a single-winner election method in which voters rank candidates in order of preference. The _____ determines the winner of an election by giving each candidate a certain number of points corresponding to the position in which he or she is ranked by each voter. Once all votes have been counted the candidate with the most points is the winner.

   a. 1-center problem
   b. 2-3 heap
   c. 120-cell
   d. Borda count

3. The mathematical concept of a _____ expresses the intuitive idea of deterministic dependence between two quantities, one of which is viewed as primary and the other as secondary. A _____ then is a way to associate a unique output for each input of a specified type, for example, a real number or an element of a given set.

   a. Grill
   b. Going up
   c. Coherent
   d. Function

4. In mathematics, an _____ is a generalization for the concept of a function in which the dependent variable has not been given 'explicitly' in terms of the independent variable. To give a function f explicitly is to provide a prescription for determining the value of the function y in terms of the input value x:

   $$y = f$$

   a. Inflection point
   b. Implicit differentiation
   c. Ordinary differential equation
   d. Implicit Function

5. In the branch of mathematics called multivariable calculus, the _____ is a tool which allows relations to be converted to functions. It does this by representing the relation as the graph of a function. There may not be a single function whose graph is the entire relation, but there may be such a function on a restriction of the domain of the relation.

   a. A Mathematical Theory of Communication
   b. A chemical equation
   c. Implicit Function Theorem
   d. Inverse function theorem

6. In statistics, _____ has two related meanings:

   - the arithmetic _____.
   - the expected value of a random variable, which is also called the population _____.

   It is sometimes stated that the '_____' _____s average. This is incorrect if '_____' is taken in the specific sense of 'arithmetic _____' as there are different types of averages: the _____, median, and mode. For instance, average house prices almost always use the median value for the average.

For a real-valued random variable X, the _____ is the expectation of X.

   a. Statistical population   b. Mean
   c. Probability   d. Proportional hazards model

7. In calculus, the _____ states, roughly, that given a section of a smooth curve, there is at least one point on that section at which the derivative of the curve is equal to the 'average' derivative of the section. It is used to prove theorems that make global conclusions about a function on an interval starting from local hypotheses about derivatives at points of the interval.

This theorem can be understood concretely by applying it to motion: if a car travels one hundred miles in one hour, so that its average speed during that time was 100 miles per hour, then at some time its instantaneous speed must have been exactly 100 miles per hour.

   a. Fundamental Theorem of Calculus   b. Calculus controversy
   c. Functional integration   d. Mean Value Theorem

8. In linear algebra, _____ is the process of finding a set of orthogonal vectors that span a particular subspace. Formally, starting with a linearly independent set of vectors $\{v_1,...,v_k\}$ in an inner product space, _____ results in a set of orthogonal vectors $\{u_1,...,u_k\}$ that generate the same subspace as the vectors $v_1,...,v_k$. Every vector in the new set is orthogonal to every other vector in the new set; and the new set and the old set have the same linear span.
   a. Indeterminate system   b. Orthogonalization
   c. Examples of vector spaces   d. Antiunitary

9. In mathematics, a _____ is a statement that can be proved on the basis of explicitly stated or previously agreed assumptions.
   a. Logical value   b. Disjunction introduction
   c. Theorem   d. Boolean function

10. A set S of real numbers is called _____ from above if there is a real number k such that k ≥ s for all s in S. The number k is called an upper bound of S. The terms _____ from below and lower bound are similarly defined.
   a. Derivative algebra   b. Descent
   c. Harmonic series   d. Bounded

11. In mathematics, the concept of a _____ tries to capture the intuitive idea of a geometrical one-dimensional and continuous object. A simple example is the circle. In everyday use of the term '_____', a straight line is not curved, but in mathematical parlance _____s include straight lines and line segments.
   a. Curve   b. Kappa curve
   c. Negative pedal curve   d. Quadrifolium

12. In calculus, a function f defined on a subset of the real numbers with real values is called monotonic (also monotonically increasing or non-_____), if for all x and y such that x ≤ y one has f(x) ≤ f(y), so f preserves the order. In layman's terms, the sign of the slope is always positive (the curve tending upwards) or zero (i.e., non-_____, or asymptotic, or depicted as a horizontal, flat line) Likewise, a function is called monotonically _____ (non-increasing) if, whenever x ≤ y, then f(x) ≥ f(y), so it reverses the order.

Chapter 29. Limits and Compact Sets

a. Dual pair
b. Decreasing
c. Circular convolution
d. Tensor product of Hilbert spaces

13. In mathematics the infimum of a subset of some set is the greatest element, not necessarily in the subset, that is less than or equal to all elements of the subset. Consequently the term _____ is also commonly used. Infima of real numbers are a common special case that is especially important in analysis.
    a. Strict weak ordering
    b. Greatest lower bound
    c. Strong antichain
    d. Supremum

14. In mathematics the infimum of a subset of some set is the greatest element, not necessarily in the subset, that is less than or equal to all elements of the subset. Consequently the term greatest lower bound is also commonly used. _____ of real numbers are a common special case that is especially important in analysis.
    a. Upper bound
    b. Order isomorphism
    c. Infinite descending chain
    d. Infima

15. In mathematics, given a subset S of a partially ordered set T, the supremum (sup) of S, if it exists, is the least element of T that is greater than or equal to each element of S. Consequently, the supremum is also referred to as the _____, lub or _____. If the supremum exists, it may or may not belong to S.
    a. Compact element
    b. Least upper bound
    c. Complete Heyting algebra
    d. Supermodular

16. In mathematics, especially in order theory, an upper bound of a subset S of some partially ordered set is an element of P which is greater than or equal to every element of S. The term _____ is defined dually as an element of P which is lesser than or equal to every element of S. A set with an upper bound is said to be bounded from above by that bound, a set with a _____ is said to be bounded from below by that bound.
    a. Monomial order
    b. Partially ordered set
    c. Cofinality
    d. Lower bound

17. In mathematics, given a subset S of a partially ordered set T, the _____ of S, if it exists, is the least element of T that is greater than or equal to each element of S. Consequently, the _____ is also referred to as the least upper bound, lub or LUB. If the _____ exists, it may or may not belong to S.
    a. Supremum
    b. Chain complete
    c. Compact element
    d. Scott topology

18. In mathematics, especially in order theory, an _____ of a subset S of some partially ordered set is an element of P which is greater than or equal to every element of S. The term lower bound is defined dually as an element of P which is lesser than or equal to every element of S. A set with an _____ is said to be bounded from above by that bound, a set with a lower bound is said to be bounded from below by that bound.
    a. Order isomorphism
    b. Upper bound
    c. Order-embedding
    d. Infinite descending chain

19. In real analysis, the _____ is a fundamental result about convergence in a finite-dimensional Euclidean space $\mathbb{R}^n$. The theorem states that each bounded sequence in $\mathbb{R}^n$ has a convergent subsequence. An equivalent formulation is that a subset of $\mathbb{R}^n$ is sequentially compact if and only if it is closed and bounded.

Chapter 29. Limits and Compact Sets 261

a. Heine-Borel theorem
b. Fundamental axiom of analysis
c. Least upper bound axiom
d. Bolzano-Weierstrass Theorem

20. In economics, the _____ functional form of production functions is widely used to represent the relationship of an output to inputs. It was proposed by Knut Wicksell, and tested against statistical evidence by Paul Douglas and Charles Cobb in 1928.
a. State price
b. Burden of proof
c. Cobb-Douglas
d. State price vector

21. In the mathematical area of order theory, the _____ or finite elements of a partially ordered set are those elements that cannot be subsumed by a supremum of any non-empty directed set that does not already contain members above the _____ element.

Note that there are other notions of compactness in mathematics; also, the term 'finite' in its normal set theoretic meaning does not coincide with the order-theoretic notion of a 'finite element'.

In a partially ordered set an element c is called _____ if it satisfies one of the following equivalent conditions:

- For every nonempty directed subset D of P, if D has a supremum sup D and c ≤ sup D then c ≤ d for some element d of D.
- For every ideal I of P, if I has a supremum sup I and c ≤ sup I then c is an element of I.

If the poset P additionally is a join-semilattice then these conditions are equivalent to the following statement:

- For every nonempty subset S of P, if S has a supremum sup S and c ≤ sup S, then c ≤ sup T for some finite subset T of S.

In particular, if c = sup S, then c is the supremum of a finite subset of S.

a. Locally regular space
b. Train track
c. Matching distance
d. Compact

22. The Condorcet candidate or _____ of an election is the candidate who, when compared with every other candidate, is preferred by more voters. Informally, the _____ is the person who would win a two-candidate election against each of the other candidates. A _____ will not always exist in a given set of votes, which is known as Condorcet's voting paradox.
a. 1-center problem
b. Psephology
c. Condorcet winner
d. 120-cell

23. In mathematics and in the sciences, a _____ (plural: _____e, formulæ or _____s) is a concise way of expressing information symbolically (as in a mathematical or chemical _____), or a general relationship between quantities. One of many famous _____e is Albert Einstein's $E = mc^2$ (see special relativity

In mathematics, a _____ is a key to solve an equation with variables. For example, the problem of determining the volume of a sphere is one that requires a significant amount of integral calculus to solve.

a. 1-center problem	b. 2-3 heap
c. Formula	d. 120-cell

24. In mathematics, an _____ is a ring-shaped geometric figure a term used to name a ring-shaped object. The adjectival form is annular.

The open _____ is topologically equivalent to both the open cylinder $S^1 \times (0, 1)$ and the punctured plane.

a. Annulus	b. Outcome
c. OMAC	d. Erlang

25. In mathematics, the _____ or Euclidean metric is the 'ordinary' distance between two points that one would measure with a ruler, which can be proven by repeated application of the Pythagorean theorem. By using this formula as distance, Euclidean space becomes a metric space. The associated norm is called the Euclidean norm.

Older literature refers to this metric as Pythagorean metric.

a. Euclidean metric	b. A chemical equation
c. A Mathematical Theory of Communication	d. Euclidean distance

26. In linear algebra, functional analysis and related areas of mathematics, a _____ is a function that assigns a strictly positive length or size to all vectors in a vector space, other than the zero vector. A seminorm, on the other hand, is allowed to assign zero length to some non-zero vectors.

A simple example is the 2-dimensional Euclidean space R^2 equipped with the Euclidean _____.

a. Leibniz formula	b. Going up
c. Compression	d. Norm

27. In mathematics, the _____ is a representation of a function as an infinite sum of terms calculated from the values of its derivatives at a single point. It may be regarded as the limit of the Taylor polynomials. _____ are named after English mathematician Brook Taylor.

a. Local linearity	b. C^r topology
c. 1-center problem	d. Taylor series

28. In mathematics, an _____ is a statement about the relative size or order of two objects, or about whether they are the same or not

- The notation a < b means that a is less than b.
- The notation a > b means that a is greater than b.
- The notation a ≠ b means that a is not equal to b, but does not say that one is bigger than the other or even that they can be compared in size.

In all these cases, a is not equal to b, hence, '_____'.

Chapter 29. Limits and Compact Sets

These relations are known as strict _____

- The notation a ≤ b means that a is less than or equal to b;
- The notation a ≥ b means that a is greater than or equal to b;

An additional use of the notation is to show that one quantity is much greater than another, normally by several orders of magnitude.

- The notation a << b means that a is much less than b.
- The notation a >> b means that a is much greater than b.

If the sense of the _____ is the same for all values of the variables for which its members are defined, then the _____ is called an 'absolute' or 'unconditional' _____. If the sense of an _____ holds only for certain values of the variables involved, but is reversed or destroyed for other values of the variables, it is called a conditional _____.

An _____ may appear unsolvable because it only states whether a number is larger or smaller than another number; but it is possible to apply the same operations for equalities to inequalities. For example, to find x for the _____ 10x > 23 one would divide 23 by 10.

a. A posteriori
b. A chemical equation
c. A Mathematical Theory of Communication
d. Inequality

29. In mathematics, a _____ is often represented as the sum of a sequence of terms. That is, a _____ is represented as a list of numbers with addition operations between them, for example this arithmetic sequence:

1 + 2 + 3 + 4 + 5 + ... + 99 + 100

In most cases of interest the terms of the sequence are produced according to a certain rule, such as by a formula, by an algorithm, by a sequence of measurements, or even by a random number generator.

a. Blind
b. Series
c. Contact
d. Concavity

30. A _____ is one of the basic shapes of geometry: a polygon with three corners or vertices and three sides or edges which are line segments. A _____ with vertices A, B, and C is denoted ABC.

In Euclidean geometry any three non-collinear points determine a unique _____ and a unique plane.

a. 1-center problem
b. Kepler triangle
c. Fuhrmann circle
d. Triangle

31. In mathematics, the _____ states that for any triangle, the length of a given side must be less than the sum of the other two sides but greater than the difference between the two sides.

In Euclidean geometry and some other geometries this is a theorem. In the Euclidean case, in both the less than or equal to and greater than or equal to statements, equality occurs only if the triangle has a 180° angle and two 0° angles, as shown in the bottom example in the image to the right.

a. Minkowski inequality
b. Greater than
c. Rearrangement inequality
d. Triangle inequality

32. _____ is a part of mathematics concerned with questions of size, shape, and relative position of figures and with properties of space. _____ is one of the oldest sciences. Initially a body of practical knowledge concerning lengths, areas, and volumes, in the third century BC _____ was put into an axiomatic form by Euclid, whose treatment--Euclidean _____--set a standard for many centuries to follow.

a. 1-center problem
b. Geometry
c. 120-cell
d. 2-3 heap

33. In calculus, the _____ is a formula for the derivative of the composite of two functions.

In intuitive terms, if a variable, y, depends on a second variable, u, which in turn depends on a third variable, x, then the rate of change of y with respect to x can be computed as the rate of change of y with respect to u multiplied by the rate of change of u with respect to x. Schematically,

$$\frac{dy}{dx} = \frac{dy}{du} \cdot \frac{du}{dx}.$$

For an explanation of notation used in this section, see Function composition.

The _____ states that, under appropriate conditions,

$$(f \circ g)'(x) = f'(g(x))g'(x),$$

which in short form is written as

$$(f \circ g)' = f' \circ g \cdot g'.$$

Alternatively, in the Leibniz notation, the _____ is

$$\frac{dy}{dx} = \frac{dy}{du} \cdot \frac{du}{dx}.$$

In integration, the counterpart to the _____ is the substitution rule.

a. Chain Rule
b. 120-cell
c. 1-center problem
d. Product rule

34. The _____ is a basic theorem used to solve maximization problems in microeconomics. It may be used to prove Hotelling's lemma, Shephard's lemma, and Roy's identity. The statement of the theorem is:

Consider an arbitrary maximization problem where the objective function (f) depends on some parameter (a):

$$M(a) = \max_{x} f(x, a)$$

where the function M(a) gives the maximized value of the objective function (f) as a function of the parameter (a.)

a. A posteriori
b. A Mathematical Theory of Communication
c. Envelope Theorem
d. A chemical equation

35. In mathematics, an _____ is a binary relation between two elements of a set which groups them together as being 'equivalent' in some way. Let a, b, and c be arbitrary elements of some set X. Then 'a ~ b' or 'a ≡ b' denotes that a is equivalent to b.

a. A chemical equation
b. Equivalence class
c. A Mathematical Theory of Communication
d. Equivalence relation

36. In the study of metric spaces in mathematics, there are various notions of two metrics on the same underlying space being 'the same', or _____.

In the following, M will denote a non-empty set and d_1 and d_2 will denote two metrics on M.

The two metrics d_1 and d_2 are said to be topologically _____ if they generate the same topology on M.

a. A posteriori
b. A chemical equation
c. A Mathematical Theory of Communication
d. Equivalent

37. _____ is a branch of mathematics which focuses on the study of matrices. Initially a sub-branch of linear algebra, it has grown to cover subjects related to graph theory, algebra, combinatorics, and statistics as well.

The term matrix was first coined in 1848 by J.J. Sylvester as a name of an array of numbers.

a. Pairing
b. Semi-simple operators
c. Segre classification
d. Matrix theory

38. _____ is the branch of mathematics that studies the properties of a space that are preserved under continuous deformations. _____ grew out of geometry, but unlike geometry, _____ is not concerned with metric properties such as distances between points. Instead, _____ involves the study of properties that describe how a space is assembled, such as connectedness and orientability.

a. Ring
b. Topology
c. 1-center problem
d. Structure

39. In mathematics, a _____ is a rectangular table of elements, which may be numbers or, more generally, any abstract quantities that can be added and multiplied. Matrices are used to describe linear equations, keep track of the coefficients of linear transformations and to record data that depend on multiple parameters. Matrices are described by the field of _____ theory.
   a. Compression
   b. Coherent
   c. Double counting
   d. Matrix

40. In several fields of mathematics the term _____ is used with different but closely related meanings. They all relate to the notion of mapping the elements of a set to other elements of the same set, i.e., exchanging elements of a set.

The general concept of _____ can be defined more formally in different contexts:

In combinatorics, a _____ is usually understood to be a sequence containing each element from a finite set once, and only once.

   a. Cyclic permutation
   b. Linearly independent
   c. Tensor product
   d. Permutation

41. In mathematics, in matrix theory, a _____ is a square-matrix that has exactly one entry 1 in each row and each column and 0's elsewhere. Each such matrix represents a specific permutation of m elements and, when used to multiply another matrix, can produce that permutation in the rows or columns of the other matrix.

Given a permutation π of m elements,

$$\pi : \{1, \ldots, m\} \to \{1, \ldots, m\}$$

given in two-line form by

$$\begin{pmatrix} 1 & 2 & \cdots & m \\ \pi(1) & \pi(2) & \cdots & \pi(m) \end{pmatrix},$$

its _____ is the m × m matrix P_π whose entries are all 0 except that in row i, the entry equals 1.

   a. Partitioned matrix
   b. Cartan matrix
   c. Permutation Matrix
   d. Hessenberg matrix

42. In mathematics, a _____ of a set X is a collection of sets such that X is a subset of the union of sets in the collection. In symbols, if

$$C = \{U_\alpha : \alpha \in A\}$$

is an indexed family of sets U_α, then C is a _____ of X if

$$X \subseteq \bigcup_{\alpha \in A} U_\alpha$$

_____s are commonly used in the context of topology. If the set X is a topological space, then a _____ C of X is a collection of subsets U_α of X whose union is the whole space X.

a. Generalised metric
b. Manifold
c. Contractible space
d. Cover

43. In geometry, a closed _____ is one of the 2^n subsets of an n-dimensional Euclidean space defined by constraining each Cartesian coordinate axis to be nonnegative or nonpositive. That is, a closed _____ is the analogue of a closed quadrant in the plane and a closed octant in three-dimensional space. A closed _____ is defined by a system of inequalities

$\varepsilon_i x_i \geq 0$ for $1 \leq i \leq n$

on the coordinates x_i, where each ε_i is +1 or −1.

a. Orthant
b. Ortsbogen theorem
c. Equal incircles theorem
d. Euclidean space

44. A _____ is a symmetrical geometrical object. In non-mathematical usage, the term is used to refer either to a round ball or to its two-dimensional surface. In mathematics, a _____ is the set of all points in three-dimensional space which are at distance r from a fixed point of that space, where r is a positive real number called the radius of the _____.

a. Differentiable manifold
b. Differential geometry of curves
c. Lie derivative
d. Sphere

45. In mathematics, a _____ is the set of points of distance 1 from a fixed central point, where a generalized concept of distance may be used; a closed unit ball is the set of points of distance less than or equal to 1 from a fixed central point. Usually a specific point has been distinguished as the origin of the space under study and it is understood that a _____ or unit ball is centered at that point. Therefore one speaks of 'the' unit ball or 'the' _____.

a. Uniform boundedness principle
b. Unit sphere
c. Extensions of symmetric operators
d. Invariant subspace problem

46. In the topology of metric spaces the _____, named after Eduard Heine and Émile Borel, states:

Chapter 29. Limits and Compact Sets

For a subset S of Euclidean space R^n, the following two statements are equivalent:

- S is closed and bounded
- every open cover of S has a finite subcover, that is, S is compact.

In the context of real analysis, the former property is sometimes used as the defining property of compactness. However, the two definitions cease to be equivalent when we consider subsets of more general metric spaces and in this generality only the latter property is used to define compactness. In fact, the _____ for arbitrary metric spaces reads:

A subset of a metric space is compact if and only if it is complete and totally bounded.

The history of what today is called the _____ starts in the 19th century, with the search for solid foundations of real analysis.

a. Heine-Borel Theorem
c. Dominated convergence theorem
b. Real projective line
d. Luzin N property

Chapter 30. Calculus of Several Variables II

1. In economics, the _____ functional form of production functions is widely used to represent the relationship of an output to inputs. It was proposed by Knut Wicksell, and tested against statistical evidence by Paul Douglas and Charles Cobb in 1928.
   a. State price vector
   b. State price
   c. Burden of proof
   d. Cobb-Douglas

2. In mathematics, a _____ is a statement that can be proved on the basis of explicitly stated or previously agreed assumptions.
   a. Disjunction introduction
   b. Boolean function
   c. Theorem
   d. Logical value

3. In the mathematical area of order theory, the _____ or finite elements of a partially ordered set are those elements that cannot be subsumed by a supremum of any non-empty directed set that does not already contain members above the _____ element.

   Note that there are other notions of compactness in mathematics; also, the term 'finite' in its normal set theoretic meaning does not coincide with the order-theoretic notion of a 'finite element'.

   In a partially ordered set an element c is called _____ if it satisfies one of the following equivalent conditions:

   - For every nonempty directed subset D of P, if D has a supremum sup D and c ≤ sup D then c ≤ d for some element d of D.
   - For every ideal I of P, if I has a supremum sup I and c ≤ sup I then c is an element of I.

   If the poset P additionally is a join-semilattice then these conditions are equivalent to the following statement:

   - For every nonempty subset S of P, if S has a supremum sup S and c ≤ sup S, then c ≤ sup T for some finite subset T of S.

   In particular, if c = sup S, then c is the supremum of a finite subset of S.

   a. Train track
   b. Locally regular space
   c. Matching distance
   d. Compact

4. The mathematical concept of a _____ expresses the intuitive idea of deterministic dependence between two quantities, one of which is viewed as primary and the other as secondary. A _____ then is a way to associate a unique output for each input of a specified type, for example, a real number or an element of a given set.
   a. Function
   b. Going up
   c. Coherent
   d. Grill

5. In mathematics, given a subset S of a partially ordered set T, the supremum (sup) of S, if it exists, is the least element of T that is greater than or equal to each element of S. Consequently, the supremum is also referred to as the _____, lub or _____. If the supremum exists, it may or may not belong to S.
   a. Complete Heyting algebra
   b. Least upper bound
   c. Compact element
   d. Supermodular

6. In mathematics, especially in order theory, an _____ of a subset S of some partially ordered set is an element of P which is greater than or equal to every element of S. The term lower bound is defined dually as an element of P which is lesser than or equal to every element of S. A set with an _____ is said to be bounded from above by that bound, a set with a lower bound is said to be bounded from below by that bound.

a. Order isomorphism
b. Infinite descending chain
c. Order-embedding
d. Upper bound

7. In mathematics, an _____ is a generalization for the concept of a function in which the dependent variable has not been given 'explicitly' in terms of the independent variable. To give a function f explicitly is to provide a prescription for determining the value of the function y in terms of the input value x:

$$y = f$$

a. Ordinary differential equation
b. Implicit Function
c. Inflection point
d. Implicit differentiation

8. In the branch of mathematics called multivariable calculus, the _____ is a tool which allows relations to be converted to functions. It does this by representing the relation as the graph of a function. There may not be a single function whose graph is the entire relation, but there may be such a function on a restriction of the domain of the relation.

a. A chemical equation
b. Implicit Function Theorem
c. Inverse function theorem
d. A Mathematical Theory of Communication

9. In economics, a consumer's _____ v(p,w) gives the consumer's maximal utility when faced with a price level p and an amount of income w. It represents the consumer's preferences over market conditions.

This function is called indirect because consumers usually think about their preferences in terms of what they consume rather than prices.

a. A Mathematical Theory of Communication
b. Expected utility hypothesis
c. A chemical equation
d. Indirect utility function

10. In statistics, _____ has two related meanings:

- the arithmetic _____.
- the expected value of a random variable, which is also called the population _____.

It is sometimes stated that the '_____' _____s average. This is incorrect if '_____' is taken in the specific sense of 'arithmetic _____' as there are different types of averages: the _____, median, and mode. For instance, average house prices almost always use the median value for the average.

For a real-valued random variable X, the _____ is the expectation of X.

a. Proportional hazards model
b. Probability
c. Statistical population
d. Mean

Chapter 30. Calculus of Several Variables II

11. In calculus, the _____ states, roughly, that given a section of a smooth curve, there is at least one point on that section at which the derivative of the curve is equal to the 'average' derivative of the section. It is used to prove theorems that make global conclusions about a function on an interval starting from local hypotheses about derivatives at points of the interval.

This theorem can be understood concretely by applying it to motion: if a car travels one hundred miles in one hour, so that its average speed during that time was 100 miles per hour, then at some time its instantaneous speed must have been exactly 100 miles per hour.

a. Fundamental Theorem of Calculus
b. Calculus controversy
c. Functional integration
d. Mean Value Theorem

12. In mathematics, the _____ or Pythagoras' theorem is a relation in Euclidean geometry among the three sides of a right triangle. The theorem is named after the Greek mathematician Pythagoras, who by tradition is credited with its discovery and proof, although it is often argued that knowledge of the theory predates him.. The theorem is as follows:

In any right triangle, the area of the square whose side is the hypotenuse is equal to the sum of the areas of the squares whose sides are the two legs.

a. 1-center problem
b. 120-cell
c. 2-3 heap
d. Pythagorean Theorem

13. _____ is a branch of mathematics which focuses on the study of matrices. Initially a sub-branch of linear algebra, it has grown to cover subjects related to graph theory, algebra, combinatorics, and statistics as well.

The term matrix was first coined in 1848 by J.J. Sylvester as a name of an array of numbers.

a. Pairing
b. Matrix theory
c. Semi-simple operators
d. Segre classification

14. In linear algebra, functional analysis and related areas of mathematics, a _____ is a function that assigns a strictly positive length or size to all vectors in a vector space, other than the zero vector. A seminorm, on the other hand, is allowed to assign zero length to some non-zero vectors.

A simple example is the 2-dimensional Euclidean space R^2 equipped with the Euclidean _____.

a. Norm
b. Compression
c. Going up
d. Leibniz formula

15. In mathematics, a _____ is an expression constructed from variables and constants, using the operations of addition, subtraction, multiplication, and constant non-negative whole number exponents. For example, $x^2 - 4x + 7$ is a _____, but $x^2 - 4/x + 7x^{3/2}$ is not, because its second term involves division by the variable x and also because its third term contains an exponent that is not a whole number.

_____s are one of the most important concepts in algebra and throughout mathematics and science.

a. Group extension
b. Coimage
c. Semifield
d. Polynomial

16. In mathematics, the _____ is a representation of a function as an infinite sum of terms calculated from the values of its derivatives at a single point. It may be regarded as the limit of the Taylor polynomials. _____ are named after English mathematician Brook Taylor.
    a. C^r topology
    b. Taylor series
    c. Local linearity
    d. 1-center problem

17. In statistics, the _____ one-way analysis of variance by ranks is a non-parametric method for testing equality of population medians among groups. Intuitively, it is identical to a one-way analysis of variance with the data replaced by their ranks. It is an extension of the Mann-Whitney U test to 3 or more groups.
    a. Kruskal-Wallis
    b. Sign test
    c. Lilliefors test
    d. P-rep

18. In mathematics, an _____ in the sense of ring theory is a subring $\mathcal{O}$ of a ring R that satisfies the conditions

    1. R is a ring which is a finite-dimensional algebra over the rational number field $\mathbb{Q}$
    2. $\mathcal{O}$ spans R over $\mathbb{Q}$, so that $\mathbb{Q}\mathcal{O} = R$, and
    3. $\mathcal{O}$ is a lattice in R.

The third condition can be stated more accurately, in terms of the extension of scalars of R to the real numbers, embedding R in a real vector space. In less formal terms, additively $\mathcal{O}$ should be a free abelian group generated by a basis for R over $\mathbb{Q}$.

The leading example is the case where R is a number field K and $\mathcal{O}$ is its ring of integers. In algebraic number theory there are examples for any K other than the rational field of proper subrings of the ring of integers that are also _____s.

    a. Order
    b. Algebraic
    c. Efficiency
    d. Annihilator

19. The Condorcet candidate or _____ of an election is the candidate who, when compared with every other candidate, is preferred by more voters. Informally, the _____ is the person who would win a two-candidate election against each of the other candidates. A _____ will not always exist in a given set of votes, which is known as Condorcet's voting paradox.
    a. 1-center problem
    b. 120-cell
    c. Psephology
    d. Condorcet winner

20. In mathematics, the concept of a _____ tries to capture the intuitive idea of a geometrical one-dimensional and continuous object. A simple example is the circle. In everyday use of the term '_____', a straight line is not curved, but in mathematical parlance _____s include straight lines and line segments.
    a. Negative pedal curve
    b. Curve
    c. Quadrifolium
    d. Kappa curve

21. In mathematics, and more specifically set theory, the _____ is the unique set having no members. Some axiomatic set theories assure that the _____ exists by including an axiom of _____; in other theories, its existence can be deduced. Many possible properties of sets are trivially true for the _____.
   a. A Mathematical Theory of Communication
   b. Inverse function
   c. Empty function
   d. Empty set

22. In mathematics, a _____ is a set that is negligible in some sense. For different applications, the meaning of 'negligible' varies. In measure theory, any set of measure 0 is called a _____.
   a. Borel-Cantelli lemma
   b. Prevalence and shyness
   c. Radonifying function
   d. Null set

23. In mathematics, especially in set theory, a set A is a _____ of a set B if A is 'contained' inside B. Notice that A and B may coincide. The relationship of one set being a _____ of another is called inclusion.
   a. Horizontal line test
   b. Cartesian product
   c. Set of all sets
   d. Subset

24. In set theory, the term _____ refers to a set operation used in the convergence of set elements to form a resultant set containing the elements of both sets. As a simple example, a _____ of two disjoint sets, which do not have elements in common results in a set containing all elements from both sets. A Venn diagram representing the _____ of sets A and B.
   a. Union
   b. UES
   c. Event
   d. Introduction

25. In mathematics, the _____ of a number n is the number that, when added to n, yields zero. The _____ of n is denoted −n. For example, 7 is −7, because 7 + (−7) = 0, and the _____ of −0.3 is 0.3, because −0.3 + 0.3 = 0.
   a. Algebraic structure
   b. Associativity
   c. Arity
   d. Additive inverse

26. An _____ is a function which does the reverse of a given function.
   a. Inverse Function
   b. Empty set
   c. A Mathematical Theory of Communication
   d. Empty function

27. In mathematics, the _____ gives sufficient conditions for a vector-valued function to be invertible on an open region containing a point in its domain. Further, the theorem shows the total derivative of the inverse function exists and gives a formula for it. The theorem can be generalized to maps defined on manifolds, and on infinite dimensional Banach spaces.
   a. Isoperimetric inequality
   b. A Mathematical Theory of Communication
   c. A chemical equation
   d. Inverse Function Theorem

28. In discrete mathematics and predominantly in set theory, a _____ is a concept used in comparisons of sets to refer to the unique values of one set in relation to another. The terms 'absolute' and 'relative' _____ refer to more specific applications of the concept, with universal _____s referring to elements unique to the universal set and the latter referring to the unique elements of one set in relation to another. In this image, the universal set is represented by the border of the image, and the set A as a disc.
   a. Derivative algebra
   b. Kernel
   c. Huge
   d. Complement

29. In mathematics, a _____ can mean either an element of the set {1, 2, 3, ...} or an element of the set {0, 1, 2, 3, ...}. The latter is especially preferred in mathematical logic, set theory, and computer science.

_____s have two main purposes: they can be used for counting, and they can be used for ordering.

a. Natural number
b. Cardinal numbers
c. Strong partition cardinal
d. Suslin cardinal

30. The _____ are the set of numbers consisting of the natural numbers including 0 and their negatives. They are numbers that can be written without a fractional or decimal component, and fall within the set {... −2, −1, 0, 1, 2, ...}.

a. A chemical equation
b. A Mathematical Theory of Communication
c. A posteriori
d. Integers

31. In mathematics, a _____ is a number which can be expressed as a ratio of two integers. Non-integer _____s are usually written as the vulgar fraction $\frac{a}{b}$, where b is not zero. a is called the numerator, and b the denominator.

a. Pre-algebra
b. Minkowski distance
c. Rational number
d. Tally marks

32. In calculus, the _____ is a formula for the derivative of the composite of two functions.

In intuitive terms, if a variable, y, depends on a second variable, u, which in turn depends on a third variable, x, then the rate of change of y with respect to x can be computed as the rate of change of y with respect to u multiplied by the rate of change of u with respect to x. Schematically,

$$\frac{dy}{dx} = \frac{dy}{du} \cdot \frac{du}{dx}.$$

For an explanation of notation used in this section, see Function composition.

The _____ states that, under appropriate conditions,

$$(f \circ g)'(x) = f'(g(x))g'(x),$$

which in short form is written as

$$(f \circ g)' = f' \circ g \cdot g'.$$

Alternatively, in the Leibniz notation, the _____ is

$$\frac{dy}{dx} = \frac{dy}{du} \cdot \frac{du}{dx}.$$

In integration, the counterpart to the _____ is the substitution rule.

a. Product rule
c. 120-cell
b. Chain Rule
d. 1-center problem

33. _____ describes the property of operations in mathematics and computer science which means that multiple applications of the operation does not change the result. The concept of _____ arises in a number of places in abstract algebra.

There are several meanings of _____, depending on what the concept is applied to:

- A unary operation is called idempotent if, whenever it is applied twice to any value, it gives the same result as if it were applied once. For example, the absolute value function is idempotent as a function from the set of real numbers to the set of real numbers: ab = ab.
- A binary operation is called idempotent if, whenever it is applied to two equal values, it gives that value as the result. For example, the operation giving the maximum value of two values is idempotent: ma = x.
- Given a binary operation, an idempotent element for the operation is a value for which the operation, when given that value for both of its operands, gives the value as the result. For example, the number 1 is an idempotent of multiplication: 1 × 1 = 1.

A unary operation f that is a map from some set S into itself is called idempotent if, for all x in S,

  f

In particular, the identity function id_S, defined by
id_S, is idempotent, as is the constant function K_c, where c is an element of S, defined by $K_c(x) = c$.

a. Idempotence
c. Antiisomorphism
b. Absorption law
d. Ordered exponential

34. In mathematics, a _____ is a rectangular table of elements, which may be numbers or, more generally, any abstract quantities that can be added and multiplied. Matrices are used to describe linear equations, keep track of the coefficients of linear transformations and to record data that depend on multiple parameters. Matrices are described by the field of _____ theory.

a. Double counting
c. Coherent
b. Compression
d. Matrix

35. This article will state and prove the _____ for differentiation, and then use it to prove these two formulas.

The _____ for differentiation states that for every natural number n, the derivative of $f(x) = x^n$ is $f'(x) = nx^{n-1}$, that is,

$$(x^n)' = nx^{n-1}.$$

The _____ for integration

$$\int x^n \, dx = \frac{x^{n+1}}{n+1} + C$$

for natural n is then an easy consequence. One just needs to take the derivative of this equality and use the _____ and linearity of differentiation on the right-hand side.

a. Standard part function
b. Power Rule
c. Periodic function
d. Functional integration

36. In mathematics, _____ is a property that a binary operation can have. It means that, within an expression containing two or more of the same associative operators in a row, the order that the operations are performed does not matter as long as the sequence of the operands is not changed. That is, rearranging the parentheses in such an expression will not change its value.

a. Unital
b. Algebraically closed
c. Associativity
d. Idempotence

37. In mathematics, a set is said to be _____ if the operation on members of the set produces a member of the set. For example, the real numbers are closed under subtraction, but the natural numbers are not: 3 and 7 are both natural numbers, but the result of 3 − 7 is not.

Similarly, a set is said to be closed under a collection of operations if it is closed under each of the operations individually.

a. Closed under some operation
b. Continuous linear extension
c. Control chart
d. Contingency table

38. The _____ is a rule which states that when you add or multiply numbers, changing the order doesn't change the result.

a. Conditional event algebra
b. Coimage
c. Commutative law
d. Semigroupoid

39. In mathematics, and in particular in abstract algebra, distributivity is a property of binary operations that generalises the _____ law from elementary algebra.

Chapter 30. Calculus of Several Variables II

a. Closure with a twist   b. Permutation
c. General linear group   d. Distributive

40. In mathematics and in the sciences, a _____ (plural: _____e, formulæ or _____s) is a concise way of expressing information symbolically (as in a mathematical or chemical _____), or a general relationship between quantities. One of many famous _____e is Albert Einstein's E = mc² (see special relativity

In mathematics, a _____ is a key to solve an equation with variables. For example, the problem of determining the volume of a sphere is one that requires a significant amount of integral calculus to solve.

a. 120-cell   b. 2-3 heap
c. 1-center problem   d. Formula

41. In mathematics, the term _____ has several different important meanings:

- An _____ is an equality that remains true regardless of the values of any variables that appear within it, to distinguish it from an equality which is true under more particular conditions. For this, the 'triple bar' symbol ≡ is sometimes used.
- In algebra, an _____ or _____ element of a set S with a binary operation Â· is an element e that, when combined with any element x of S, produces that same x. That is, eÂ·x = xÂ·e = x for all x in S.
    - The _____ function from a set S to itself, often denoted id or id$_S$, s the function such that i = x for all x in S. This function serves as the _____ element in the set of all functions from S to itself with respect to function composition.
    - In linear algebra, the _____ matrix of size n is the n-by-n square matrix with ones on the main diagonal and zeros elsewhere. This matrix serves as the _____ with respect to matrix multiplication.

A common example of the first meaning is the trigonometric _____

$$\sin^2 \theta + \cos^2 \theta = 1$$

which is true for all real values of θ, as opposed to

$$\cos \theta = 1,$$

which is true only for some values of θ, not all. For example, the latter equation is true when $\theta = 0$, false when $\theta = 2$

Chapter 30. Calculus of Several Variables II

The concepts of 'additive _____' and 'multiplicative _____' are central to the Peano axioms. The number 0 is the 'additive _____' for integers, real numbers, and complex numbers. For the real numbers, for all $a \in \mathbb{R}$,

$$0 + a = a,$$

$$a + 0 = a, \text{ and}$$

$$0 + 0 = 0.$$

Similarly, The number 1 is the 'multiplicative _____' for integers, real numbers, and complex numbers.

    a. ARIA   b. Action
    c. Identity   d. Intersection

42. In mathematics, an _____ is a complex number whose squared value is a real number less than or equal to zero. The imaginary unit, denoted by i or j, is an example of an _____. If y is a real number, then iÂ·y is an _____, because:

$$(i \cdot y)^2 = i^2 \cdot y^2 = -y^2 \leq 0.$$

They were defined in 1572 by Rafael Bombelli.

    a. A posteriori   b. A Mathematical Theory of Communication
    c. Imaginary number   d. A chemical equation

43. In mathematics the concept of a _____ generalizes notions such as 'length', 'area', and 'volume'. Informally, given some base set, a '_____' is any consistent assignment of 'sizes' to the subsets of the base set. Depending on the application, the 'size' of a subset may be interpreted as its physical size, the amount of something that lies within the subset, or the probability that some random process will yield a result within the subset.

    a. Measure   b. Lattice
    c. Cusp   d. Congruent

44. In mathematics, a _____ is a natural number which has exactly two distinct natural number divisors: 1 and itself. An infinitude of _____s exists, as demonstrated by Euclid around 300 BC. The first twenty-five _____s are:

    2, 3, 5, 7, 11, 13, 17, 19, 23, 29, 31, 37, 41, 43, 47, 53, 59, 61, 67, 71, 73, 79, 83, 89, 97.

    a. Pronic number   b. Perrin number
    c. Highly composite number   d. Prime number

Chapter 30. Calculus of Several Variables II

45. In mathematics, the _____s may be described informally in several different ways. The _____s include both rational numbers, such as 42 and −23/129, and irrational numbers, such as pi and the square root of two; or, a _____ can be given by an infinite decimal representation, such as 2.4871773339...., where the digits continue in some way; or, the _____s may be thought of as points on an infinitely long number line.

These descriptions of the _____s, while intuitively accessible, are not sufficiently rigorous for the purposes of pure mathematics.

   a. Tally marks
   b. Pre-algebra
   c. Real number
   d. Minkowski distance

46. In statistics and mathematical epidemiology, _____ is the risk of an event relative to exposure. _____ is a ratio of the probability of the event occurring in the exposed group versus a non-exposed group.

$$RR = \frac{p_{\text{exposed}}}{p_{\text{non-exposed}}}$$

For example, if the probability of developing lung cancer among smokers was 20% and among non-smokers 1%, then the _____ of cancer associated with smoking would be 20.

   a. Relative risk
   b. Statistical epidemiology
   c. 1-center problem
   d. Mendelian randomization

47. _____ is a concept in economics, finance, and psychology related to the behaviour of consumers and investors under uncertainty. _____ is the reluctance of a person to accept a bargain with an uncertain payoff rather than another bargain with a more certain, but possibly lower, expected payoff.

The inverse of a person's _____ is sometimes called their risk tolerance.

   a. Ruin theory
   b. Stochastic modelling
   c. Life table
   d. Risk aversion

48. In linear algebra, _____ is the process of finding a set of orthogonal vectors that span a particular subspace. Formally, starting with a linearly independent set of vectors $\{v_1,...,v_k\}$ in an inner product space, _____ results in a set of orthogonal vectors $\{u_1,...,u_k\}$ that generate the same subspace as the vectors $v_1,...,v_k$. Every vector in the new set is orthogonal to every other vector in the new set; and the new set and the old set have the same linear span.
   a. Orthogonalization
   b. Indeterminate system
   c. Antiunitary
   d. Examples of vector spaces

49. In mathematics the infimum of a subset of some set is the greatest element, not necessarily in the subset, that is less than or equal to all elements of the subset. Consequently the term _____ is also commonly used. Infima of real numbers are a common special case that is especially important in analysis.
   a. Strict weak ordering
   b. Supremum
   c. Strong antichain
   d. Greatest lower bound

50. In mathematics, especially in order theory, an upper bound of a subset S of some partially ordered set is an element of P which is greater than or equal to every element of S. The term _____ is defined dually as an element of P which is lesser than or equal to every element of S. A set with an upper bound is said to be bounded from above by that bound, a set with a _____ is said to be bounded from below by that bound.

a. Partially ordered set
c. Cofinality
b. Monomial order
d. Lower bound

51. In mathematics and logic, a _____ is a way of showing the truth or falsehood of a given statement by a straightforward combination of established facts, usually existing lemmas and theorems, without making any further assumptions. In order to directly prove a conditional statement of the form 'If p, then q', it is only necessary to consider situations where the statement p is true. Logical deduction is employed to reason from assumptions to conclusion.

a. Minimal counterexample
c. Proofs from THE BOOK
b. Proof by exhaustion
d. Direct proof

52. In mathematics, a _____ is a convincing demonstration that some mathematical statement is necessarily true. _____s are obtained from deductive reasoning, rather than from inductive or empirical arguments. That is, a _____ must demonstrate that a statement is true in all cases, without a single exception.

a. Germ
c. Conchoid
b. Proof
d. Congruent

53. The _____ is a basic theorem used to solve maximization problems in microeconomics. It may be used to prove Hotelling's lemma, Shephard's lemma, and Roy's identity. The statement of the theorem is:

Consider an arbitrary maximization problem where the objective function (f) depends on some parameter (a):

$$M(a) = \max_x f(x, a)$$

where the function M(a) gives the maximized value of the objective function (f) as a function of the parameter (a.)

a. A posteriori
c. Envelope Theorem
b. A Mathematical Theory of Communication
d. A chemical equation

54. In propositional logic, contraposition is a logical relationship between two statements of material implication. A proposition Q is materially implicated by a proposition P when the following relationship holds:

$$(P \to Q)$$

In vernacular terms, this states 'If P then Q', or, 'If Socrates is a man then Socrates is human.' In a conditional such as this, P is called the antecedent and Q the consequent. One statement is the _____ of the other just when its antecedent is the negated consequent of the other, and vice-versa.

a. Continuous signal
c. Control chart
b. Contrapositive
d. Contour map

Chapter 30. Calculus of Several Variables II

55. In the study of metric spaces in mathematics, there are various notions of two metrics on the same underlying space being 'the same', or _____.

In the following, M will denote a non-empty set and d_1 and d_2 will denote two metrics on M.

The two metrics d_1 and d_2 are said to be topologically _____ if they generate the same topology on M.

   a. A chemical equation
   b. A Mathematical Theory of Communication
   c. A posteriori
   d. Equivalent

56. _____, in logic and fields that rely on it such as mathematics and philosophy, is a biconditional logical connective between statements. In that it is biconditional, the connective can be likened to the standard material conditional ('if') combined with its reverse ('only if'); hence the name. The result is that the truth of either one of the connected statements requires the truth of the other.
   a. Enumerative definition
   b. Algebraic logic
   c. Existential graph
   d. If and only if

57. The _____ governs the differentiation of products of differentiable functions.
   a. Reciprocal Rule
   b. 1-center problem
   c. 120-cell
   d. Product Rule

58. In abstract algebra, a _____ is an algebraic structure in which the operations of addition, subtraction, multiplication and division may be performed in a way that satisfies some familiar rules from the arithmetic of ordinary numbers.

All _____s are rings, but not conversely. _____s differ from rings most importantly in the requirement that division be possible, but also, in modern definitions, by the requirement that the multiplication operation in a _____ be commutative.

   a. Chord
   b. Functional
   c. Field
   d. Blind

59. _____ is the word given to a number of similar team sports, all of which involve (to varying degrees) kicking a ball with the foot in an attempt to score a goal. The most popular of these sports worldwide is association _____, more commonly known as just '_____' or 'soccer'. The English language word '_____' is also applied to 'gridiron _____' (a name associated with the North American sports, especially American _____ and Canadian _____), Australian _____, Gaelic _____, rugby _____ (rugby league and rugby union), and related games.
   a. 120-cell
   b. Football
   c. 1-center problem
   d. 2-3 heap

60. _____ reductio ad impossibile is a type of logical argument where one assumes a claim for the sake of argument and derives an absurd or ridiculous outcome, and then concludes that the original claim must have been wrong as it led to an absurd result.

It makes use of the law of non-contradiction -- a statement cannot be both true and false. In some cases it may also make use of the law of excluded middle -- a statement must be either true or false.

a. 1-center problem
b. 120-cell
c. Reductio ad absurdum
d. 2-3 heap

61. In mathematics, a _____ is often represented as the sum of a sequence of terms. That is, a _____ is represented as a list of numbers with addition operations between them, for example this arithmetic sequence:

$1 + 2 + 3 + 4 + 5 + ... + 99 + 100$

In most cases of interest the terms of the sequence are produced according to a certain rule, such as by a formula, by an algorithm, by a sequence of measurements, or even by a random number generator.

a. Blind
b. Concavity
c. Contact
d. Series

62. _____ is a method of mathematical proof typically used to establish that a given statement is true of all natural numbers. It is done by proving that the first statement in the infinite sequence of statements is true, and then proving that if any one statement in the infinite sequence of statements is true, then so is the next one.

The method can be extended to prove statements about more general well-founded structures, such as trees; this generalization, known as structural induction, is used in mathematical logic and computer science.

a. Ground expression
b. Herbrand structure
c. Finitary
d. Mathematical induction

63. _____ is a mathematical system attributed to the Greek mathematician Euclid of Alexandria. Euclid's Elements is the earliest known systematic discussion of geometry. It has been one of the most influential books in history, as much for its method as for its mathematical content.

a. Infinitely near point
b. Analytic geometry
c. Equidimensional
d. Euclidean geometry

64. _____ is a part of mathematics concerned with questions of size, shape, and relative position of figures and with properties of space. _____ is one of the oldest sciences. Initially a body of practical knowledge concerning lengths, areas, and volumes, in the third century BC _____ was put into an axiomatic form by Euclid, whose treatment--Euclidean _____--set a standard for many centuries to follow.

a. 2-3 heap
b. 120-cell
c. 1-center problem
d. Geometry

65. In linear algebra, two n-by-n matrices A and B over the field K are called _____ if there exists an invertible n-by-n matrix P over K such that

Chapter 30. Calculus of Several Variables II

$$P^{-1}AP = B.$$

One of the meanings of the term similarity transformation is such a transformation of a matrix A into a matrix B.

Similarity is an equivalence relation on the space of square matrices.

_____ matrices share many properties:

- rank
- determinant
- trace
- eigenvalues
- characteristic polynomial
- minimal polynomial
- elementary divisors

There are two reasons for these facts:

- two _____ matrices can be thought of as describing the same linear map, but with respect to different bases
- the map $X \mapsto P^{-1}XP$ is an automorphism of the associative algebra of all n-by-n matrices, as the one-object case of the above category of all matrices.

Because of this, for a given matrix A, one is interested in finding a simple 'normal form' B which is _____ to A -- the study of A then reduces to the study of the simpler matrix B.

a. Similar
c. Dense
b. Blinding
d. Coherence

66. A _____ is a simple shape of Euclidean geometry consisting of those points in a plane which are at a constant distance, called the radius, from a fixed point, called the center. A _____ with center A is sometimes denoted by the symbol A.

A chord of a _____ is a line segment whose two endpoints lie on the _____.

a. Malfatti circles
c. Circumcircle
b. Circle
d. Circular segment

67. In mathematics, a _____ is a circle with a unit radius. Frequently, especially in trigonometry, 'the' _____ is the circle of radius 1 centered at the origin in the Cartesian coordinate system in the Euclidean plane. The _____ is often denoted S^1; the generalization to higher dimensions is the unit sphere.

a. Open unit disk
c. Unit circle
b. Excircle
d. Inscribed angle theorem

284 *Chapter 30. Calculus of Several Variables II*

68. In trigonometry, the _____ is a function defined as $\tan x = \sin x / \cos x$. The function is so-named because it can be defined as the length of a certain segment of a _____ (in the geometric sense) to the unit circle. In plane geometry, a line is _____ to a curve, at some point, if both line and curve pass through the point with the same direction.

    a. Hopf conjectures   b. Conformal geometry
    c. Projective connection   d. Tangent

69. In geometry, an _____ is a triangle in which all three sides have equal lengths. In traditional or Euclidean geometry, _____s are also equiangular; that is, all three internal angles are also equal to each other and are each 60°. They are regular polygons, and can therefore also be referred to as regular triangles.

    a. A Mathematical Theory of Communication   b. A chemical equation
    c. Isotomic conjugate   d. Equilateral triangle

70. A _____ is one of the basic shapes of geometry: a polygon with three corners or vertices and three sides or edges which are line segments. A _____ with vertices A, B, and C is denoted ABC.

In Euclidean geometry any three non-collinear points determine a unique _____ and a unique plane.

    a. Fuhrmann circle   b. Kepler triangle
    c. Triangle   d. 1-center problem

71. The Gompertz-Makeham law states that death rate is a sum of age-independent component and age-dependent component, which increases exponentially with age. In a protected environment where external causes of death are rare the age-independent mortality component is often negligible, and in this case the formula simplifies to a _____ of mortality with exponential increase in death rates with age.

The Gompertz-Makeham law of mortality describes the age dynamics of human mortality rather accurately in the age window of about 30-80 years.

    a. 1-center problem   b. Gompertz law
    c. 120-cell   d. Gompertz-Makeham law of mortality

72. The _____ is the distance around a closed curve. _____ is a kind of perimeter.

The _____ of a circle is the length around it.

    a. Brascamp-Lieb inequality   b. Compactness measure of a shape
    c. Circumference   d. Flatness

73. The _____ is a unit of plane angle, equal to 180/π degrees, or about 57.2958 degrees. It is the standard unit of angular measurement in all areas of mathematics beyond the elementary level.

The _____ is represented by the symbol 'rad' or, more rarely, by the superscript c.

    a. 2-3 heap   b. 1-center problem
    c. Radian   d. 120-cell

Chapter 30. Calculus of Several Variables II

74. In mathematics, a _____ is a polynomial equation of the second degree. The general form is

$$ax^2 + bx + c = 0,$$

where a ≠ 0.

The letters a, b, and c are called coefficients: the quadratic coefficient a is the coefficient of x^2, the linear coefficient b is the coefficient of x, and c is the constant coefficient, also called the free term or constant term.

a. Linear equation
b. Quartic equation
c. Difference of two squares
d. Quadratic equation

75. A quadratic equation with real solutions, called roots, which may be real or complex, is given by the _____: x = $\frac{-b \pm \sqrt{b^2 - 4ac}}{2a}$.

a. Parametric continuity
b. Quotient
c. Differential Algebra
d. Quadratic formula

76. In mathematics, the _____ of a complex number is given by changing the sign of the imaginary part. Thus, the conjugate of the complex number

$$z = a + ib$$

(where a and b are real numbers) is

$$\bar{z} = a - ib.$$

The _____ is also very commonly denoted by z *. Here $\bar{z}$ is chosen to avoid confusion with the notation for the conjugate transpose of a matrix (which can be thought of as a generalization of complex conjugation.)

a. Complex conjugate
b. 120-cell
c. Real part
d. 1-center problem

77. In mathematics, the _____s are an extension of the real numbers obtained by adjoining an imaginary unit, denoted i, which satisfies:

$$i^2 = -1.$$

Every _____ can be written in the form a + bi, where a and b are real numbers called the real part and the imaginary part of the _____, respectively.

_____s are a field, and thus have addition, subtraction, multiplication, and division operations. These operations extend the corresponding operations on real numbers, although with a number of additional elegant and useful properties, e.g., negative real numbers can be obtained by squaring _____s.

a. 1-center problem
c. Real part
b. 120-cell
d. Complex number

78. In algebra, a _____ of an element in a quadratic extension field of a field K is its image under the unique non-identity automorphism of the extended field that fixes K. If the extension is generated by a square root of an element r of K, then the _____ of $a + b\sqrt{r}$ is $a - b\sqrt{r}$ for $a, b \in K$, and in particular in the case of the field C of complex numbers as an extension of the field R of real numbers, the complex _____ of a + bi is a − bi.

Forming the sum or product of any element of the extension field with its _____ always gives an element of K.

   a. Real structure
   c. Conjugate
   b. Relation algebra
   d. Trinomial

79. In mathematics, the _____ of a complex number z, is the second element of the ordered pair of real numbers representing z,. It is denoted by Im or $\Im\{z\}$, where $\Im$ is a capital I in the Fraktur typeface. The complex function which maps z to the _____ of z is not holomorphic.
   a. A posteriori
   c. Imaginary part
   b. A chemical equation
   d. A Mathematical Theory of Communication

80. In mathematics, the _____ of a complex number z, is the first element of the ordered pair of real numbers representing z. It is denoted by Re{z} or $\Re\{z\}$, where $\Re$ is a capital R in the Fraktur typeface. The complex function which maps z to the _____ of z is not holomorphic.
   a. 120-cell
   c. 1-center problem
   b. Complex number
   d. Real part

81. In mathematics, the _____ is a geometric representation of the complex numbers established by the real axis and the orthogonal imaginary axis. It can be thought of as a modified Cartesian plane, with the real part of a complex number represented by a displacement along the x-axis, and the imaginary part by a displacement along the y-axis.

The _____ is sometimes called the Argand plane because it is used in Argand diagrams.

   a. 1-center problem
   c. 2-3 heap
   b. 120-cell
   d. Complex plane

82. In mathematics, a _____ is, informally, an infinitely vast and infinitely thin sheet. _____ s may be thought of as objects in some higher dimensional space, or they may be considered without any outside space, as in the setting of Euclidean geometry
   a. Group
   c. Blocking
   b. Bandwidth
   d. Plane

83. In mathematics, the _____ of a real number is its numerical value without regard to its sign. So, for example, 3 is the _____ of both 3 and −3.

The _____ of a number a is denoted by $|a|$.

Chapter 30. Calculus of Several Variables II

Generalizations of the _____ for real numbers occur in a wide variety of mathematical settings.

a. Area hyperbolic functions
b. A Mathematical Theory of Communication
c. A chemical equation
d. Absolute value

84. In several fields of mathematics the term _____ is used with different but closely related meanings. They all relate to the notion of mapping the elements of a set to other elements of the same set, i.e., exchanging elements of a set.

The general concept of _____ can be defined more formally in different contexts:

In combinatorics, a _____ is usually understood to be a sequence containing each element from a finite set once, and only once.

a. Permutation
b. Tensor product
c. Linearly independent
d. Cyclic permutation

85. In mathematics, in matrix theory, a _____ is a square-matrix that has exactly one entry 1 in each row and each column and 0's elsewhere. Each such matrix represents a specific permutation of m elements and, when used to multiply another matrix, can produce that permutation in the rows or columns of the other matrix.

Given a permutation π of m elements,

$$\pi : \{1, \ldots, m\} \to \{1, \ldots, m\}$$

given in two-line form by

$$\begin{pmatrix} 1 & 2 & \cdots & m \\ \pi(1) & \pi(2) & \cdots & \pi(m) \end{pmatrix},$$

its _____ is the m × m matrix P_π whose entries are all 0 except that in row i, the entry equals 1.

a. Hessenberg matrix
b. Cartan matrix
c. Partitioned matrix
d. Permutation Matrix

86. In mathematics, the _____ system is a two-dimensional coordinate system in which each point on a plane is determined by an angle and a distance. The _____ system is especially useful in situations where the relationship between two points is most easily expressed in terms of angles and distance; in the more familiar Cartesian or rectangular coordinate system, such a relationship can only be found through trigonometric formulation.

As the coordinate system is two-dimensional, each point is determined by two _____s: the radial coordinate and the angular coordinate.

Chapter 30. Calculus of Several Variables II

a. Sir Isaac Newton
c. Sequence alignment
b. Polar coordinate
d. Vampire

87. Exponentiation is a mathematical operation, written a^n, involving two numbers, the base a and the _____ n. When n is a positive integer, exponentiation corresponds to repeated multiplication:

$$a^n = \underbrace{a \times \cdots \times a}_{n},$$

just as multiplication by a positive integer corresponds to repeated addition:

$$a \times n = \underbrace{a + \cdots + a}_{n}.$$

The _____ is usually shown as a superscript to the right of the base. The exponentiation a^n can be read as: a raised to the n-th power, a raised to the power [of] n or possibly a raised to the _____ [of] n, or more briefly: a to the n-th power or a to the power [of] n, or even more briefly: a to the n.

a. Exponential sum
c. Exponentiating by squaring
b. Exponent
d. Exponential tree

88. In complex analysis, a branch of mathematics, the _____ of a complex-valued function g is a function whose complex derivative is g. More precisely, given an open set U in the complex plane and a function $g : U \to \mathbb{C}$, the _____ of g is a function $f : U \to \mathbb{C}$ that satisfies $\frac{df}{dz} = g$.

As such, this concept is the complex-variable version of the _____ of a real-valued function.

a. Integral
c. Indefinite integral
b. Antiderivative
d. Integration by parts

89. In calculus, an antiderivative, primitive or _____ of a function f is a function F whose derivative is equal to f. The process of solving for antiderivatives is antidifferentiation. Antiderivatives are related to definite integrals through the fundamental theorem of calculus, and provide a convenient means for calculating the definite integrals of many functions.

a. Integral
c. Integral test for convergence
b. Integration by parts operator
d. Indefinite integral

90. In commutative algebra, the notions of an element _____ over a ring, and of an _____ extension of rings, are a generalization of the notions in field theory of an element being algebraic over a field, and of an algebraic extension of fields.

The special case of greatest interest in number theory is that of complex numbers _____ over the ring of integers Z.

The term ring will be understood to mean commutative ring with a unit.

a. Arc length
b. Antidifferentiation
c. Integral test for convergence
d. Integral

91. In grammatical theory, definiteness is a feature of noun phrases, distinguishing between entities which are specific and identifiable in a given context (_____ noun phrases) and entities which are not (indefinite noun phrases Examples are:

- Free form: English the boy.
- Phrasal clitic: as in Basque: Cf. emakume ('woman'), emakume-a (woman-ART: 'the woman'), emakume ederr-a (woman beautiful-ART: 'the beautiful woman')
- Noun affix: as in Romanian: om ('man'), om-ul (man-ART: 'the man'); om-ul bun (man-ART good: 'the good man')
- Prefix on both noun and adjective: Arabic اﻟﻜﺘﺎب اﻟﻜﺒﻴﺮ (al-kitāb al-kabīr) with two instances of al- (DEF-book-DEF-big, literally, 'the book the big')

Germanic, Romance, Celtic, Semitic, and auxiliary languages generally have a _____ article, sometimes used as a postposition. Many other languages do not.

a. Syntax
b. 1-center problem
c. Sentence diagram
d. Definite

92. _____ is a core concept of basic mathematics, specifically in the fields of infinitesimal calculus and mathematical analysis. Given a function f

$$\int_a^b f(x)\,dx,$$

is equal to the area of a region in the xy-plane bounded by the graph of f, the x-axis, and the vertical lines x = a and x = b, with areas below the x-axis being subtracted.

The term 'integral' may also refer to the notion of antiderivative, a function F whose derivative is the given function f.

a. Integration
b. OMAC
c. Epigraph
d. Apex

93. In calculus, and more generally in mathematical analysis, _____ is a rule that transforms the integral of products of functions into other, hopefully simpler, integrals. The rule arises from the product rule of differentiation.

If u = f[x], v = g[x], and the differentials du = f '[x] dx and dv = g'[x] dx; then in its simplest form the product rule is:

a. Integration by parts
c. Integration by parts operator
b. Arc length
d. Integral test for convergence

94. _____ is a branch of mathematics that includes the study of limits, derivatives, integrals, and infinite series, and constitutes a major part of modern university education. Historically, it has been referred to as 'the _____ of infinitesimals', or 'infinitesimal _____'. Most basically, _____ is the study of change, in the same way that geometry is the study of space.
   a. Test for Divergence
   c. Calculus
   b. Hyperbolic angle
   d. Partial sum

95. The _____ specifies the relationship between the two central operations of calculus, differentiation and integration.

The first part of the theorem, sometimes called the first _____, shows that an indefinite integration can be reversed by a differentiation.

The second part, sometimes called the second _____, allows one to compute the definite integral of a function by using any one of its infinitely many antiderivatives.

   a. Standard part function
   c. Maxima and minima
   b. Hyperbolic angle
   d. Fundamental Theorem of Calculus

96. Georg Friedrich Bernhard _____ was a German mathematician who made important contributions to analysis and differential geometry, some of them paving the way for the later development of general relativity.

_____ was born in Breselenz, a village near Dannenberg in the Kingdom of Hanover in what is today Germany. His father, Friedrich Bernhard _____, was a poor Lutheran pastor in Breselenz who fought in the Napoleonic Wars.

   a. Paul C. van Oorschot
   c. Riemann
   b. Gustave Bertrand
   d. Brook Taylor

97. In mathematics, a _____ is a method for approximating the total area underneath a curve on a graph, otherwise known as an integral. It may also be used to define the integration operation. The sums are named after the German mathematician Bernhard Riemann.
   a. Solid of revolution
   c. Riemann sum
   b. Singular measure
   d. Multiple integral

98. The term surplus is used in economics for several related quantities. The _____ is the amount that consumers benefit by being able to purchase a product for a price that is less than they would be willing to pay. The producer surplus is the amount that producers benefit by selling at a market price mechanism that is higher than they would be willing to sell for.
   a. Marginal rate of technical substitution
   c. Returns to scale
   b. Producer surplus
   d. Consumer surplus

Chapter 30. Calculus of Several Variables II

99. _____ is the probability of some event A, given the occurrence of some other event B. _____ is written P[A|B], and is read 'the probability of A, given B'.

Joint probability is the probability of two events in conjunction. That is, it is the probability of both events together. The joint probability of A and B is written $P(A \cap B)$ or $P(A,B)$.

    a. Sample space
    b. Renewal theory
    c. Conditional probability
    d. Quantile

100. In probability theory, an _____ is a set of outcomes to which a probability is assigned. Typically, when the sample space is finite, any subset of the sample space is an _____. However, this approach does not work well in cases where the sample space is infinite, most notably when the outcome is a real number.

    a. Audio compression
    b. Information set
    c. Event
    d. Equaliser

101. In simple terms, two events are _____ if they cannot occur at the same time.

In logic, two _____ propositions are propositions that logically cannot both be true. To say that more than two propositions are _____ may, depending on context mean that no two of them can both be true, or only that they cannot all be true.

    a. Determinism
    b. Philosophy of mathematics
    c. Philosophy
    d. Mutually exclusive

102. _____ is the likelihood or chance that something is the case or will happen. Theoretical _____ is used extensively in areas such as statistics, mathematics, science and philosophy to draw conclusions about the likelihood of potential events and the underlying mechanics of complex systems.

The word _____ does not have a consistent direct definition.

    a. Discrete random variable
    b. Probability
    c. Statistical significance
    d. Standardized moment

103. In statistics, a _____ is a subset of a population. Typically, the population is very large, making a census or a complete enumeration of all the values in the population impractical or impossible. The _____ represents a subset of manageable size.

    a. Dispersion
    b. Boussinesq approximation
    c. Duality
    d. Sample

104. In probability theory, the _____ or universal _____, often denoted S, Ω of an experiment or random trial is the set of all possible outcomes. For example, if the experiment is tossing a coin, the _____ is the set {head, tail}. For tossing a single six-sided die, the _____ is {1, 2, 3, 4, 5, 6}.

    a. Marginal distribution
    b. Martingale central limit theorem
    c. Sample space
    d. Markov chain

105. In microeconomics, a consumer's _____ specifies what the consumer would buy in each price and wealth situation, assuming it perfectly solves the utility maximization problem. Marshallian demand is sometimes called Walrasian demand or uncompensated demand function instead, because the original Marshallian analysis ignored wealth effects.

According to the utility maximization problem, there are L commodities with prices p.

a. Hicksian demand function
b. 1-center problem
c. Precautionary demand
d. Marshallian demand function

106. In economics, game theory, and decision theory the _____ theorem or _____ hypothesis predicts that the 'betting preferences' of people with regard to uncertain outcomes can be described by a mathematical relation which takes into account the size of a payout, the probability of occurrence, risk aversion, and the different utility of the same payout to people with different assets or personal preferences. It is a more sophisticated theory than simply predicting that choices will be made based on expected value.

Daniel Bernoulli described the complete theory in 1738.

a. A Mathematical Theory of Communication
b. Indirect utility function
c. A chemical equation
d. Expected utility

107. In probability theory and statistics, the _____ of a random variable is the integral of the random variable with respect to its probability measure. For discrete random variables this is equivalent to the probability-weighted sum of the possible values, and for continuous random variables with a density function it is the probability density -weighted integral of the possible values.

The _____ may be intuitively understood by the law of large numbers: The _____, when it exists, is almost surely the limit of the sample mean as sample size grows to infinity.

a. Infinitely divisible distribution
b. Event
c. Illustration
d. Expected value

108. In mathematics, _____ are used in the study of chance and probability. They were developed to assist in the analysis of games of chance, stochastic events, and the results of scientific experiments by capturing only the mathematical properties necessary to answer probabilistic questions. Further formalizations have firmly grounded the entity in the theoretical domains of mathematics by making use of measure theory.

a. Random variables
b. Median polish
c. Statistical dispersion
d. Statistics

109. In linear algebra, a row vector or _____ is a 1 × n matrix, that is, a matrix consisting of a single row:

$$\mathbf{x} = \begin{bmatrix} x_1 & x_2 & \ldots & x_m \end{bmatrix}.$$

The transpose of a row vector is a column vector:

$$\begin{bmatrix} x_1 \\ x_2 \\ \vdots \\ x_m \end{bmatrix} = \begin{bmatrix} x_1 & x_2 & \ldots & x_m \end{bmatrix}^T.$$

The set of all row vectors forms a vector space which is the dual space to the set of all column vectors.

Row vectors are sometimes written using the following non-standard notation:

$$\mathbf{x} = \begin{bmatrix} x_1, x_2, \ldots, x_m \end{bmatrix}.$$

- Matrix multiplication involves the action of multiplying each row vector of one matrix by each column vector of another matrix.

- The dot product of two vectors a and b is equivalent to multiplying the row vector representation of a by the column vector representation of b:

$$\mathbf{a} \cdot \mathbf{b} = \begin{bmatrix} a_1 & a_2 & a_3 \end{bmatrix} \begin{bmatrix} b_1 \\ b_2 \\ b_3 \end{bmatrix}.$$

a. Row Matrix
c. Woodbury matrix identity
b. Gram-Schmidt process
d. Dual vector space

110. In probability theory and statistics, _____ is a measure of how much two variables change together.

If two variables tend to vary together, then the _____ between the two variables will be positive. On the other hand, when one of them is above its expected value the other variable tends to be below its expected value, then the _____ between the two variables will be negative.

a. Minimum distance estimation
c. Median
b. Meta-analysis
d. Covariance

111. In mathematics and statistics, _____ is a measure of difference for interval and ratio variables between the observed value and the mean. The sign of _____, either positive or negative, indicates whether the observation is larger than or smaller than the mean. The magnitude of the value reports how different an observation is from the mean.

a. Filter
b. Conchoid
c. Functional
d. Deviation

112. In probability and statistics, the _____ is a measure of the dispersion of a collection of numbers. It can apply to a probability distribution, a random variable, a population or a data set. The _____ is usually denoted with the letter σ.
   a. Failure rate
   b. Standard deviation
   c. Null hypothesis
   d. Statistical population

113. In probability theory and statistics, the _____ of a random variable, probability distribution averaging the squared distance of its possible values from the expected value. Whereas the mean is a way to describe the location of a distribution, the _____ is a way to capture its scale or degree of being spread out. The unit of _____ is the square of the unit of the original variable.
   a. Nonlinear regression
   b. Kendall tau rank correlation coefficient
   c. Probability distribution
   d. Variance

114. The _____ of a material is defined as its mass per unit volume:

$$\rho = \frac{m}{V}$$

Different materials usually have different densities, so _____ is an important concept regarding buoyancy, metal purity and packaging.

In some cases _____ is expressed as the dimensionless quantities specific gravity or relative _____, in which case it is expressed in multiples of the _____ of some other standard material, usually water or air.

In a well-known story, Archimedes was given the task of determining whether King Hiero's goldsmith was embezzling gold during the manufacture of a wreath dedicated to the gods and replacing it with another, cheaper alloy.

   a. 1-center problem
   b. 2-3 heap
   c. 120-cell
   d. Density

115. In mathematics, specifically in combinatorial commutative algebra, a convex lattice polytope P is called _____ if it has the following property: given any positive integer n, every lattice point of the dilation nP, obtained from P by scaling its vertices by the factor n and taking the convex hull of the resulting points, can be written as the sum of exactly n lattice points in P. This property plays an important role in the theory of toric varieties, where it corresponds to projective normality of the toric variety determined by P.

The simplex in R^k with the vertices at the origin and along the unit coordinate vectors is _____.

   a. Polytetrahedron
   b. Hypercube
   c. Demihypercubes
   d. Normal

116. In mathematics, a _____ is a function that represents a probability distribution in terms of integrals.

Formally, a probability distribution has density f, if f is a non-negative Lebesgue-integrable function $\mathbb{R} \to \mathbb{R}$ such that the probability of the interval [a, b] is given by

$$\int_a^b f(x)\, dx$$

for any two numbers a and b. This implies that the total integral of f must be 1.

a. Law of total variance
b. Quantile
c. Pseudocount
d. Probability density function

Chapter 1
1. d   2. a   3. d   4. d   5. d   6. a   7. b   8. b   9. d   10. c
11. b   12. a   13. a   14. b   15. d   16. a   17. d

Chapter 2
1. d   2. d   3. d   4. b   5. c   6. d   7. d   8. d   9. d

Chapter 3
1. b   2. c   3. d   4. d   5. d   6. d   7. b   8. d   9. a   10. c
11. d   12. b   13. b   14. d   15. d   16. d   17. d   18. d   19. d   20. b
21. d   22. b   23. b   24. c   25. c   26. a   27. d   28. d   29. c   30. a
31. b   32. d   33. b   34. c   35. d   36. b   37. d   38. d   39. d   40. d
41. a   42. b   43. a   44. d   45. b   46. d   47. b   48. a   49. d   50. c

Chapter 4
1. b   2. d   3. a   4. d   5. b   6. d   7. d   8. d   9. b   10. d
11. c   12. a   13. d   14. b   15. d   16. d

Chapter 5
1. d   2. a   3. d   4. d   5. d   6. d   7. a   8. a   9. b   10. d
11. d   12. c   13. d   14. d   15. d   16. c

Chapter 6
1. d   2. d   3. d   4. b   5. b   6. b   7. d   8. d   9. d   10. d
11. d   12. c   13. d   14. d   15. a   16. c   17. a   18. d   19. d   20. c
21. d   22. b   23. d   24. c   25. d   26. b   27. d   28. d   29. a   30. a
31. d   32. c   33. d   34. c   35. c   36. c   37. d   38. d   39. c   40. b
41. b   42. d   43. d   44. c   45. b

Chapter 7
1. d   2. a   3. b   4. a   5. d   6. d   7. a   8. c   9. a   10. a
11. c   12. a   13. c   14. d   15. d   16. c   17. b   18. c   19. d   20. d
21. d   22. d   23. d   24. d   25. a   26. d   27. a   28. b   29. d   30. b
31. d   32. d   33. a   34. d   35. c   36. d   37. c   38. c   39. d   40. d
41. c   42. c   43. d   44. d   45. d   46. a

Chapter 8
1. d   2. d   3. d   4. d   5. c   6. b   7. d   8. d   9. d   10. d
11. d   12. b   13. b   14. a   15. a   16. c   17. d   18. d   19. d   20. d
21. a   22. d   23. d   24. a   25. a   26. a   27. d   28. c   29. b   30. d
31. a   32. b   33. b   34. d   35. b   36. c   37. d   38. c   39. d   40. d
41. d   42. c   43. d   44. d   45. d   46. d   47. c   48. a   49. b   50. d
51. d   52. a   53. d   54. d   55. d   56. c

ANSWER KEY

Chapter 9
1. c 2. b 3. d 4. d 5. d 6. c 7. d 8. c 9. d 10. d
11. b 12. a 13. a 14. d 15. c

Chapter 10
1. d 2. a 3. c 4. d 5. c 6. b 7. d 8. a 9. a 10. d
11. a 12. c 13. b 14. d 15. d 16. d 17. d 18. a 19. a 20. b
21. d 22. b 23. d 24. d 25. d 26. b 27. d 28. d 29. d 30. d
31. a 32. b 33. d 34. b 35. d 36. d 37. a 38. b 39. d 40. d
41. b 42. d 43. a 44. c 45. c 46. b 47. c 48. b 49. b 50. b
51. b 52. a 53. b 54. a 55. a 56. d 57. d 58. c

Chapter 11
1. b 2. d 3. a 4. d 5. b 6. d 7. c 8. b 9. c 10. d
11. d 12. c 13. d 14. d 15. d

Chapter 12
1. c 2. b 3. c 4. d 5. c 6. d 7. d 8. d 9. d 10. d
11. d 12. a 13. d 14. d 15. d 16. a 17. d 18. a 19. c 20. a
21. d 22. d 23. b 24. c 25. d 26. d 27. d 28. c 29. d 30. b
31. d 32. d 33. d 34. d

Chapter 13
1. c 2. d 3. a 4. d 5. d 6. d 7. b 8. d 9. d 10. a
11. c 12. a 13. d 14. c 15. a 16. d 17. c 18. b 19. d 20. d
21. d 22. d 23. a 24. c 25. a 26. a 27. c 28. b 29. a 30. d
31. c 32. d 33. b 34. d 35. d 36. d 37. d 38. d 39. c 40. b
41. d 42. d 43. b 44. d 45. d 46. d 47. b

Chapter 14
1. c 2. c 3. a 4. b 5. a 6. c 7. a 8. c 9. d 10. a
11. b 12. d 13. d 14. d 15. d 16. c 17. d 18. d 19. d 20. d
21. d 22. a 23. d 24. d 25. b 26. d 27. d 28. a 29. c 30. d
31. b 32. b 33. b 34. d 35. b 36. d 37. a 38. d 39. d 40. a
41. d 42. b 43. b 44. b 45. c 46. a 47. d 48. d

Chapter 15
1. d 2. d 3. c 4. a 5. d 6. b 7. d 8. a 9. d 10. d
11. d 12. d 13. a 14. d 15. d 16. d 17. a 18. d 19. d 20. d
21. c 22. a 23. b 24. d 25. b 26. d 27. b 28. d 29. d 30. d
31. d 32. b 33. d 34. d 35. a

Chapter 16

1. d	2. a	3. c	4. d	5. c	6. d	7. a	8. d	9. b	10. b
11. d	12. b	13. c	14. a	15. d	16. d	17. d	18. d	19. d	20. c
21. a									

Chapter 17

1. d	2. d	3. b	4. d	5. d	6. a	7. a	8. d	9. d	10. b
11. c	12. a	13. a	14. a	15. d	16. c	17. b	18. d	19. a	20. b
21. d	22. d	23. b	24. a	25. b	26. c	27. c	28. d	29. d	30. d

Chapter 18

1. d	2. a	3. a	4. d	5. a	6. d	7. a	8. c	9. d	10. a
11. b	12. d	13. d	14. d	15. c	16. d	17. d	18. d	19. d	20. c
21. d	22. d	23. d	24. c	25. d	26. b	27. d	28. c	29. c	30. d
31. d	32. d	33. d							

Chapter 19

| 1. c | 2. a | 3. d | 4. d | 5. d | 6. d | 7. b | 8. b | 9. d | 10. d |
| 11. d | 12. d | 13. d | 14. d | 15. d | 16. d | 17. a | | | |

Chapter 20

1. d	2. c	3. d	4. b	5. d	6. d	7. d	8. d	9. b	10. b
11. a	12. d	13. d	14. d	15. a	16. d	17. d	18. b	19. a	20. c
21. c	22. a	23. d	24. d	25. d	26. b	27. c	28. d	29. d	30. d
31. a	32. d	33. c	34. b	35. a	36. b	37. d			

Chapter 21

1. d	2. d	3. b	4. d	5. d	6. c	7. d	8. c	9. b	10. d
11. d	12. d	13. c	14. c	15. c	16. c	17. d	18. d	19. d	20. b
21. d	22. c	23. d	24. c	25. d	26. d				

Chapter 22

1. c	2. d	3. c	4. d	5. a	6. d	7. d	8. c	9. d	10. d
11. d	12. a	13. b	14. d	15. c	16. d	17. a	18. d	19. c	20. d
21. c	22. b	23. b	24. d	25. c	26. b	27. d	28. b	29. d	30. b
31. b	32. d	33. b	34. d	35. c	36. d	37. b	38. a		

Chapter 23

1. d	2. d	3. c	4. d	5. a	6. d	7. d	8. b	9. d	10. d
11. c	12. d	13. d	14. d	15. b	16. c	17. c	18. c	19. a	20. d
21. a	22. c	23. c	24. a	25. a	26. d	27. c	28. d	29. d	30. b
31. b	32. b	33. d	34. b	35. d	36. d	37. d	38. d	39. a	40. d
41. d	42. b	43. d	44. b	45. d	46. d	47. b	48. d	49. d	50. d
51. d	52. d	53. d	54. a	55. d	56. a	57. a	58. b	59. d	60. d
61. b	62. d	63. c	64. c	65. d	66. a	67. b	68. d	69. d	70. b
71. d	72. d								

Chapter 24

1. d	2. b	3. d	4. d	5. d	6. b	7. a	8. d	9. c	10. d
11. d	12. d	13. c	14. d	15. c	16. d	17. a	18. d	19. b	20. b
21. c	22. b	23. d	24. d	25. d	26. d	27. d	28. d	29. a	30. b
31. a	32. a	33. d	34. b	35. d	36. d	37. c	38. d	39. d	40. d
41. d	42. d	43. d	44. d	45. b	46. d	47. b	48. c	49. d	50. d
51. d	52. a	53. d	54. c	55. c	56. c	57. d	58. d	59. d	60. c
61. b	62. d	63. d	64. a	65. d	66. a	67. d	68. d	69. b	

Chapter 25

1. a	2. b	3. a	4. d	5. d	6. b	7. d	8. d	9. d	10. c
11. d	12. a	13. a	14. c	15. c	16. d	17. b	18. a	19. d	20. b
21. d	22. d	23. d	24. d	25. c	26. b	27. d	28. d	29. d	30. b
31. d	32. c	33. d	34. b	35. a	36. c	37. b	38. d	39. d	40. d
41. a	42. b	43. a	44. b	45. c	46. d	47. d	48. d	49. a	50. a
51. a	52. c	53. d	54. a	55. a	56. a	57. c	58. b		

Chapter 26

1. d	2. d	3. d	4. a	5. d	6. d	7. d	8. d	9. d	10. d
11. b	12. a	13. d	14. c	15. d	16. d	17. b	18. d	19. d	20. b
21. a	22. d	23. d	24. d	25. c	26. d	27. c	28. a	29. c	30. b
31. d	32. b	33. c	34. a	35. a	36. b	37. d			

Chapter 27

1. b	2. a	3. d	4. d	5. d	6. d	7. c	8. d	9. d	10. d
11. d	12. b	13. b	14. a	15. b	16. d	17. d	18. d	19. a	20. d
21. d	22. d	23. d	24. d	25. d	26. d	27. d	28. c	29. d	30. d
31. d	32. b	33. d	34. d	35. c	36. d	37. a	38. a	39. b	40. d
41. d	42. c	43. d	44. a	45. d					

Chapter 28

1. d	2. d	3. a	4. d	5. a	6. d	7. c	8. b	9. c	10. d
11. b	12. c	13. c	14. a	15. d	16. d	17. b	18. d	19. d	20. b
21. d	22. c	23. c	24. a	25. d	26. d	27. d			

Chapter 29

1. d	2. d	3. d	4. d	5. c	6. b	7. d	8. b	9. c	10. d
11. a	12. b	13. b	14. d	15. b	16. d	17. a	18. b	19. d	20. c
21. d	22. c	23. c	24. a	25. d	26. d	27. d	28. d	29. b	30. d
31. d	32. b	33. a	34. c	35. d	36. d	37. d	38. b	39. d	40. d
41. c	42. d	43. a	44. d	45. b	46. a				

Chapter 30

1. d	2. c	3. d	4. a	5. b	6. d	7. b	8. b	9. d	10. d
11. d	12. d	13. b	14. a	15. d	16. b	17. a	18. a	19. d	20. b
21. d	22. d	23. d	24. a	25. d	26. a	27. d	28. d	29. a	30. d
31. c	32. b	33. a	34. d	35. b	36. c	37. a	38. c	39. d	40. d
41. c	42. c	43. a	44. d	45. c	46. a	47. d	48. a	49. d	50. d
51. d	52. b	53. c	54. b	55. d	56. d	57. d	58. c	59. b	60. c
61. d	62. d	63. d	64. d	65. a	66. b	67. c	68. d	69. d	70. c
71. b	72. c	73. c	74. d	75. d	76. a	77. d	78. c	79. c	80. d
81. d	82. d	83. d	84. a	85. d	86. b	87. b	88. b	89. d	90. d
91. d	92. a	93. a	94. c	95. d	96. c	97. c	98. d	99. c	100. c
101. d	102. b	103. d	104. c	105. d	106. d	107. d	108. a	109. a	110. d
111. d	112. b	113. d	114. d	115. d	116. d				

www.ingramcontent.com/pod-product-compliance
Lightning Source LLC
Chambersburg PA
CBHW080543230426
43663CB00015B/2699